Slouching towards Gaytheism

SUNY series in Queer Politics and Cultures
Cynthia Burack and Jyl J. Josephson, editors

SLOUCHING TOWARDS GAYTHEISM

Christianity and Queer Survival in America

W. C. HARRIS

Cover design by Philip Pascuzzo

Published by State University of New York Press, Albany

© 2014 State University of New York

For information, contact State University of New York Press, Albany, NY
www.sunypress.edu

Production by Diane Ganeles
Marketing by Anne M. Valentine

Library of Congress Cataloging-in-Publication Data

Harris, W. C. (William Conley)
    Slouching towards gaytheism : Christianity and queer survival in America / W. C.
Harris.
        pages cm. — (SUNY series in queer politics and cultures)
    Includes bibliographical references and index.
    ISBN 978-1-4384-5111-4 (hardcover : alk. paper) — ISBN 978-1-4384-5112-1
(pbk. : alk. paper) 1. Homosexuality—Religious aspects—Christianity. 2. Homosexuality—United States. I. Title.
    BR115.H6H365 2014
    241'.664--dc23
                                            2013021457

            10 9 8 7 6 5 4 3 2 1

for Karl

"That," I said, "is the straightest name I ever heard."
"What's a gay name?" asked Alex.
"Dorrinda Spreddem," I offered.
                    —Ethan Mordden, "The Straight"

I tell you, the function of a homosexual is to make you uneasy.

—Martha Shelley, "Gay Is Good"

CONTENTS

Acknowledgments   ix

Introduction:
Where Gays Lie   1

1. "The End of the Rainbow, My Pot of Gold":
The Queer Erotics of Purity Balls and Christian Abstinence Culture   41

2. Breeding Fraternities:
Ex-Gay Ministries, Barebacking, and Alternative Models of Relation   65

3. Jesus Needs Gays, Yes He Does:
Gay Religion, Queer Spirituality, and the Recalcitrance of Ideology   87

4. Slouching towards Gaytheism:
*Gay Suicide, "It Gets Better," and Religion's Stranglehold
on Queer Survival*   141

Conclusion:
Before the Cock Crows   177

Notes   209

Works Cited   245

Index   263

ACKNOWLEDGMENTS

As always, my first and greatest debt is to Karl Woelz. His love, intellect, humor, and insight continue to make for a partnership rewarding and sustaining beyond my ability to imagine. Karl, along with colleague and partner-in-crime Dawn Vernooy, was the first to see these pages. Their patience with successive drafts and occasional (and, one hopes, now absent) opacities was surpassed only by the acuity of their suggestions and their willingness to talk through moments of conceptual or diagnostic impasse. I cannot thank or repay them enough. Together with Dawn, Fred Kogan and Craig Bierman went beyond the call of duty in assisting the transition of Karl, me, and our feline dependents to Philadelphia and continue to provide sustenance, laughter, camp commiseration, and a shared love and disdain for all the right things. My mother, Judy Harris, yet again proved her devotion and her proofreading chops. She has supported my work and my life with equal fidelity. Others, in person or through felicitous online connections, supplied the camaraderie and diversion essential to making it through: Laurie and Matthew Cella, Jen Clements, Patrick Dilley, Larry Douglas, Flip Eikner, Scott Hightower, Kim Justis, Roger Loveday, Larry McMahan, Eric Moore, Andrew Owens, Andy Saunders, Mary Stewart, Christopher Strenge, Kate von Goeler, and Bernard Welt.

It has been a pleasure to work a second time with State University of New York Press. The editorial and production team, including Beth Bouloukos, Rafael Chaiken, Diane Ganeles, Fran Keneston, and Anne

Valentine, were encouraging, adroit, and continually helpful. Special thanks go to Cynthia Burack and Jyl Josephson, editors of the Queer Politics and Cultures series, for their advice and support. Sincere, constructive feedback from internal as well as outside readers coupled rigorous criticism with inspiring intellectual generosity and was key in realizing the book's present state.

INTRODUCTION

Where Gays Lie

Queer Americans were one of many groups buoyed by the election of Democratic candidate Barack Obama to the presidency in 2008. Eight years of the Bush administration saw the attempted and successful curtailment of civil liberties and rights—through measures as disparate as the violation of wire-tapping laws, the detention of citizens and foreigners in the name of safeguarding national security, and, particularly germane to queer Americans, the passage of state laws and referenda defining marriage heterosexually and depriving same-sex couples of the numerous civil, economic, and social rights enjoyed by straight spouses. By 2010, gay and lesbian Americans and those who support them, as well as an array of progressives, Democrats, independents, and even some Republicans, were ready for change: the reversal of foreign and domestic policies put forward during the previous eight years and true progress on issues of social, economic, and civil equity that had languished under, if not been actively opposed by, the Bush administration and the GOP. "Change—Yes, We Can" was the Obama campaign's progressive-leaning slogan, after all. Like Clinton in the 1992 presidential race, Obama courted the favor of the GLBT community among other ethnic minorities, political liberals, and other historically Democratic groups. He promised to lift the 1993 ban on gay military service ("Don't Ask, Don't Tell," or DADT), to pass a version of the Employment Non-Discrimination Act (ENDA) inclusive of gays and lesbians, and, more reservedly, to work for the repeal of the 1996 Defense of Marriage Act (DOMA), which defined marriage heterosexually, blocked marriage benefits for gay and lesbian couples, and exempted states from having to honor the marriage licenses granted to same-sex couples in another state.

In the first two years of Obama's first term, however, the administration appeared to break, actively block, or allow to drift into limbo these promises to the gay and lesbian community. In terms of understanding the neoliberal antipathy to gays and lesbians that has endured through the past several Democratic *and* Republican administrations, it's important to recall that Bill Clinton, a Democratic president, signed DADT into law and did so *before* the 1994 Republican takeover of both congressional houses. DOMA became law after that "revolution," but Clinton did not employ his veto power. Furthermore, many Democratic senators and representatives fell into lockstep with the Republican majority and voted with it in significant numbers: Democratic senators cast 30 out of 85, or 35 percent, of the "yea" votes for DADT, and the Democratic approval margin in the House was 118 out of 183, or 64 percent. As if DOMA had not sufficiently codified homophobia on the federal level, George W. Bush endorsed the proposed Federal Marriage Amendment (FMA), a similarly hostile piece of legislation. The preexistence of DOMA, which the FMA would have merely duplicated, explains the latter measure's repeated failure, and it reveals the FMA as the most extreme form of homophobia. Had it succeeded, it would have enshrined antigay discrimination in the Constitution, a form of legislative homophobia more difficult to eradicate than that of DOMA. Further, the amendment was nothing more than a billy club to whip up homophobia among the GOP's base as well as conservative Democrats in the lead-up to the 2004 elections. The FMA's antigay cultural force is undiminished by the fact that, since its first proposal in 2002, it has repeatedly been defeated in the House by strong majorities and has consistently failed to garner enough Senate votes even to be considered on the floor. In spite of being a dismal legislative failure *federally* speaking, the proposed amendment was a concrete rhetorical success, and, on the level of individual states, a practical victory. Although the FMA came to nothing, its endorsement by the White House and the GOP made gay and lesbian Americans once again a political football. Reviving this wedge issue stoked the fires of homophobia nationally and arguably contributed, in that same election year, to the passage of constitutional amendments or bans against gay marriage in eleven states.

In 2010, two years after Obama's election and despite Democratic majorities in both congressional houses since 2006, the outlook on change for American queers did not look much more promising. Protracted legal wrangling over both DADT and Prop 8 seemed, pending appeals, to threaten defeat for gay and lesbian equality. By contrast, 2011 and 2012 brought definite movement forward on one of these fronts and promise of the same on the other. The eventual success of DADT's repeal by Congress in December 2010, which took effect in September 2011, marks concrete progress on one of these fronts—as does the June 2011 victory for marriage equality in New York State. Yet that progress is not guaranteed to be permanent. It remains to be seen whether growing popular support for marriage equality, as with the successful DADT repeal, will translate into substantial, far-reaching action on the federal level. While DADT's repeal seemed to pass, relatively speaking, with little fanfare or attention from the political and religious right, at least two Republican hopefuls for the 2012 presidential race, Herman Cain and Texas governor Rick Perry, stated that they would seek to reinstitute DADT if elected.[1]

In 2011 and 2012, the Obama administration's position on gay marriage began to show distinct signs of forward movement. In February 2011 the president instructed the Department of Justice not to defend DOMA in the event of legal challenges. In May 2012, prompted by Vice President Biden's expression of strong support for gay marriage on *Meet the Press*, Obama soon made his own endorsement of gay marriage, an announcement many gay and lesbian Americans had been waiting for. The tides turned more strongly toward gay equality when the 2012 elections saw three more states (Maine, Maryland, and Washington) approve same-sex marriage, raising the total of such states, as of 2013, to thirteen plus the District of Columbia.[2] There's no arguing that these historic developments constitute unquestionable advances for an American president. Equally of note is the U.S. Supreme Court's announcement that it would hear two cases involving same-sex marriage in March 2013. In one, the court has the chance to uphold the 2010 repeal of Prop 8 by federal Judge Vaughn Walker and legalize gay marriage in California. In the other, the justices could strike down the provision of DOMA that limits federal benefits to heterosexual couples and, arguably, violates the Constitution's equal protection clause; a gay-positive victory here not only would extend those benefits to gay and lesbian couples but also could undermine the constitutionality of DOMA as a whole and strengthen the path to gay equality via marriage. The possibility exists, however, that the Court could hand down narrow rulings that affirm gay rights in specific instances without endorsing the right to marry.

Given the progress made on these fronts, I wish to clarify the purpose of highlighting, as much of my account does, moments of legislative, executive, and judicial resistance and inaction in the struggles over Prop 8, DOMA, and DADT. To emphasize the period *leading up* to more recent, positive changes is not to mount a personal attack against Obama or his administration, nor is it to bemoan unnecessarily the time he took to, as he put it, "evolve" on the gay marriage issue. Much less is the intent to deny the magnitude of the steps forward in policy and shifting public opinion between 2010 and 2012. My desire in focusing on the period of stagnation is, instead, to make a case in point. This is the same case one could make regarding the spate of anti-gay state and federal measures passed or proposed under the previous two presidents: namely, the tendentious, malign influence exerted on political discourse by religious rhetoric, by the invocation of religiously couched moral arguments in issues of civil rights, and the extent to which such rhetoric and its associated values can hamper *anti*homophobic action by well-meaning officials and sympathetic allies.

In view of the currently improved prospects for gays and lesbians following from these changes, it's worth putting my rationale in yet stronger terms. Positive developments in the quest for gay rights do not meaningfully alter my argument but instead enable a more nuanced, equally forceful version of it: even if some of the major roadblocks to queer equality are being removed, persistent, religiously fueled homophobia continues to shape public perception and treatment of queer people. The likelihood or actuality of gay marriage's becoming legal does not make society less heteronormative or heterosexual norms any less antagonistic at their core to the shape of queer lives, of any life that seeks to move outside hetero culture's imaginative confines. Queer theorist David Halperin puts the matter plainly in his ingenious, paradigmatic work on camp and gay culture, *How to Be Gay* (2012):

Social acceptance, the decriminalization of gay sex, the legalization of homosexual social and sexual institutions, the removal of barriers to same-sex marriage, to military service, to the priesthood and psychoanalysis, along with other previously off-limits professions, should not be confused with the end of sexual normativity, let alone the collapse of heterosexual culture.

Some gay people, to be sure, may see social equality as tacitly implying an affirmation of the essential normativity of lesbigay folks. That is indeed what it signifies to many people, straight as well as gay, for better or worse. And of course the release of gay people from social oppression, as well as the breakdown of once-universal consensus about the fundamental pathology of homosexuality, which served to justify that oppression, represent absolutely momentous developments, of wide scope and astonishing rapidity, whose significance cannot be overstated. . . . Nonetheless, gay liberation and . . . the gay rights movement have not undone the social and ideological dominance of heterosexuality, even if they have made its hegemony a bit less secure and total. (442–443)

Citing as precedent Michael Warner's incisive 1999 intervention *The Trouble with Normal*, Halperin reminds queers that "what heteronormativity involves is not only the normativity of a specific sexual practice, but also the obviousness and self-evidence of a style of social existence which carries with it an unquestioned prestige and normative power. . . . It embodies an imaginative structure that imparts meaning to the form of individual existence" (451). In short,

the end of discrimination, the rectification of social injustice, and the leveling of all differential treatment of sexual minorities—even should it occur—would not be the same thing as the end of the *cultural dominance* of heterosexuality, the disappearance of heterosexuality as a set of cultural norms. . . .

The dominance of heteronormativity depends on the pervasiveness and inescapability of that ethos—much more than it does on compulsory heterosexuality as a sexual practice. (448, 452)

This is not to minimize the historic advance that full legalization of gay marriage would constitute, given the rights that happen to be bound up with marriage. But a pro–gay marriage position on the part of queers is hardly a radical one. Again, Halperin captures the concern shared by myself and many other gays over rushing into the normative clutches of institutions like marriage in order to obtain the desired equal rights that, unfortunately, seem moored to it and it alone: "rushing to embrace heterosexual forms of life, including heterosexual norms" amounts to "accepting the terms in which heterosexual dominance is articulated . . . and positively promoting them" (443). One might even explain a good deal of the resistance to gay marriage as the continued influence of Christianity and its deep-seated homophobia if not the heteronormativity of religion in general. What could be more conservative and reassuring a move than individuals seeking not to oppose an institution but to *join* it? The risk of gay marriage, or at least of its fervent, intemperate embrace by queers, is the possible loss of a valuable critical perspective once vital to the queer community but currently much out of vogue: a heightened awareness of the numbing, sanctimonious effect of embracing heteronorms. (Now, embracing heteronorms is not the same as being included by them; that is true of us all, gay, bi, trans, or straight.) What else could explain the charge on the part of same-sex marriage opponents that more people adhering to an institution threatens its destruction rather than its expansion and perpetuation? Marriage is an institution saturated in heteronormativity, bearing the marks of the state and the church. This does not limit its meanings or prevent its alteration. It does, however, lend it a rigidity, a core constellation of values that, though gays and lesbians may be included in its numerical ranks, remains ideologically inimical to nonheterosexuals, to irony, abjection, nonmonogamy, gender dissonance—in short, to the dissident values at the core of an authentic gay culture and queer life.

The most important point I'm seeking to make is that, time and again, the core and impetus of homophobic rhetoric, laws, and violence facing American queers is religion. As an illustration of the degree to which religion reinforces both legal discrimination against queers and heteronormativity more generally, let's return for a moment to the trials of the marriage equality battle in California. Proposition 8 was a ballot measure, passed in November 2008, that successfully banned gay marriage in California after that state's Supreme Court had ruled only months earlier that denying marriage licenses to same-sex couples violated the state constitution's equal protection clause. Conservative religious and political groups such as the National Organization for Marriage (NOM), Focus on the Family (FOF), the American Family Association (AFA), the Union of Orthodox Jewish Congregations of America, and a cohort of evangelical Christians aggressively voiced their support for Prop 8, encouraging followers and congregants to contribute financially to ProtectMarriage, the ballot measure's official proponent. Monetary donations by organizations and individuals from across the country were heavy on both sides of the issue, setting a record for the highest-funded nonpresidential campaign in any state. NoOnProp 8, the movement to defeat the measure, raised almost $40 million, and ProtectMarriage raised just over $43 million. While one might take some comfort in the near parity of the fundraising efforts, it's noteworthy that almost *half* of contributions to Protect-Marriage originating outside California came from Mormon sources in Utah, where the Church of Latter-Day Saints mounted an ardent crusade in favor of the referendum. Between 80 and 90 percent of the volunteers collecting door-to-door for the measure were Mormon.[3] Between financial support and verbal endorsements, it's indisputable that the drive for, and successful passage of, Prop 8 was fueled by religious—rather than (merely?) political—motives. Although a number of political organizations supported Prop 8 along with religious groups, many of the former were organizations who had previously defined themselves as political vehicles for religiously defined agendas or who expressed their opposition to gay marriage in religious terms.

It was against this background of amplified attention to gay rights and heightened antigay sentiment that, in September and October 2010, a series of tragic, violent incidents involving gay Americans unfolded—events expressing, in a condensed, even more personal fashion, an upsurge in homophobic animosity. Multiple gay bashings in New York City as well as in Denver, Colorado, made headlines, as did the deaths of several gay teens who, within the span of a few weeks, committed suicide after enduring repeated, brutal antigay verbal and physical harassment, harassment that had often gone unaddressed by school officials. For introductory purposes, a brief discussion of just three recent outcroppings of homophobia in American commercial and political life during the same period of time will suffice to epitomize the persistent or periodically renewed national upwelling of antigay feeling—a zeitgeist that conservatives feel increasingly entitled to voice as merely their "opinion" or, more grandiosely, as a tenet of their faith and values. Whether singly or together, it may seem overstated to some to claim any of the following events (the gay bashings, teen suicides, and legislative contests) as the bellwether of cultural homophobia. Nonetheless, each serves as an index—from minor to severe—of the parlous state of queer existence in a country where religious belief is exempt from criticism and thus where the homophobic discrimination and violence so intimately allied with and nourished by conservative Christianity appears indomitable.

In early October 2010 *QSaltLake* reported Walmart's plans to sell an ex-gay parenting book in over one hundred of its stores in the Western United States. The book, titled *Chased by an Elephant: The Gospel Truth about Today's Stampeding Sexuality*, is by Janice Barrett Graham, wife to the president of Mormon-oriented educational foundation Standard of Liberty and mother to an ex-gay son. According to her introduction, Graham's declared intention is to "help shed the clear light of truth on today's dark and tangled ideas about male and female, proper gender roles, the law of chastity, and the God-given sexual appetite" (qtd. in *QSaltLake* staff par. 1).[4] Graham also writes about her son, Andrew, who claims to have "overcome" his homosexuality and is now "happily" married to a woman (par. 5). In his own book, *Captain of My Soul*, Andrew claims to expose "the deceitful and predatory nature of the 'gay' lifestyle" (qtd. in par. 7). More troublesome is the fact that *Chased by an Elephant* is a children's book. Explicitly targeting children, teenagers, and their parents and educators, Janice Graham extends to her readers the presumptuous and homophobic assurance that young queers' stories, like her son's, can "end . . . happily with . . . deliverance and healing through family support, expert professional counseling, truth, and repentance through the Atonement of Jesus Christ" (qtd. in par. 8). Graham's words exemplify the clichéd nature of the Right's leitmotif that homosexuality is a choice paired with the conservative Christian notion that one can choose to be heterosexual with Christ. Furthermore, Walmart's plans to carry her book lay bare the trifecta of how people like Republican leaders want to see America, the America they speak to: conservatives, Christians, and consumers.

Political campaigns may be a more predictable site for homophobic proclamations than the shelves of American retailers. Republican Rebecca Kleefisch certainly made no secret of her opposition to same-sex marriage during her campaign for lieutenant governor of Wisconsin.

In a baffling return to the logical fallacy that helped make a laughingstock of former representative Rick Santorum (R.-PA), Kleefisch reiterated her support for the state's 2006 constitutional marriage ban, upheld in 2010 by Wisconsin's Supreme Court. Where Santorum compared homosexuality to pedophilia and bestiality (in his words "man on child [and] man on dog"), Kleefisch altered her examples only slightly, omitting pedophilia. She retained the comparison to bestiality and the same basic premise: that legalizing gay marriage would lead to implicitly ludicrous demands for marriage rights by other, similarly perverted populations. Kleefisch opined, "This is a slippery slope. . . . [A]t what point are we going to be okay marrying inanimate objects? Can I marry this table or this, you know, clock? Can we marry dogs? This is ridiculous and biblically, again, I'm going to go right back to my fundamental Christian beliefs [that] marriage is between one man and one woman" (qtd. in Tedder, "WI Lt. Gov. Hopeful" par. 1). Like many conservative Christians, Kleefisch openly sports the notion that religious doctrine should be the primary, if not sole, basis for political policy. More galling is her refusal to see anything inappropriate about dictating civil law and infringing civil rights on the basis of religion. Far from issuing a retraction when criticized for her comment, Kleefisch told an audience at University of Wisconsin-Waukesha that "I was talking about the slippery slope and what we would have to do in legislation in order to define and redefine what marriage is. If I sounded insensitive, that's wrong" (qtd. in Tedder, "WI Lt. Gov. Hopeful" par 2). The first sentence nonsensically restates her previous statement without altering its content. The second sentence, while it may sound like an apology— and was lapped up as such by the press, without a modicum of editorial scrutiny— cleverly evades culpability. If she had said "I was being insensitive, that was wrong" or "If what I said was insensitive, that was wrong," then she would have actually been apologizing for an offensive statement. Instead, she said "If I *sounded* insensitive, that's wrong." This may sound like an apology, but it's not. Rather, it ascribes the offensiveness of her words and the comparison to bestiality to *misperception* on the part of others rather than to her own prejudice and hatemongering. She's saying, in a non-apology apology, "I wasn't being insensitive; you merely misinterpreted me."

Most relevant to my argument, Kleefisch armored herself in that most unassailable American discourse, her "fundamental Christian beliefs." One has to concede her cunningly ambiguous use of the word "fundamental" to speak not only to fundamentalist Christians, whose religious identities have routinely hinged on an opposition to homosexuality for the past few decades, but also to moderate Christians who consider their beliefs fundamental, or integral, to their lives.[5] If mining the shallow well of logical fallacy injured Santorum's 2008 reelection effort, the same strategy failed to harm Kleefisch's bid for office. Kleefisch was technically carried into office by the success of her running mate, Republican gubernatorial candidate Scott Walker, who won with 52 percent of the vote. Winning the Republican primary for the lieutenant governor slot automatically earned Kleefisch her spot on the final ticket. While the Waukesha campus organized a rally to protest what one student called Kleefisch's "dehumaniz[ing]" remarks, there was little indication that her comments affected the election's outcome, and they may even have helped ("Kleefisch's Comments Draw Protest" par. 4).

That same October, a fouler, more disturbing incident, involving a Midland, Arkansas school board member, revealed the murderous impulse characteristic of religious homophobia and its impact on political culture and social discourse. Some context first: LGBTQ Spirit Day was a campaign started online by a Canadian teenager that quickly spread across the internet and media, encouraging people to wear purple on October 20, 2010. Wearing purple on this day was meant to commemorate the six gay teens, including Asher Brown and Tyler Clementi, whose suicides within the span of a few weeks had brought antigay bullying and harassment to national attention that summer. As a display of tolerance, solidarity, and support for queer teens, LGBTQ Spirit Day became popular among many adults as well as schoolchildren. It was to this campaign, then, that Arkansas school board member Clint McCance was responding on his Facebook page. One assumes from McCance's comments that school board members may have been invited to participate as well; given the school environment in which most of the dead teens were harassed, this seems only fitting. McCance wrote as his Facebook status: "Seriously they want me to wear purple because five queers committed suicide. The only way im wearin it for them is if they all commit suicide. I cant believe the people of this world have gotten this stupid. We are honoring the fact that they sinned and killed thereselves because of their sin. REALLY PEOPLE" (qtd. in Broverman, "School Official Wants Gays Dead" par. 2).[6] As Broverman reports, "Initially, six people 'liked'

[the] message. He also received supportive comments, though some challenged" him (par. 3). Prompted by one comment that McCance interpreted as judgmental ("Because hatred is always right"), he added another offensive comment to the thread:

> No because being a fag doesn't give you the right to ruin the rest of our lives. If you easily get offended by being called a fag then dont tell anyone you are a fag. Keep that shit to yourself. I dont care how people decide to live their lives. They dont bother me if they keep it to thereselves. It pisses me off though that we make a special purple fag day for them. I like that fags cant procreate. I also enjoy the fact that they often give each other aids and die. (qtd. in Broverman, "School Official Wants Gays Dead" par. 3).

After another commenter took him to task for being unchristian, McCance responded: "I would disown my kids if they were gay. They will not be welcome at my home or in my vicinity. I will absolutely run them off. Of course my kids will know better. My kids will have solid christian beliefs. See it infects everyone" (qtd. in par. 5). Leaving aside the damning comment on the U.S. educational system represented by McCance's use of "thereselves"—not even the commonly mistaken "theirselves"—one has to be struck by the brazen hostility, ignorance, and, particularly for a public education official, inappropriateness.

Although the Arkansas Department of Education quickly criticized McCance's words, which of themselves might constitute the sort of harassment prohibited to Arkansas students, teachers, and school board members whether on or off campus, as an elected official McCance was immune to removal for reasons other than felony conviction or absenteeism. Fortunately, after several bloggers prompted a barrage of criticism and threats by posting his home and work phone numbers and addresses, McCance resigned after less than a week. It's karmically fitting that McCance felt the same threat and blunt animosity he so freely directed at gay teens.

McCance's words resonate long after his resignation, as do the discouraging realities they convey about the power of religion to warp one's sense of ethics and about the hectoring invective that many queers still hear regularly voiced by peers, parents, educators, religious figures, and politicians. McCance relies on one of the homophobe's most tried and true ploys: espousing indifference regarding other people's sexuality but demanding that anyone who isn't heterosexual stay in the closet. Enforcing silence and invisibility by veiled or overt threats is a transparent bid not just to marginalize queer culture but to eradicate queer life. Interestingly, McCance, like the Grahams, combines the clichéd homophobic notion that homosexuality is a choice ("my kids will know better") with the possibility—or fear?—that his children might in fact be gay, in which case he confirms another fear of closeted gay teens ("I would disown [them] . . . run them off"). Most corrosive of all is the brutal animus toward gays: he "enjoy[s]" the fact that AIDS claims gay men's lives. He also relies on the hostile equation of homosexuality and disease ("See it infects everyone"). If one might have thought that rhetoric of homosexuality as a risk to the nation's health, if not to the future of civilization, was a relic of the homophobic past, McCance's words attest to the contrary. After all, it was as recently as the 1980s, during the first onslaught of the AIDS crisis, that Americans—not just private citizens but pundits, journalists, politicians, and religious leaders—relied on the same vicious, ignorant imagery.[7]

As evidence toward this book's central argument, McCance pointedly places homosexuality in opposition to religion, which is implicitly characterized as heterosexual. He assumes that his kids—whom he says "know better" than to be gay, or at least know better than to come out to him—are insulated from the "infect[ion]" of gayness by their "solid Christian beliefs." In calling homosexuality a "sin," McCance lays bare the religious and specifically Christian basis of his antigay stance. Now, some might seek to counter McCance's harangue with a plea for the tolerant character of so-called true Christianity, some authentic version uncontaminated by deforming hatred. But seeking a gentler version of religion is feckless and gets us nowhere; such an endeavor does nothing to alter or diminish the force or impact of antigay conservative Christian positions. The more sensible counter would be to insist that religion no longer be part of the discussion where legal parity, public policy, or civil rights are concerned. McCance's harangue should serve as a flash point for the toxicity, inappropriateness, and utter incompatibility of religion to public discourse. What animates *Chased by an Elephant* and the comments of Kleefisch and McCance is a violent core of religiously galvanized disgust—a disgust echoed and realized in the verbal and physical violence of antigay bullies and gay bashers. It's *this* disgust that gay suicidal teens such as Tyler Clementi and Asher Brown felt could not be successfully dodged or overcome. It's *this* culturally inescapable pulse that gay-positive voices and developments in politics, culture, and even religion seemed unable to match.

Intelligent arguments have been made, most recently by Christopher Hitchens and Sam Harris, that religion in general obstructs progress, rational discourse, and the humane treatment of others—and, inasmuch as it fuels war, terrorism, and genocide, endangers humankind's survival.[8] My focus is not that wide, in terms of geography, culture, or religious sect. I am interested in the consistently antagonistic, often murderous impact of religious discourse in America on its queer constituents. Christianity is hardly the only religion practiced in America, but from its conservative evangelical strains to its more moderate embodiments it's the single faith with the greatest influence on public discourse, domestic political policy, and cultural life. Obviously, public discourse about Islam, from across the political and religious spectrums, bears a great deal of weight in the life of Americans in the twenty-first century. But, brute occurrences like 9/11 aside, the source and stimulus for much of the rhetoric about Islam is arguably Christianity—that is, not just various religious figures' attacks on or pleas for tolerance of Muslims or Muslim Americans but the extent to which Christianity itself, notwithstanding the constitutional "wall" of church-state separation, saturates, restricts, and dictates American discussion of and action on political, social, and civil rights issues. While the present discussion confines itself to the homophobic cultural reverberations generated or fueled by Christianity, I would allege that my observations apply to most, if not all, other religious traditions in the United States. The case for religion's pernicious impact on human life, its inhibition of ethical, reasonable, humane treatment of others, has been made adequately by others such as Hitchens and Harris but not exclusively in relation to homosexuality. The illuminating work of mapping the coercive as well as sustaining ramifications of religion for queer existence in other religions or places remains to be done, though it lies beyond the scope of my project. Far from suggesting the ease with which these incidents and the intersecting issues of religious rhetoric, sexuality, and civil rights can be addressed, much less resolved, this book points to the urgency of starting that conversation and doing so in a way that gets us beyond the stifling position of being unable to criticize or exclude discourse grounded in religious "values" discourse. *Slouching towards Gaytheism* simultaneously argues for full enfranchisement of and freedom from verbal and physical harassment for a population whose lives, dignity, and rights America's culturally ascendant religious discourse either disdains or exhorts the destruction of.

It is within these parameters that *Slouching towards Gaytheism* examines a number of interrelated artifacts, contexts, and issues relating to queer and/or Christian quests for purity and ethical progress. These contexts include purity balls, abstinence culture, ex-gay "therapy," projects of gay Christianity and gay spirituality, and the sexual subculture of barebacking. The following chapters worry at the present intersection of religion, political/civil rights, and conservative and moderate-to-liberal Christianity. They also explore the brighter ethical possibilities queers might find in alternative models of relation and identity as inspired by atheism, barebacking subculture, and the troubled confines and confining power of the Christian closet. A number of previous volumes analyze one or more of these elements individually— Tanya Erzen's *Straight to Jesus*, Michelle Wolkomir's *Be Not Deceived*, Cynthia Burack's *Sin, Sex, and Democracy*, Christopher Hitchens's *God Is Not Great*, and Janet Jakobsen and Ann Pellegrini's *Love the Sin*, to name a few examples. *Slouching towards Gaytheism* attempts to frame a broader discussion by linking contexts that are often discussed discretely or from a particular perspective: Burack's dissection of Christian Right rhetoric, Hitchens's atheist polemic on the general toxicity of religion, Jakobsen and Pellegrini's recommendation of "secular morality," Erzen's and Wolkomir's sociological studies of ex-gay and gay Christian ideology and group dynamics.[9] Examining these topics from a broader cultural studies stance will, I hope, render the discussion accessible to readers coming from a variety of theoretical backgrounds. In analyzing the sometimes toxic, sometimes generative relations between these contexts—their relations to queerness and to each other—my hope is to gesture toward a rhetorical exit for American queers, a sustaining intellectual as well as practical solution for their besieged, disenfranchised condition.

— —

To return to Christopher Hitchens, an arena of American culture that especially discourages one's "chainless mind [from] do[ing] its own thinking" is that of conservative Christianity—in particular, the

Christian purity movement with which this book initiates its discussion. Typically religiously inflected, purity cults are most invested in women's bodies, primarily those of prepubescent and pubescent girls.[10] In 1998, Randy and Lisa Wilson held the first purity ball. Since that time, Randy has served as director of the Generations of Light ministry and also worked for the Family Research Council. The purity ball is a disturbing variation on the father-daughter dance where fathers and daughters mutually pledge to guard the latter's chastity in a ceremony involving the exchange of rings between father and daughter. The idea is that, after the pledge, the girl will channel her interest in men through the father-daughter relationship until marriage. At this point, the father, who has promised "protection in all areas of purity," hands over the purity ring to the groom, the husband now taking charge of the young woman's sexuality. Here, parental care dovetails all too easily and worryingly with the exchange of women, an insight made famous by Gayle Rubin's feminist take on Lévi-Strauss in "The Traffic in Women." Like the abstinence movement in general, purity ball culture relies on outmoded, reductive Freudian notions about gender and sexuality.[11]

Chapter 1 starts by focusing on a little-discussed corollary to the purity ball: what Christian purity culture has to say to young men. What limits does it impose and what loopholes does it fail to spot when addressing male teens, some of whom who are likely to be queer or protoqueer? Purity literature abounds in books advising teens to refrain from premarital sex so as not to cheapen their bodies or their relationships or damage their self-esteem. "Save yourself for marriage," the stale baseline of this unimaginative rhetoric, might seem rather dated advice for reaching contemporary teens. Yet this approach seems to appeal to teens, at least to those who are part of the sizeable Christian youth culture—a culture exemplified by Young Life, a highly successful youth ministry that runs camps, clubs, and contemporary Christian music concert tours. Part of this book's argument is that the appeal of the purity cult for queer or questioning teens might lie less in the rhetoric of abstinence and more in the movement that accompanies it, the "queer" (in the sense of "uneasy" or "odd") fellowship provided by other young gay men struggling to be pure, straight, and Christian—or just wanting to be closer to other attractive young men. The success of such organizations has been fueled by the rise and popularity of "abstinence only" sex education programs. Initiated by the Clinton administration in 1996 and expanded by George W. Bush in 2000 into the Community-Based Abstinence Education program, abstinence education made the preaching of abstinence by health educators and outreach programs a condition for receiving federal funding. After studies in 2004 and 2007, however, Congress announced that abstinence education was almost entirely a failure. Not only did such programs fail to significantly impact teen pregnancy and STD infection rates, they irresponsibly spread outright lies about the effectiveness of condom usage, countertruths designed to make not having sex at all the only viable option. It's not implausible that misinformation of this type might lead purity-cult teens to have unsafe sex, risk pregnancy, and contract STDs when they fall off the wagon, as many inevitably do. Desires, whether represented as natural or unnatural, can be suppressed only for so long.

What interests me is investigating the extent to which the purity cult movement addresses male sexuality *outside the context of heterosexual insertive intercourse.* How does the movement address male sexuality other than by telling boys and young men not to have sex with women until marriage? How is male sexuality addressed by these movements *other than* in relation to women? Are male teens told not to masturbate? How are homoerotic urges dealt with in protogay and curious teens? Does purity literature address the possibility that forbidding sexual contact with girls until marriage might make sexual contact with boys more appealing or available than otherwise? After all, in a number of cultures outside the United States and within some ethnic subcultures inside the United States, male homosexual activity is explicitly or implicitly condoned as a legitimate premarital outlet—an alternative that is seen perhaps as relatively innocuous inasmuch as it conserves a culturally fetishized female sexuality.

The more pointed question in chapter 1 regards what gay and bisexual male Christian youths find it necessary to avoid, what they are required to repress in order to survive a hostile environment that necessitates adherence to external moral directives or internal impulses. The Jezebel-like temptation of women is not a likely issue for most of them. In looking at religious self-help literature surrounding the purity movement, as well as sociological accounts of ex-gay ministries and non-APA-approved therapies, this book outlines the cultural dimensions and force of what I call the "purity closet," the direct and the more oblique consequences and objectives of corseting male sexuality within specific, narrow bounds.[12] Perhaps to the surprise of religious homophobes loyal to purity cults, the effect is not to shut out homosexuality physically and psychologically but rather to immure homoeroticism between gay or straight-identified men safely beyond what is thinkable, to enshrine it firmly as heterosexuality's antipodean other—the fearful engine that, far from threatening, in fact drives and sustains it.

Purity balls and abstinence rhetoric focus so much on daddy's little girl, on creepy daddy-daughter cathexis, that one must wonder where the mothers and sons have disappeared to. Rather than an oedipal worry, my question is what are the boys doing all this time, while they wait for daddies to hand off their daughters' hymens on far-distant wedding days? Is purity culture doubly closeting for gay youth? Or might it, on the contrary, serve as a convenient refuge? Perhaps so, if no sex means not having to confront queer sex if all sex outside the sanctioned bounds is queer or queering. Might abstinence become the perfect cover story for a queer-desiring double agent, side-by-side with not only the sacralized female flesh it doesn't really care to touch, that it earns praise *not* touching, but also a fraternity of hormonally surging boyflesh? Purity-striving male adolescents can admire each other's restraint, commiserate over the struggles of waiting, share fantasies about what straight sex will be like. The trouble is, these fantasies may start out pure and safely scaffolded within the abstract paradise of hetero marriage. Without practical access to marriage or heterosexuality, abstaining youth *are* queer in a sense. They are queer by default, by their inexperience, by their lack of entry. Fantasies of what sex with women will be like might easily slide sideways into what, for the pubescent and untried, can be as good as hetero sex: any sex at all.

Lest this seem a simplistic argument that restraint, perforce, leads to indulgence—a slippery Manichean slope by way of Oscar Wilde—my aim is to tease out those proxy spaces where queer youth may pine, those lay-bys where queer teens might not just escape gay pasts and access straight futures but where they might *sustain* gay pasts and augur queer futures. What unanticipated interstices does purity culture offer where queerness is not extinguished but suspended in solution, where straight interpellation can be postponed? How might queer youth access purity culture not to turn straight but rather to escape being deciphered, found out, and outed, to evade being dissolved fully in Christ *or* queerness, to shirk being crucially fixed within or by the crux of normativity?

Faced with what many will find to be the puzzling nature of queer Christian identity, another objective—and the topic of chapter 2—emerges: thinking through the patent as well as the cryptic possibilities of subjectivity for the conflicted gay Christian. Why are there so many gay men in the ranks of the antigay new Right? For merely one recent addition to the Vichy Hall of Closet Case Fame, consider George Rekers, board member of NARTH (the National Association for Reparative Therapy) and, with James Dobson, cofounder of the Family Research Council. In 2010 Rekers was seen in the Miami airport returning from a ten-day vacation with "Lucien," a male escort he found on the website Rentboys.com.[13] Now, queer activists might think it axiomatic that gay Christian youth, especially in the purity track, can only suffer the ache of split subjectivity, and queer theorists might tout such youths as proof of the riches lying beyond identitarianism's core poverty. But I'm suggesting that these youths' pleasures may be more enthralling, and their pain more disabling, than either of the two camps would allow. Informed by psychoanalytic theory, we might begin to consider modalities of being, fucking, or fellowshipping that avoid the "othering" pitfall to which "identification politics" are prone, according to Tim Dean in *Unlimited Intimacy: Reflections on the Subculture of Barebacking* (2009). "Grounded in recognition," identification politics is the "politics of the ideal image," and ideals, in Dean's view, constrain our alliances to those founded on "empathy, identification, and recognition," on one's "capacity to imagine [oneself] in the other's place" (21). Although he is writing about gay barebacking subculture, Dean's analysis seems of use in parsing subcultural dynamics like those associated with conservative queer Christianity. If these dynamics initially defy our capacity to understand them, that's because, Dean would argue, our understanding has been trained to operate on the restricted basis of empathy and recognition. The alternative Dean offers is "an impersonal ethics" based, by contrast, on "the *failure* to identify others as persons and [on] seeing how otherness remains irreducible to other persons, as well as to social categories of difference" (25). Rather than struggling to find within conservative Christian experience some basis for identification, considering it a modality of otherness enables us to sketch a framework for identity that eludes the positive and negative

representational effects of identity politics as they have informed both
gay and lesbian and conservative Christian experience in the United
States for at least the past half century. Within different contexts, the
following chapters explore the negative and positive effects of gay
Christian identity and the overt as well as more cloaked possibilities
its various permutations hold for obscuring diversity, for inhibiting
divergence, for generating either false or strategic opportunities for cultural consolidation and identitarian leverage.[14] The varied intersections
between gay and Christian identity afford exceptional illustrations of
the competing demands and rewards for queer life of constructionist
critiques of identity on the one hand and, in the words of David Van
Leer, "identifiable cultural difference[s]" and the "social reality behind
constructed categories" on the other (9).[15]

Chapter 2 investigates queer Christians as not merely a subcultural
group but as what Dean refers to as "post-subcultural," in the sense of
being a "social grouping . . . not characterized by the epistemologi-
cally reassuring coherence, homogeneity, or boundedness that the term
subculture often implies" (43).[16] Such *resistance* to crystallization might
seem a welcome counter to identity's more perniciously normalizing
effects. In the context of the gay Christian closet, it is a construct that
abrades as well as preserves. On the one hand, it dissolves Christian
teens' homosexuality within a cloying doctrinal compound aggressively
hostile to core erotic desires; on the other hand, the Christian closet
undermines the reparative Christian project by solidifying homosexuality as one's cross to bear in a religiously mandated heterosexual world.
Gay conservative Christianity, then, hails the dissolution of the oppressive program whose norms simultaneously hail (or co-opt) them in
an Althusserian sense. In an ex-gay organization such as New Hope
ministries, where "queer conversions" confront the reality that sexual
"falls" will continue to occur and that gay desire may never be overcome
or supplanted by hetero desire, this recalcitrance yields a model of
identity sufficiently nuanced, complex, and conflicted enough to per-
mit provisional escape from the rigidities of conservative Christian as
well as gay identity. This is not to say that gay conservative Christians
are not subjected themselves to unwarranted pain and self-loathing,
or that homophobic Christianity's relentless reproach and expansive
grasp will not finally outstrip the endurance of gay participants or
overwhelm queer acts of defiance. In an ex-gay movement generally
preaching that change is possible,[17] however, homosexuality ironically

remains ingrained at the conservative Christian movement's political and theological heart. It has become so firmly lodged there, one might venture, that it will take much to displace or replace it, with the consequence that gay teens struggling either to overcome their homosexual urges or to reconcile themselves to being gay *and* religious have already accepted a version of homosexuality that is by definition incompatible with religious doctrine. Thus conservative religious positions about homosexuality and, more broadly, religious positions in general do not constitute a tincture, a way of resolving the conflict since homosexuality by principle is not, and operationally *cannot* be, miscible with hetero Christianity. Rather, they are an emulsion, a hostile suspension of the other in their midst, with little sincere intent—or, I would argue, capability—of resolution or reconciliation.[18]

Given the diversity of religious organizations and denominations on the antigay as well as progay sides, it's important to clarify the evidentiary choices and considerations that shape chapters 2 and 3. In her account of gay and ex-gay Christian groups, Michelle Wolkomir refers to these groups, respectively, with the general labels "Accept" and "Expell," a shorthand whose utility I have embraced. For illustrative and analytical purposes, however, I have focused on specific organizations characteristic of these more general types. Obviously, neither New Hope nor the Metropolitan Community Church, the ex-gay and gay-positive Christian groups I focus on, can be taken as wholly representative of either conservative or liberal American Christianity. Nonetheless, New Hope and MCC are the most well-known groups within their respective camps and have been the subject of in-depth sociological analysis; therefore, they seem ideal candidates for discussion, even if they fail to represent every conservative or progay group. Progay Christian groups exist other than MCC, of course: among others, the LGBT-inclusive Evangelicals Concerned; its Evangelical Lutheran analog, ReconcilingWorks; and DignityUSA, the progay Catholic group that defies church doctrine regarding gay sex as sinful, unlike its conservative analog, Courage International. Conversely, one can locate mainstream Christian sects and congregations that are apathetic or unfriendly to queers. It has been most useful for my immediate purposes, though, to highlight not only those organizations with greater public recognition but those also that, due to their size or connection to other conservative evangelical or progressive political movements, wield more salient cultural cachet or influence. For example, while arguably more liberal and queer-friendly than many mainstream sects—certainly more so than conservative Christianity—MCC illustrates the failure of even a liberal Christian sect to question broader cultural narratives of homosexuality, heteronormative priorities that compromise, even if without overtly counteracting, the organization's progay commitments. For example, members of MCC typically refute homophobic interpretations of the Bible. At the same time, their failure (in general) to question theological authority more broadly denotes an incomplete commitment to institutional transformation. It is this incomplete commitment to institutional transformation that, despite sincere liberalizing intentions, leaves unquestioned other heteronormative religious and social values such as the valorization of monogamy over casual intimacy, which is spurned as promiscuity. And if a liberal denomination like MCC retains such compromising commitments, mainstream Christian sects, though vocally tolerant of homosexuality, are equally, perhaps more, likely to do so. Examining the conservative and liberal extremes of American Christianity cannot claim to be representative of all mainstream sects that fall in between, but my polemic aims to be argumentatively forceful and representative rather than encyclopedic.

Despite its simplicity as a pun, this chapter's title, "Where Gays Lie," demarcates two important realities explored in the following pages. In one sense, gay and queer/questioning male adults and teenagers involved in purity and abstinence culture "lie" in the Christian closet in the sense of existing in it, by choice or under some kind of physical, psychological, and ideological duress. Similarly, their participation in ex-gay therapy or gay Christian support groups may locate them within the Christian closet: either indefinitely, as they fight to quarantine their gay behaviors and desires from ostensibly authentic Christian selves; or temporarily, as they seek to find a path out of this divided feeling, relearning or reconstructing their faith traditions in order to merge areas of a life they have long experienced as disjunct. Whether their presence in any of these worlds is coerced or whether they seek these precincts willingly, their tenure there may be characterized by gradations of pain, pleasure, or amalgams of the two—feelings derived from modeling or imposture, from sanctioned or forbidden physical actions or emotional investments ranging from nonsexual male friendship to gay sex. The second sense of "where gays lie" is equally resonant. Queer boys and men must dissimulate in the Christian closet. To meet the demands of purity and abstinence, of ex-gay or gay Christian identity, or to shirk those demands while feigning observance, they may find it necessary to prevaricate, to dissemble, to deceive others or themselves.

Chapter 3 follows a third edge of my inquiry into gay Christian identity. What drives the Christian who is happily gay, who's not seeking to become straight? What rewards him, keeps him sane? Many gay Christian projects home in on gay *spirituality*, whose favor among many GLBT persons suggests that religion's structures and strictures have grown inextricable over the centuries with intolerance and homophobia, whereas spirituality can sidestep such conflict by a manner of Neoplatonic transcendence. Gay Christians who seek to strike a truce between the homophobic religious values by which they were raised and the liberal religious, political, and sexual values to which they're equally, if not more deeply, loyal have attempted to do so through two distinct avenues: gay religion, the rehabilitation of traditional Western religious institutions exemplified by MCC, the Metropolitan Community Church; and gay spirituality, or redefinitions of spirituality outside traditional institutionalized religion.

Chapter 3 builds on representative studies in these areas—Michelle Wolkomir's *Be Not Deceived* (2006), Melissa Wilcox's *Coming Out in Christianity* (2003), Toby Johnson's *Gay Spirituality* (2000), and Marcella Althaus-Reid's *The Queer God* (2003)—to suggest some of the limitations that hinder the ultimate progressiveness of such recuperative endeavors. Such a compromise ultimately turns out to be a ruse, a false solution that diverts us from the actual problem. The real problem, unaddressed by many forms of gay spirituality and religion, by deinstitutionalized and institutionalized religions alike, is the intolerance seemingly ingrained in Western social formations and religious systems in general, their shared yet—despite localized areas of liberalization—intransigent tendencies toward the reactionary and the heterocentric.

According to critics like Sam Harris and Christopher Hitchens, attempts by moderate and liberal Christians to distance themselves from the excesses of more conservative incarnations do little to blunt the force of the latter. Indeed, they seem to inflame it. Their own reliance on even humane articulations of moral or religious authority compromise their license to question other articulations of religious or moral prerogative, no matter how fanatical or distasteful. Moderate and liberal endorsement of religion and spirituality tends to sanction, despite itself sometimes, the idea that religion has credibility beyond the individual, that even its strictly ethical jurisdiction extends to the political discourse and civil life of others. It's worth asking, as I do in chapter 4 and the conclusion, what ends are served by queers going to church. Are personal spiritual ends enough? Mustn't larger political and ethical goals be acknowledged as well, if not heeded first? As religious queers, are we trying to fit in? Are we seeking to prove how normal we are, how law-abiding, how traditional? Are we trying to get God—Father—Daddy—to love us at last? Are we courting the blessing of an authority we don't need, the imprimatur of norms we would do best to be more skeptical of? For those whose spiritual needs are nonnegotiable, my proposal can be taken on a purely pragmatic basis. As with the unquestioning normativity of most arguments for same-sex marriage, we should scrutinize the extent to which designs larger than our own—norms larger than our own limited scope and sometimes inimical to our desire and well-being—drive the argument. Is queer energy that we invest in religious social encounters energy that is misspent or misdirected, that would be more beneficially directed elsewhere? It might appear an impious or reductive joke to say that gay bars and clubs serve as "gay church," but it's not completely off the mark. If bars, bath houses, or tea dances are not themselves capable of fostering similar spaces for contemplation and sociability, for transcendental or erotic exchange—and I would contend they *are* generative in these, if not more, ways—then they point toward and are prolific of spaces in which such practices might be developed, needs met, identities discovered, restored, and ruptured. In making a categorical bid for gay atheism, the questions I offer are essentially these: whose approval are gay Christians seeking? Whose approval do gays and gay Christians need or require? Even if a bid to be loved does not *mean* to include a bid to be fixed—indeed, even though it may expressly *exclude* such an idea—my grievance would be that, intentions aside, the result is the same.

Chapter 4 frames this discussion with an analysis of the "It Gets Better" video campaign initiated by sex columnist Dan Savage in response to a wave of gay teen suicides in September and October 2010. Relevant to this discussion are not only the questions of how to counsel harassed gay teens and combat antigay bullying but also reactions to the suicides by antigay figures such as the Family Research Council's Tony Perkins and Exodus International's Alan Chambers. Following this chapter's outline of the continued, detrimental consequences of religious beliefs to queer life and survival, and the weight those beliefs wield in American public discourse, the conclusion discusses President Obama's own "It Gets Better" video, parsing what it said, as well as what it quite heteronormatively failed to address, about the unabated rancor and legally sanctioned antagonism of American culture toward its queer constituents. Rounding out the argument for the continued necessity for queers to opt out of religion, the conclusion also begins to outline gaytheism's benefits as well as possibilities for forging gay community in ways beyond the poisonously normative reach of religion in institutionalized as well as deinstitutionalized forms.

At the outset it seems desirable to distinguish parts of my analysis that critique conservative Christianity from those that lodge a broader critique of institutional religion in general. It's certainly possible to differentiate moments when my critique targets conservative Christianity from segments of mainstream and liberal Christianity examined in chapters 3 and 4. It's true that chapters 1 and 2 focus on American conservative Christianity's vituperative crusade against gays and lesbians, its obsessive, seemingly constitutive opposition of Christian, heterosexual purity to queer *im*purity and the notion that faith stipulates straight sexual behavior or queer celibacy. But my overall argument runs on a sliding scale from forms of Christianity many readers might easily agree are homophobic, such as conservative Christianity, to incarnations of institutional religion such as mainstream Christian sects and liberal denominations like the Metropolitan Community Church (MCC). It's these latter groups that, while tolerant and/or liberal toward homosexuality, may nonetheless participate in larger, more subtly reactionary cultural narratives—narratives that are, at their base, heteronormative. Central to *Slouching towards Gaytheism* are not just reservations about queer efforts to compromise with conservative Christianity but a critical dissent from queer efforts to inhabit mainstream as well as liberalized forms of institutional religion. Admittedly, the term "conservative Christianity" denotes a definable though internally diverse group. On the other hand, "Christianity" and "religion" naturally refer to gradually wider, much more heterogeneous categories and belief systems. In the first two chapters my focus is mainly on certain organizations and individuals under the aegis of conservative Christianity, and my use there of the term "religion" as an identitarian synonym for conservative Christianity is intentional. For as odd or imprecise as the equation might seem to an outside observer, conservative Christians, including those dedicated to battling the cultural "normalization" of homosexuality, are likely to view their beliefs and actions as embodying the most authentic form of Christianity, a religiosity to which others fail to measure up. Chapters 3 and 4 query the extent to which liberal strains of Christianity and even nonsectarian spirituality might not also be inhibitive of progress on queer issues of equality, inclusion, and thus survival. My demurral from deinstitutionalized as well as institutionalized religion, from liberal as well as conservative forms of Christianity, is pragmatically as well as ideologically motivated. Even if liberal Christians advocate proqueer stances or policies and thus oppose their conservative counterparts on these issues, liberal defenses of religion thwart the attempt to disconnect religion from civil life. Such defenses undermine the ability not just to refute *certain* religious assertions, like the more overt, violent homophobic claims of conservative Christians but to repudiate religious belief as a suitable facet of political debate. Liberal and moderate reclamations of religion muddy the ability to see it for the contaminating adjunct and deforming parameter it is in regard to ethical equity and civil democracy. There is a second and related ideological objection: liberal strains of Christianity as well as nonsectarian styles of spirituality may share or retain some basic structural assumptions of the more reactionary belief systems they have attempted to move beyond—hierarchical, heterocentric assumptions such as the valorization of marriage, monogamy, reproduction, and the opposition of marriage to an implicitly and comparatively impoverished promiscuity.

In chapters 3 and 4, my use of the term "Christianity" to denote conservative, mainstream, and liberal strains and the term "religion" to denote the wider phenomenon is not meant to suggest complete interchangeability. Rather, the intent is to point to their continuity along a graduated scale of relative characteristics shared by religion and Christianity where they diverge as well as where they overlap: not merely a scale running from homophobia to tolerance but a complex range of structural issues that impede, often unintentionally, an authentic, untrammeled commitment to queers free from heteronormativity's hierarchies and normative valuations. For those valuations remain at some level queerphobic. What lurks within institutionalized and deinstitutionalized religion alike is not only ideological homophobia but residual heteronormative biases—a recalcitrance that often has more to do with Western religion's long history than with the intent of individual, modern practitioners, a constitutive, generic resistance that renders not merely conservative Christianity but Christianity and religion in general as innately inhospitable to queer Americans seeking political justice, civil equity, or cultural recognition. My bid is to leave behind the noxious realm of religion and religiously polluted social and political discourse and to insist on a nonreligious ethical system where the concern is with sublunary right action and humane justice rather than salvation and extramundane justice. Because this book is a polemic, its core proposal is that, given the heteronormativity deeply ingrained in so many institutions (including American Christianity in general) and their intellectual and affective structures, queers should demur from religion as a reactionary framework, that they should cease attempts to rehabilitate forms of religion and seek forms of community and ethical sustenance outside religious strictures. My suggestion is sure to discomfit those gays, lesbians, and allies who seek to reconcile institutionalized religion with nonnormative sexuality or who seek a nontoxic space of spirituality. This book's polemic, however, is a reaction to the continued influence of religiously justified homophobic rhetoric on public debate about queers' rights and humanity. As long as religious belief in America is exempted from rational argument, it endangers queer existence.

My demurral in the face of liberal as well as conservative gay Christianity rests on a queer critical suspicion of ideologically laden heteronormative structures. Here, *Slouching towards Gaytheism* follows, in regard to religion, Michael Warner's lead in *The Trouble with Normal*, which questions the gay marriage movement as a largely uncritical embrace of what constitutes a structurally exclusionary institution and what will remain one even after gay and lesbian inclusion. In regard to my own argument, I don't mean to callowly posit that any received or nonce structure can escape *all* ideological trappings. I merely advocate a healthy cognizance of normativity's pernicious compatibility with ostensibly progressive narratives like liberationism, tolerance, self-discovery, and self-authentication. The book's title contains a coinage, "gaytheism," pointing to two possibly but not necessarily overlapping meanings. On the one hand, "gaytheism" gestures toward a belief in gayness or queerness as a sustaining construction, however embedded within or intersected by contrary and conflicting positionalities. On the other hand, the term points to an advocacy for atheism, for disengagement with religious discourse, as a productive way forward for those who find themselves in need of queer communal belonging, who long for a sustaining queer context. My argument is not likely to convince all readers, particularly those who derive emotional sustenance from religion. In most cases, their sustenance may more accurately be said to be humanist or ethical rather than religious in nature. Much more good—and much less harm—would be done by more precise labeling. If these unconvinced readers are queer, or if they are supportive straights and care about the health, lives, and fair treatment of their queer relatives, friends, neighbors, or fellow citizens, I would ask them to consider the following questions, at least for the duration of this book. Might not the needs they find met by religion be met by other ideas, forms of community, and social venues that do not impede our collective social and political progress, that do not harass or malign gay and lesbian Americans? Might the needs currently met by religion be equally met by ethical systems standing apart from the pressure historically exerted by religious institutions, by forms of community and social venues that do not actively oppose gays' and lesbians' *civil* enfranchisement and just treatment under the laws of a secular nation? Christopher Hitchens concedes that the loss or even reevaluation of beliefs one has formerly held to be true or meaningful can initially produce a feeling of irreparable loss. Yet based on his own disenchantment after years of staunch faith in the tenets of Marxism, Hitchens promises, "you will feel better too . . . once you leave hold of the doctrinaire and allow your chainless mind to do its own thinking" (153).

The reasoning behind the frankness of my polemic is that sometimes the strongest form of an argument is necessary, rhetorically as well as practically. If my argument strikes some as tendentious, as insufficiently measured—if I seem to encourage throwing out the spiritual or religious baby with the toxically homophobic conservative Christian bathwater—scaling back my quarrel to the more easily agreed-upon target of conservative Christianity in order to dodge such a reaction would be insincere. The critique of conservative American Christianity's mass of falsehoods, hypocrisies, and excesses in its recent war against homosexuality has been elegantly and convincingly made by others. *Slouching towards Gaytheism* makes the perhaps impolitic yet fair objection that countering the hate speech and refuting the lies of antigay conservative Christians may not be the whole battle, and that the extent to which religion generally is relied on in making political arguments, the degree to which implicitly religious "values" are exempt from debate or criticism in American culture, is an equally urgent, if less conspicuous, obstacle to queer parity and survival. Those who are firm in their political and/or religious opinions have nothing to fear from a critique of homophobic, conservative religion, for such a critique plays, with obvious exceptions, to a relatively wide and receptive audience. But they also have nothing to fear from a critique of religion and spirituality *in general* as an inappropriate, damaging adjunct to queer life or entrée to social equality and cultural inclusion. A clarion call needs to be strong and emphatic when conditions are critical, as they are for queer Americans. Apologists for more tolerant instantiations of religion and spirituality will balk. But the imbrication of religion and politics must be addressed if queers and queer rights are to survive, if this is to be a civil nation. This book is my way of addressing it.

———

Many, though not all, of the cultural and political phenomena discussed previously stem from the summer and fall of 2010, when a cluster of gay teen suicides received prolonged media focus and public attention, precipitating vehement exchanges between progay and antigay audiences. In 2012, the next election year, gay rights and their opponents were again prominently in the national spotlight. More importantly, gay equality more often than not made significant headway. Despite, or maybe because of, that progress, cultural rhetoric related to homosexuality remained mixed, retaining a good deal of religiously driven toxicity. For example, attempted boycotts against two large companies—Starbucks and JCPenney—ended up backfiring, therefore underscoring growing tolerance on gay issues by more American corporations, and revealed net gains not just in recognition of gay and lesbian relationships and families as valid but also in support for attempts to secure gay and lesbian rights, including marriage. By contrast, a boycott of Chick-fil-A spurred, along with widespread criticism of the company, considerable, and perniciously profitable, antigay consumer support, making vexingly palpable the toxic effects of conservative religion's deep, continued entanglement with American politics.

In May 2012 Boston's First Circuit Court of Appeals ruled DOMA unconstitutional. A similar ruling was handed down in July by a U.S. district judge in Hartford, Connecticut, making for a total of six judicial decisions against the federal law. Starbucks was one of forty-eight companies, including Microsoft, Nike, and Time Warner, to file a brief in the Boston case "arguing that the law negatively affected their businesses"—a strong and admirable stand on a "once-risky" issue (Phillip pars. 3, 1). Starbucks had gone further still in January of that year, siding with a bill that proposed legalizing same-sex marriage in the company's home state of Washington. Particularly irksome to right-wing religious and political organizations was Starbucks's assertion in a press release that same-sex marriage is "core to who we are as a company" (qtd. in Garber, "Starbucks Supports" par. 7).[19] Two spokespersons from the National Organization for Marriage (NOM) questioned Starbucks CEO Howard Schultz at a stockholders' meeting, disingenuously posing as stockholders concerned that such a position might negatively impact stock value. Without hedging or faltering for a moment, Schultz reaffirmed his company's embrace of tolerance:

> The senior team of Starbucks discussed this, and it was, to be candid with you, not something that was a difficult decision for us. And we did share this with some members of the Board as well. . . . I don't want to answer the question in a way that would be disrespectful to you or other people who might see it differently. I think Starbucks has many constituents, and from time to time we are going to make a decision that we think is consistent with the heritage and tradition of the company that perhaps may be inconsistent with one's group view of the world. . . . But we made that decision, in our view, through the lens of humanity and being the kind of company that embraces diversity. . . . [And] shareholder value has increased significantly in large part because management has made the right kind of decisions that [are] in the best interest of the entire company. ("Starbucks Shareholders Ask CEO Schultz About Controversial Gay Marriage Stance")

Schultz's subtle phrasing deserves note. Though invoking the concept of respect for beliefs that one disagrees with, he makes no concession to the conservative Christian position that often underwrites homophobic political arguments. He doesn't say "I respect your views" or "I don't disrespect your beliefs"; rather, he says that he doesn't "want to answer . . . in a way that would be disrespectful"—even though, of course, the answer *refuses* to accord respect, much less offer any concession, to a viewpoint it deeply disagrees with on political and ethical grounds. Addressing the NOM interlocutors and their supporters as "people who might see it differently" casts a wide net, contrasting the company's ethically motivated stance with a mere matter of (mis)perception.

Another attempted boycott, this time of department store chain JCPenney in January 2012, centered on criticism of gay-positive ads and media campaigns by a group called One Million Moms (OMM), an arm of the American Family Association (AFA), a conservative Christian and right-wing political advocacy group. Through its AFA-sponsored website as well as through a Facebook page of the same name, One Million Moms, whose name invokes exponentially more supporters than evidenced by its Facebook group, criticized JCPenney for hiring openly lesbian Ellen DeGeneres as its new spokesperson. Claiming that "most of [its] customers are traditional families," OMM called on the retail chain to nix the deal. The threat that "jumping on the pro-gay bandwagon . . . will lose [them] customers with traditional values" is an ideologically pernicious co-optation of tradition, normality, and heterosexuality, all too familiar from its repeated invocations by the Christian Right and the GOP (qtd. in "Ellen DeGeneres' JCPenney Partnership" pars. 3, 4). When the company refused to renege on the deal, OMM called for a boycott by "traditional"-values consumers. Not only did JCPenney refuse to buckle in the face of criticism by OMM's parent organization, the AFA—a group that the Southern Poverty Law Center has classified as a hate group, along with NOM, Americans for the Truth about Homosexuality, Concerned Women for America, the Family Research Council, and the Traditional Values Coalition.[20] The company escalated its commitment to gay consumers by featuring photos, a few months later, of lesbian and gay couples with their children in its Mother's Day and Father's Day catalogs. These were not images that, in the tradition of marketing queer consumers have seen in the past, *could* be read as *sub rosa* messages to gays and lesbians. These photographs were accompanied by copy explicitly identifying the adult models as lesbian or gay couples and parents, under the tag lines "freedom of expression" and "first pals." Claiming "we will not be ignored" (one presumes the camp invocation of Glenn Close's crazed femme fatale from *Fatal Attraction* was unintentional), OMM responded to the ads by accusing the chain of "promoting sin" and asking followers to write "Return to Sender" on their JCPenney catalogs (qtd. in "One Million Moms Condemns" par. 4; qtd. in "'One

Million' Moms Responds" par. 2). Clearly, OMM's equation of so-called "Biblical values [with] truth"—the "truth that homosexuality is wrong"—is not one with which the company concurs. Given a choice between "not tolerat[ing] this sinful nature," as OMM's website put it, and embracing a diverse consumer base on ethical principles rather than prejudice, JC Penney reassuringly chose the latter (qtd. in "'One Million' Moms Responds" par. 3).[21] Despite repeated shrill and homophobic criticism, the chain stood by its ads, as they had the DeGeneres partnership. Threatened right-wing boycotts of both Starbucks and JCPenney failed to materialize in any substantial way or at least showed no signs of impacting either company's profits or public image.

Anecdotally, these corporate refusals to concede ground to homophobic invective even when couched in religious, "family values" rhetoric manifest not only an admirable ethical stand but also a decreasing concern in the business community over the negative PR and profit impact incurred by a brand that brushes aside such rhetoric. After all, even if hollow, such rhetoric can be inflammatory. The queer-friendly marketing of these companies speaks to a confidence in the shifting landscape of public opinion on gay issues. Similarly, the fizzled boycotts indicate that the tide is turning against opponents of same-sex marriage and GLBT rights, that their rhetoric is losing its sting and, consequently, its brawn. However, another corporate-related gay rights controversy that followed on the heels of these two, centering this time around fast-food franchise Chick-fil-A, produced a more ambivalent result, energizing gay marriage opponents as much as its supporters and intimating that Christian-allied antigay rhetoric is far from losing its power to mobilize a significant sector of American consumers and voters even as more Americans are questioning the self-proclaimed purity of that rhetoric's motives.

Chick-fil-A president and chief operating officer Dan Cathy ignited a storm of both criticism and defense with comments he made during an interview with the *Biblical Recorder*'s Allan K. Blume in July 2012. Reprinted on the *Baptist Press* website, the interview, as one might expect from the venue, showcased the "biblical principles" on which the business runs (Blume par. 7). Other than the obvious signs—the strict Sabbath observance of being closed on Sundays imposed by company founder S. Truett Cathy in 1946 and retained by his son despite changing times—Cathy asserts that "Christians are missionaries in the workplace," and so "'our performance in the workplace should be the focus of how we build respect, rapport, and relationships with others that opens the gateway to interest in people knowing God'" (par. 9). Apparently, a chicken sandwich and waffle fries instills a yearning for old-time religion; rather than direct proselytism, Cathy is talking about "'being evangelistic in the *quality* of work you do'" (par. 10; emphasis added). This assertion is doubly disingenuous, of course. For one, Cathy's ambassadorship for the Lord hawking high-calorie eats happens to yield a neat profit—though this is hardly out of line with the prosperity gospel dear to more conservative Christian evangelists. Second, Cathy's interview evangelizes more directly and potently than his daily business activities, for the intent and possible reach of an interview in such a venue is not to proselytize unsaved souls but to spread a gospel of religiously fueled homophobia to an already saved audience, to cement and further inflame antigay feeling and opposition to gay rights initiatives among Christian heterosexuals.

The portion of the interview that makes this intent clear, and that garnered national attention well beyond its original readership, comes at the end of Blume's interview with Cathy for the *Biblical Recorder*. "Some have opposed the company's support of the traditional family," Blume notes:

> "Well, guilty as charged," said Cathy when asked about the company's position.
> "We are very much supportive of the family—the biblical definition of the family unit. We are a family-owned business, a family-led business. . . ."
> . . . "We intend to stay the course," he said. "We know that it might not be popular with everyone, but thank the Lord, we live in a country where we can share our values and operate on biblical principles." (pars. 27–28, 30)

Although a far-right media outlet like the *Washington Times* might attempt to discredit gay and gay-friendly critics by claiming Cathy never explicitly mentioned same-sex marriage, such a defense would be mendacious—or rather, correct only on the level of child-like semantics. Denouncing homosexuality is precisely the intent of barely coded rhetoric like "the biblical definition of the family unit," one of the religious and political right's go-to slogans in their fight against gay rights. Cathy responded to the initial round of criticism by strengthening the religious tone of his remarks and clarifying their antigay intent during an appearance on *The Ken Coleman Show*, broadcast by WDUN in Gainesville, Georgia: "I think we are inviting God's judgment on our nation when we shake our fist at Him and say 'we know better than you as to what constitutes a marriage' and I pray God's mercy on our generation that has such a prideful, arrogant attitude to think that we have the audacity to define what marriage is about" (qtd. in Hooper, "With Latest Comments" par. 2).[22] Following Cathy's comments and the ensuing reactions from both sides via print, television, internet, and social media, the debate's scope and volume accelerated with the call for a Chick-fil-A "Appreciation Day" spearheaded by Mike Huckabee, former Republican Arkansas governor, GOP presidential runner-up in the 2008 primaries, Baptist minister, and FOX talk show host. Held on August 1, 2012, the event—which sported a disarmingly sunny title for an event explicitly opposing gay and lesbian civil rights—generated unspecified but, according to the company, record profits in a single day as family-values, antigay customers thronged to their local Chick-fil-A. During a FOX News interview two days later, Republican presidential hopeful Herman Cain, who had terminated his own campaign several months earlier after persistent allegations of sexual harassment, claimed that the one-day event generated sales "in excess of $30 million" (Badash, "Herman Cain" par. 2). Whatever the financial bottom line, media footage showed long lines and massive crowds at franchises across the country. In response, a few days later numerous gays, lesbians, and allies organized a "kiss-in," a playful, if somewhat less concretely effective, counterevent that harkened back to the 1990s when queer activists initiated "zaps" in public spaces—political direct actions like ACT UP's "die-ins" and Queer Nation's "kiss-ins" that protested the expense of HIV medication, demanded prompter approval of new treatments, and challenged the normativity privileging heterosexual public displays of affection.

Media coverage of the interview and the ensuing controversy bandied about the notion of hampering Cathy's right to free speech, as if gay and gay-friendly critics disputed Chick-fil-A's, or any company's, right to hold or espouse specific beliefs. Yet as more perceptive evaluations by Ryan Ebersole, Lucas Grindley, and Zinnia Jones noted, what galled so many gays, lesbians, and allies was the company's record of having donated a total of $5 million to antigay religious and political organizations such as the Family Research Council, Focus on the

Family, and Exodus International. These three groups, among others, actively seek to block or reverse gay rights legislation and lobby politicians to pass antigay legislative measures. All three have been classified as hate groups by the Southern Poverty Law Center for disseminating "falsehoods" about homosexuality (that it leads to pedophilia and disease but can be cured with prayer) and seeking to influence public opinion as well as governmental policy. Funding such groups is doing more than claiming one's right to free speech. Many would accept that Cathy is well within his rights in directing his own WinShape Foundation, which funds college scholarships, Christian marriage counseling programs, and international ministries with Chick-fil-A profits. But funding an organization like Exodus doesn't merely oppress gays or spread hatred; it advocates murder.[23]

Exodus International, the high-profile ex-gay ministry to which Cathy donated heavily, has provided financial and political backing for a proposed law in Uganda popularly known as the "Kill the Gays" bill. This bill would reclassify homosexuality—which is already punished in that country, as in much of Africa, by life imprisonment—as a capital offense. When the controversial measure came to the attention of the American government, Exodus lobbied Congress *not* to pass a resolution condemning the bill. While Cathy was hardly the only supporter of the law or the sole donor to the Ugandan and American campaigns for its passage, it's undeniable—and instructive for my argument—that the initiative originated among American evangelicals: specifically, Scott Lively, president of Abiding Truth Ministries; Caleb Lee Brundidge, an ex-gay counselor of gay men seeking to go straight; and Don Schmierer, Exodus International board member. Beginning as early as 2002 but augmenting their efforts after a Ugandan High Court ruling asserting that gays and lesbians merited equal legal protection, the three held a 2009 workshop in the country's capital on the so-called evils of homosexuality. By touting the usual laundry list of homosexuality's supposed dangers, including predation, pedophilia, sexual compulsion, and disease, they drummed up enough support among legislators to have the bill introduced in the national parliament within eight months. During a PR campaign in support of the law, a Ugandan newspaper ran a story in October 2010 headlined "Hang Them: They Are After Our Kids!" along with a picture of Ugandan gay activist David Kato. Kato's murder by stabbing four months later, while viewed by many as a media-incited hate crime, was dismissed by Lively as the result of a dispute with a male prostitute over money. It's some comfort, at least, that Ugandan authorities saw it differently, sentencing Kato's killer to thirty years in prison. Meanwhile, international criticism from human rights watch groups, governments, and churches stalled the bill's progress and led to at least one Ugandan official promising to drop the capital punishment clause—a concession later denied by the sponsoring MP. I do not mean to minimize widespread opposition to the bill among political officials and religious leaders. Their demonstration of antihomophobia, decency, and ethical integrity are heartening in the face of virulent homophobia and the Christian Right's preying on prejudice and religious fear through the abuse of spiritual authority and basic logic.[24] My point is simply that, although religion is not *always* incompatible with tolerance, ethics, or justice, it has historically, perhaps inherently, been intolerant, compositionally heteronormative, and generative of emotional and physical violence toward queers. Religion seems particularly adept at fueling belief-based hate, thereby rendering it an unsuitable component of civil debate and queer life. The "Kill the Gays" bill elucidates the magnitude of homophobic Christians' thirst for gay blood and the lengths to which religiously fueled hatred can drive individuals, sects, even an entire country. Barred from slaking their thirst for gay blood in the United States, Lively and the brigades of American evangelicals who supported him, which includes major donors like Dan Cathy, went all the way to Africa to do so.[25]

The controversy surrounding Chick-fil-A's financial support of groups advocating or funding antigay legislative efforts produced *some* heartening results. Widespread attention to Chick-Fil-A's antigay stance and the hatemongering, sometimes life-threatening efforts of groups like Exodus and the FRC ended up provoking heightened support for gay rights. Among many activists, business leaders, politicians, journalists, and ordinary citizens, the support entailed more than a backlash against a single company; it augured a repudiation of discrimination masquerading as religious freedom. The Jim Henson Company, having made a previous merchandising agreement with Chick-fil-A, "end[ed] its business relationship . . . over the restaurant chain's public stance against gay marriage. . . . [According to] an announcement on Facebook, Jim Henson company CEO Lisa Henson . . . 'is personally a strong supporter of gay marriage and has directed [her company] to donate the payment we received from Chick-fil-A to GLAAD,'" the

Gay and Lesbian Alliance Against Defamation (Pfeiffer pars. 1–2). Mayors in Boston, Chicago, and San Francisco "put Cathy on notice that his company was not welcome in their cities" (Howell par. 8). More explicitly, Chicago alderman Joe Moreno went so far as vowing to "block the company from building a restaurant in his ward. . . . Unless [it] comes up with a written anti-discrimination policy, Chick-fil-A will not open its first free-standing restaurant in the city as it plans to do" (Babwin pars. 1-2). Even though these officials were forced to "quickly . . . backpedal" when it became clear that the bans had no legal standing, their unalloyed rebuke of discrimination can be nevertheless appreciated (Howell par. 9). At the same time, the Chick-fil-A incident had one disheartening short-term result: the Appreciation Day yielded that much *more* profit for Cathy and, consequently, more sizeable donations to his favorite antigay organizations.

Like previous years, then, 2012 was a year of conflicting indications regarding the prospects for advancing tolerance or securing gay and lesbian rights. To some observers, however, the tone might have seemed shriller, the tenor more menacing. In April "[v]irulently antigay North Carolina preacher Sean Harris . . . told his congregation to attack young boys who act effeminate" (Broverman, "Hateful Pastor" par. 1). Delivering a sermon encouraging congregants to vote for Amendment One, a proposed, ultimately successful state constitutional amendment banning gay marriage, Harris

> deride[d] parents who don't "squash like a cockroach" the gay out of their children. . . .
>   . . . [I]f their four-year old boy, for example, "starts acting a little 'girlish'" . . . [he] added that parents should tell their four-year olds to "man up, son, get that dress off you [,] get outside and dig a ditch because that's what boys do."
>   "Can I make it any clearer? Dads, the second you see that son dropping the limp wrist, you walk over there and crack that wrist. Give them a good punch. OK? You're not going to act like that—you were made by God to be male and you're going to be a male." (Badash, "Beat the Gay Out of Kids Pastor Apology" pars. 3-4)

A thinking person has to assume that Harris, as homophobes so often do, has drawn a reductively crude correspondence between effeminacy and male homosexuality; thus "you were made . . . male" means "you were made heterosexual." The *trans*phobia as well as homophobia of Harris's encouragement of child abuse and gay bashing is made still *more* disturbing by its deplorable abuse of religious authority to encourage such actions.[26] Although Harris was merely *advocating* gay bashing, the incident was reminiscent of several months earlier, in October 2011, when the pastor at Grace Fellowship Church in Fruitland, Tennessee, "instruct[ed] deacons and members of his congregation to physically attack a [gay] couple arriving in the church parking lot" (Gilbert par. 2). While the coincidence of the town's name may be risible—had living in "Fruitland" made these gay bashers overly sensitive?—the incident was certainly not funny, nor was the fact that one of the two men attacked "happened to be the *Pastor's own son*, Jerry Pittman, Jr." (par. 3; emphasis added). In Jerry's words, after his father yelled "SICK 'EM!" his "uncle and two other deacons came over to the car. . . . My uncle smashed me in the door as the other deacon knocked my boyfriend back . . . punching him in his face and his chest. The other deacon . . . hit me through my car window in my back" (qtd. in Gilbert pars. 4–5). Both episodes suggest with vicious irony that the conservative Christian injunction to "pray the gay away" apparently requires the supplement of physical violence.

Drawing attention to incidents like these is not meant to deny other, much more positive developments regarding gay equality in the same period. Gay rights have recently made great strides and have found wider support in overcoming previous legal and social hurdles. In addition to Maine, Maryland, and Washington's joining, in 2012, the list of states where gay marriage is legal, early in 2013 similar bills were put forward in Rhode Island, Delaware, and Illinois, passing in the first two but failing to receive a vote in the third in that year's legislative session. New Jersey's legislature approved a similar measure, but Governor Chris Christie vetoed it. And Freedom to Marry sought a 2013 referendum to overturn Ohio's gay marriage ban. The Maine vote was especially significant for its revisiting and reversal of a 2009 referendum *banning* gay marriage, a referendum that itself had overturned the state's approval of gay marriage earlier that year. During the 2012 election Minnesotans cleared the way for a bill legalizing gay marriage to take effect in 2013 by voting down a proposed constitutional ban. On the federal level, Vice President Joe Biden and President Obama made separate statements in favor of same-sex marriage, and the

Democratic National Committee unanimously approved an endorsement of gay marriage in its platform for the 2012 national convention. The 2012 election, in which Obama sought reelection against Republican challenger Mitt Romney, presented Americans with a stark differentiation between Democrats and Republicans on numerous issues; on the question of gay equality, however, voters were confronted with a clear difference between the parties *for the first time*. The steps toward gay equality leading up to the election were cemented by Obama's resounding victory. The GOP's retrograde mentality—epitomized by but hardly limited to its "war on women," its resistance to gay rights, or its hostile take on immigration—faced an emphatic repudiation in the president's reelection. Although right-wing religious and political organizations have hardly folded their tents, gay and lesbian Americans can take some pleasure in the chagrin of those like James Dobson. Dobson, an evangelist and founder of two powerful conservative lobbying groups, Focus on the Family and the Family Research Council, wrote in January 2013 that he felt "discouraged in the aftermath of the National Elections, especially in view of the moral and spiritual issues that took such a beating on November 6th. Nearly everything I have stood for these past 35 years went down to defeat" (qtd. in Steveningen par. 2).

The announcement in June 2013 that Exodus International would close its doors seemed to confirm Dobson's fears, although this development hardly guaranteed the cessation of the ex-gay movement. The apology Exodus president Alan Chambers issued for any harm he might have caused to "people in the LGBTQ community who have been hurt by the Church, Exodus International, and me" was undercut by the fact that Exodus was dissolving merely to *re*-form as the Restored Hope Network—an attempt more to dodge the negative publicity accrued by Exodus than to sincerely make amends (Chambers par. 6). More thoroughgoing signs that the far Right's political quest to block gay rights may inevitably be doomed came just two days after the Exodus announcement with the U.S. Supreme Court's verdicts in the Proposition 8 and DOMA cases. The justices allowed the California supreme court's repeal of Prop 8 to stand, thus rendering gay marriage once again legal in that state. Regarding DOMA, SCOTUS invalidated *part* of the federal law, extending federal recognition and thus federal benefits to same-sex marriages performed in states where such marriages are legal. The decision stopped short, however, of compelling states with laws *against* gay marriage to recognize licenses from other states. While the decision seemed a half-victory to some observers—by leaving DOMA's exception to the full faith and credit clause intact—it quickly became clear that the same decision prepared the ground for legalizing gay marriage *nationally* before long, and cases arguing to overturn state bans on gay marriage were almost immediately filed in state federal courts in Arkansas, Nevada, North Carolina, Ohio, Pennsylvania, Utah, Virginia, and elsewhere. SCOTUS and California's supreme court both rejected nonsensical requests, made by Prop 8 proponents immediately after the verdict against them, to halt the distribution of same-sex marriage licenses in California until they could lodge another appeal. Most tellingly of all, perhaps, was the announcement, shortly after the SCOTUS verdicts, that the U.S. House of Representatives—which had spent $2.3 million dollars defending DOMA at the federal level—would not move to defend any remaining mini-DOMAs (state laws or constitutional bans on gay marriage).

Encouraging developments aside, however, queer Americans continue to be the target of verbal abuse, physical violence, and legal discrimination from many quarters. Whether personal or legislative, these attacks are almost always clothed in the garb of *religious belief.* Granted, the originators of such attacks are often conservative Christians, or they access the language of religious conservatism. Though many moderate and liberal religious Americans may not be persuaded or mobilized, others *may* be. At the very least, queer Americans' lives—and, one might add, American lives generally—would be made no *worse*, no *less* safer, no *less* equal under the law if queers and allies excised religious rhetoric, reasoning, and appeals from their appeals for equity, if they refused to engage with liberal religious rhetoric in a typically futile attempt to refute conservative points or redeem spiritual identity structures, if they protested the acceptability of religious discourse in debates on queer public policy. Some will refuse to entertain, much less follow, this suggestion. Nonetheless: given the rancor, crisis, and ideological stalemate into which religious debates on gay rights have led us, queer lives cannot be much diminished by leaving religion and the yen for religious belonging behind, by steering away from unwinnable disputes under systems that, like religion and spirituality, embrace norms hostile to gay insights, that intrinsically refuse to engage with reason. On the contrary, queers have much to gain by steering toward a non-sectarian ethical counterpublic that appeals to logic, where the *terminus ad quem* is humane treatment in the here and now, not the awarding or denying of points on some otherworldly scoreboard.

ONE

"THE END OF THE RAINBOW, MY POT OF GOLD"

The Queer Erotics of Purity Balls and Christian Abstinence Culture

A s a gay man who has managed to skirt most of the weddings he's been invited to—a boycott against not just marriage's legal and political exclusion of queers but the economic inequities embodied and maintained by the purchase of wedding gifts—I was initially surprised to discover the extent of father-daughter fetishizing in and beyond the world of purity balls. Of course, I had little reason to be surprised. Certain reactionary heteronormative ideals are hypostatized in any wedding ceremony, though perhaps in religious ceremonies more so than in civil ones. The father giving away the bride, the father-daughter dance, and the now less common tradition of the bride's family paying for the wedding (a modern version of the dowry)—all these features underscore the transition of a woman from her parents' household to her own. To put it less nicely, what's being enacted is the handing off of the bride, an exchange of the bride-as-property between two men—the father and the groom.[1] This late in the day, such observations are far from newsworthy. In the essays "Thinking Sex" (1984) and "The Traffic in Women" (1975), Gayle Rubin radicalized Claude Lévi-Strauss's work on women's historic status as property. Influenced by Rubin's work, innumerable historians, social scientists, and feminist, Marx-ist, and queer critics have mapped out these and corollary ideas. This chapter examines how the purity ball sexualizes the father-daughter "couple," already a particular aspect of mainstream heterosexual mar-riage culture, and turns that pairing into the linchpin of conservative Christian marriage subculture. It also analyzes how the disproportion-ate cultural burden placed on this relationship produces a claustral, incongruous marriage of giddy eroticism and ascetic zealotry. Having examined father-daughter purity balls, this chapter turns next to what appears to be a blind spot in such ceremonies but is amply addressed by Christian purity literature: the purity movement as it targets young men. Specifically, I discuss how Stephen Arterburn and Fred Stoek-er's *Every Young Man's Battle: Strategies for Victory in the Real World of Sexual Temptation* (2002), one of the more popular Christian purity advice manuals for young men, tries to corral male sexuality and how the forces it summons to accomplish that end—(homo)phobia and (homo)eroticism—alternately enforce and problematize that project.[2]

As merely one of the numerous Christian purity manuals published over the past decade or so, *Every Young Man's Battle* is one book in a series created by Arterburn, founder of New Life Ministries (formerly New Life Treatment Centers) and host of the radio show *New Life Live*. The spate of companion volumes by Arterburn, Stoeker, and their purity-shepherding surrogates include *Every Man's Battle: Winning the War on Sexual Temptation One Victory at a Time* and *Every Man's Mar-riage: An Every Man's Guide to Winning the Heart of a Woman*, both by Arterburn and Stoeker; *Every Heart Restored: A Woman's Guide to Healing in the Wake of a Husband's Sexual Sin*, by Stoeker and his wife Brenda; *Every Young Man, God's Man: Confident, Courageous, and Completely His* and *Every Day for Every Man: 365 Readings for Those Engaged in the Battle*, both by Arterburn and Kenny Luck; *Every Woman's Battle: Discovering God's Plan for Sexual and Emotional Fulfill-ment*, by Shannon Ethridge; and *Every Young Woman's Battle: Guarding Your Mind, Heart, and Body in a Sex-Saturated World*, by Ethridge and Arterburn. Many of these titles come with companion workbooks and guides for talking to one's children about sexual purity. For use as a lens to investigate Christian purity culture as it might be experienced by gay men, *Every Young Man's Battle* seems optimal for a number of reasons: while a significant majority of purity manuals address a young female audience, *Every Young Man's Battle* is exemplary of those that target young men. Another factor is the mini-empire Arterburn has managed to build over the past twenty-two years, geared toward issues of sexual purity and fidelity for an evangelical constituency. In addition to offering workshops based on the *Battle* series, New Life Ministries oversees a network of 840 counselors nationwide, runs Christian drug and alcohol rehab programs and treatment centers for women and girls with eating disorders, and hosts conferences annually drawing attendees in the hundreds of thousands. Finally, Arterburn's series seems best to represent the religious content, ideological underpinnings, risible techniques, and—most importantly—the queer erotics that are my focus. By "queer erotics" I mean the unintentional eroticism of purity subculture, impulses both beyond its control and of its own creation that seem to undermine the declared ends of Christian purity culture and create spaces for queer desires (in the sense of gay and more generally nonnormative) to inhabit, stow away, burgeon, and perhaps obstruct hegemonic regimes of identity, desire, and personhood.

—

Composed in 1949 by Bobby Burke with lyrics by Horace Gerlach, the song "Daddy's Little Girl" was repeatedly recorded by various groups and artists throughout the 1950s and 1960s. After the Mills Brothers' initial recording in 1950, Al Martino's 1967 version proved the most popular, reaching #2 on the Billboard Adult Contemporary Chart. Michael Bolton released his own version as recently as 2005. A success in its own right, the song's longevity has been enhanced through its popularity as a song for the father-and-bride dance at wedding receptions. What makes the song and its association with this staple of heterosexual culture more disquieting is the barely veiled subtext of its lyrics. Even if mainstream wedding ceremonies do not feature the bride's father handing over a purity ring to the groom as proof of her virginity, any reception at which the bride and her father dance to "Daddy's Little Girl" says, or implies, much the same thing. The song's lyrics offer much for analysis, especially from the vantages of Marxist, feminist, and queer theory. The first line makes explicit how concerns typical of these perspectives are yoked together in this moment: "You're the end of the rainbow, my pot of gold, / You're daddy's little girl to have and hold." However one might describe conventional parent-child intimacy—as supportive, pedagogical, protective—here it becomes claustrophobic, infantilizing, and sexualized. By mirroring the marriage vows between bride and groom, the phrase "to have and to hold" suggests that the bride has been married to her father till now. Referring to a daughter as "the end of the rainbow" both installs a frankly oedipalized heterosexuality as the cultural telos and locates that telos safely beyond the reach of homosexuality. The line also exposes heterosexuality's simultaneously acquisitive and solipsistic nature, its drive for extension and replication. Further, the overdetermined desire for the bride, sexualized cynosure of both father and groom, daddy and darling, lends itself to a genocidal reading of the "*end* of the rainbow." The fantasy embedded here of the symbolic erasure or actual destruction of gays and lesbians is what Eve Sedgwick describes as "the phobic . . . trajectory toward imagining a time *after the homosexual*," "the hygienic Western fantasy of a world without any more homosexuals in it" (128, 127). Calling a daughter her father's "pot of gold" and "a precious gem" underscores the centrality of marriage to capitalism and recalls the cross-cultural misogynist tradition by which women's virginity possesses cultural and monetary value, even if such value accrues to her father and subsequently her husband rather than to herself. Furthermore, the song associates daughters with two American holidays that are at once Christian and capitalist ("you're the spirit of Christmas," "the Easter bunny to mommy and me")—Christmas and Easter being occasions marked as much as by shopping and chocolate consumption as by rituals commemorating the birth and resurrection of Christ.

By comparison, the rituals enacted in purity balls state overtly the same core ideas, literalizing the commitment to virginity for the most part only symbolized in mainstream weddings by the white wedding dress. Cementing a conservative arc for female life, the purity ball amalgamates structural elements of proms with those of weddings. Nancy Gibbs, writing for *Time* in 2008, describes one such event held by Randy and Lisa Wilson in Colorado Springs and attended by father-daughter "couples" with the daughters "rang[ing] in age from college down to . . . 4-year[s]-old" (par. 1). "Kneeling beneath raised swords" meant to symbolize the father's pledge to protect his daughter's chastity, the girl vows to abstain from premarital sex and accepts a purity ring representing this pledge. This is the same ring that her father will take off and hand to her groom at her wedding, crudely literalizing the "traffic in women." The fathers recite a promise "'before

God to cover my daughter as her authority and protection in the areas of purity,' to practice fidelity, shun pornography and walk with honor through a 'culture of chaos' and by doing so guide their daughters as well" (par. 5). Though written in 1998 at the height of the Clinton-Lewinsky scandal, the vows remain relevant for the Wilsons as well as for others, like Stephen Arterburn, who view mainstream culture as a morass of pornography and permissiveness that potentially threatens all youth and all marriages. Along with the obvious phallicism of the raised sword, such ceremonies typically include a "21st century version of a chastity belt": the girls receive a locket, and their fathers get the key to that locket (Gibbs and Johnson par. 3). Next to the wedding-like vows, the purity ball's prom-inspired elements may seem comparatively harmless. Father-daughter dances have existed for quite some time as an element of wedding receptions and as middle school social activities. Yet whether the Wilsons' innovation has been to introduce a chastity pledge into such events or, rather, to make explicit a subtext that had long been lurking there, father-daughter dances become irredeemably creepy when promises surrounding the integrity of a girl's hymen are involved.

According to Gibbs, purity balls are a growing phenomenon: "The Abstinence Clearinghouse estimates there were more than 4,000 purity events across the country [in 2007], with programs aimed at boys now growing even faster" (par. 6).[3] Purity balls focus almost exclusively on young women, their fathers, and an atavistic estimation for virginity.[4] Comparable events for young men and boys are less common but usually involve a pledge to help young women remain pure by not pressuring them to have sex. This is scarcely the same promise female attendees are making. An industry that *does* focus on both male and female teenagers, if still not quite equally, is the abstinence movement, a necessary apparatus for keeping the ideal of purity within reach. First federally funded in 1999 under President Clinton, abstinence-only programming received increased spending under George W. Bush. After an initial budget of $50 million under Clinton in 1999, President Bush sought to award these programs over five times as much in 2005, or $270 million, an amount Congress cut back to $168 million. This brought the running total of expenditures to $900 million in five years. At the same time, abstinence initiatives have met some roadblocks despite support from political and evangelical conservatives. Early on, three states turned down the funds because of the strings attached: not discussing safe sex or homosexuality.[5] By 2008 more than half the states refused federal funds. The same period saw a cycle of actual or attempted cuts and increases. Although the federal budget reduced abstinence education funding by $14.2 million in 2009, a measure in the House proposed restoring $50 million to such programs the following year. President Obama's 2011 budget proposed eliminating abstinence-only educational spending and redirecting it to "a pregnancy-prevention initiative [to] finance programs that have been shown in scientific studies to be effective"—the implication being that abstinence-only programs, despite protests from abstinence advocates who cite their own favored studies, have not been scientifically proven to be effective (Lewin par. 6).[6]

The moment of abstinence education's greatest public prominence, however, may have been the congressional reports and hearings in 2004 and 2008 unmasking the wealth of misinformation and bald-faced lies that such programs presented to children and teenagers as facts.[7] Some of the more outlandish mistruths revealed in the 2004 report by Rep. Henry A. Waxman (D-CA) were that "HIV . . . can be spread via sweat or tears," that "condoms fail to prevent HIV transmission as often as 31 percent of the time," that "abortion can lead to sterility and suicide," and that "half the gay male teenagers in the United States have already tested positive for the AIDS virus" (Connolly pars. 6, 1). These falsehoods aim to scare gay, protogay, and curious children and teens away from same-sex bodies, terrifying them into remaining in the erotic, psychological, and social closet. Eleven out of thirteen abstinence programs investigated grossly inflated condom failure rates and mentioned gay sex solely as a surefire path to HIV infection. The lies were thus homophobic and increased the likelihood that, when abstinent teens eventually did have sex, it would inevitably be unsafe. More striking than the six years and repeated debunkings it took to curtail federal funding of such manifest nonsense is the way abstinence-only curricula marginalize gay sexuality by discouraging condom use and the discussion of safer sex practices. As Abbie Kopf writes on *Change.org*, the abstinence-only mantra of no sex before marriage ignores the fact that "some youth are not allowed to get married. For adolescent gays, these sex-ed classes aren't only a complete waste of time but a tacit acknowledgment that gay relationships aren't valid or acceptable. . . . [T]he ACLU reports that most [programs] 'address same-sex behavior only within the context of promiscuity and disease.' In fact, some curricula go as far as to say that HIV and AIDS are simply the results of the (sinful and dirty!) homosexual 'lifestyle'" (par. 3). While certainly guilty of misleading teens in general, abstinence-only classes enact the erasure of queer teens in particular.[8] This erasure goes deeper, however, than repression; as this chapter suggests, purity culture may also have, despite itself, protective or generative repercussions that shield queers in ways at ideological odds with the official homophobic, heteronormative project.

Purity culture easily embraces abstinence education, invisible or pathologized queers, and quasi-romantic father-daughter coupling. Pledging to purity may backfire in any number of ways, of course. Straight teens coddled in the purity movement may lapse, have sex, get pregnant, or contract sexually transmitted diseases including HIV. Purity culture thus *needs* compulsive masturbating straights and oversexed, disease-ridden fags as much as, if not more than, it needs abstinence education for its catalyst and propulsive nucleus. Yet to pin these fixations on conservatives alone is unfair; they saturate the culture at large. What abstinence programs and queer exclusion do, and what the purity ball crystallizes in the fetish of the daddy-daughter "couple," is subtend and nourish that cynosure of heteronormative culture across the political and religious spectrum: the married couple. The religious Right's notable addition has been to position fathers as *sexual* guardians. Theirs is not a generic, prefeminist model of fathers shielding their daughters from young male libidos but a frantic eroticizing of the father-daughter relationship, placing filial affection and eroticism in such close proximity. When filial eroticism threatens to become a substitute for parent-child affection, the fervor of embattled fundamentalism, fueled by McCarthy-era gender roles, creates a volatile mixture of puritanical zeal and patriarchal consolidation. The ultimate and most tragic victims are not simply the daughters and the fathers but the sons and mothers, as well as young gays and lesbians, who have been excluded from the picture. All are held in thrall to the wounding agenda of purity and abstinence culture, although it is difficult to know whether they will ultimately be more damaged by the mandated, misdirected erotic energies or by the dehumanizing interdiction of the elemental, healthy human desire for sex. Here, abstinence culture exemplifies Tim Dean's assertion that "purity may be considered as an

enemy of the intellect" (5). "Sexual adventurousness," Dean continues, "gives birth to other forms of adventurousness—political, cultural,
intellectual," and it's precisely this sort of adventurousness, autonomy,
and self-nourishment that the stifling parameters of purity balls and
abstinence education seem designed to extinguish (5).[9]

If purity balls focus on controlling female sexuality, purity culture
seeks to co-opt human sexuality as a whole. The tactics for corralling
young *male* sexuality in particular, however, fail to erase straight or gay
eroticism entirely and tend to engage both in surprisingly visceral ways.
One of the more popular male abstinence guides is Stephen Arterburn
and Fred Stoeker's *Every Young Man's Battle: Strategies for Victory in
the Real World of Sexual Temptation* (2002). With his wife Shannon
Etheridge, Arterburn has spawned an entire line of books for young
and adult men and women along with workbooks for church group
discussion. Before turning to how Arterburn and Stoeker address
homosexuality, it's worth noting some of the rhetoric used in counseling male teens on purity. While enraging, ridiculous, and infuriatingly
backward to anyone with a marginally realistic attitude toward sex,
Arterburn and Stoeker's advice seems counterproductively erotic in
both content and style. Although it would be next to impossible for
Every Young Man's Battle to extol sexual purity *without* talking about
sex, one is likely to be surprised at just *how much* sex gets talked about.
Erotic accounts of spirituality are nothing new; think Donne's Holy
Sonnet XIV, "Batter My Heart, Three Person'd God," Edward Taylor's
Preparatory Meditations, or the vision of St. Teresa of Ávila immor-
talized in marble by Gian Lorenzo Bernini. Yet when sex migrates
from metaphor to sweaty, throbbing reality as it has for present-day
abstinence advocates, the relationship between eros and spirituality,
between body and mind, appears radically less stable. The technolo-
gies of mediation and management *Battle* assembles in its fight against
sexual desire are calculated to extinguish human happiness and fulfill-
ment under any auspices other than church and spouse, the prescribed
outlets of proper social interaction and sexual pleasure. More striking,
and more relevant to my project, is *Battle's* attempt, on the one hand, to
corral all sex that is not vaginal-insertive, heterosexual intercourse with
an opposite-sex spouse and, on the other hand, its sexualizing of God,
spirituality, and purity itself. Even though much of the time Arterburn
and Stoeker seem to target a putatively straight male audience, their

ideal for heterosexuality both obliquely and directly invokes a world that gay teens—or anyone with a less than truncated view of sexuality—are likely to find inhospitable.

There are both practical as well as ideological reasons for *Battle's* attempt to enclose human sexuality rather than exclude it. Practically speaking, young men are naturally sexual (read: sinful) beings, so it would be unrealistic to act as if sex and sexual desire can be escaped altogether. The ideological motivation, which also turns out to also be a practical one, is institutional sustenance. If either abstinence education or the conservative church is to survive, it requires an enemy. In addressing young men, *Battle* portrays sex as a monster that must be tamed early, lest one carry adolescence's enslaving habits of masturbation and lustful fantasy over into the sanitary preserve of married adulthood.

One of the chief weapons in *Battle's* arsenal against "sexual bondage" (38)—a phrase the authors use without apparent irony—is deflating the raging male libido by "starving" it of stimuli (143). "Bouncing the eyes," or looking away from arousing sights, supposedly deprives the male libido of the excess excitement that leads to impure thoughts and impure actions, to fantasy and pre- or extramarital sex (145). Arterburn and Stoeker's examples of what their young male audience is likely to find stimulating reveal a somewhat dated sensibility. A man's eyes, they write, are

> ravenous heat-seekers searching the horizon, locking on any target with sensual heat [such as:] Young mothers in shorts, leaning over to pull children out of car seats . . . Foxy babes wearing tank tops . . . reveal[ing] skimpy bras . . . Joggers in spandex, jiggling merrily down the sidewalk . . . [and] Smiling secretaries in low-cut blouses . . . (42)

Even if Arterburn and Stoeker, the authors of this passage, are writing about their own erotic touchstones, the references seem a bit mature for a teenage audience. As a telling miscalculation, this failure to connect with the audience is indicative of other tensions within the abstinence project. Averting teenage eyes is meant to starve the male libido of visual stimulation's "sexual chemical highs" (63). In yet another inadvertent nod to the unexamined Freudian underpinnings of their own (dis)engagement with sexuality, Arterburn and Stoeker imply that "kill[ing] every hint of immorality" effectively requires blinding oneself, like a Christianized Oedipus (53).

As a substitute or perhaps a consolation for proscribed sexual contact with other people, *Battle* consciously eroticizes the relationship with God. Reflecting on his own struggle with impurity, Stoeker declares that "in order to get closer to Him, I had to be not so close to the women in my life" (20). If it remains unclear how to resolve this apparent conflict *after* marriage, Arterburn and Stoeker present sexual impurity, which creates "distance from God," to their teen audience as antithetical to "intimacy with God" (109, 169). As one girl confesses to her youth pastor, "'I'm really in love with Jesus, but I have to admit that sexual temptation is still a struggle for me with my boyfriend" (48). Remarkably, the language employed by *Battle* to describe a relationship with God partakes of the lustful or erotic: "I'd ignored [God's] voice repeatedly as He prodded me in these areas" (43). That an erotic reading of such a line might feel strained is entirely to the point and lends weight precisely to that kind of reading. The somatic intensity of the abstinence movement, its fervid clasp of the body, guarantees that a determination to repudiate the pleasures of the body, to suppress much of what is *bodily* about our bodies, is accompanied by a vigilance for lustful eruptions and excretions. Even when *Battle* does not speak directly about sex, sexuality courses throughout the text. This is not a simple return of the repressed, since sex, here, has not been repressed. To the contrary, it has been enshrined—demonized, yes, but barely contained. If the demon of lust, the beast that pulses within our loins, were not liable at any moment to break out, to overtake and destroy us, the conservative Christian abstinence movement would lack an essential engine or at least would have to discover some other fuel. One particular phrase *Battle* uses more than once to describe the cost of sexual impurity is viscerally sexual: "God is aching for you to be one with Him"; "God is aching for you to be one with Him, that He might use you. He wants to give you a voice in His kingdom. He wants to show you His power" (22, 80). Expressive of unsatisfied sexual longing, the word "aching" in conjunction with "to be one with" someone evokes the accrued tension of blood-engorged genitals and of undischarged fluids and foreshadows their release through orgasm. But in this case those organs and climax are attributed to God. Historically speaking, sexualizing divine possession is far from an innovation, but one gets the sense from Arterburn and Stoeker that this is not what they're aiming for.

In an autobiographical passage where Stoeker, Arterburn's coauthor, relates his own struggle with pornography and premarital sex, he casts God in the role of jealous lover. In a quest to steel one *against* sexual desire, the somatic pungency of Stoeker's language would seem counterintuitive: "When I . . . couldn't put my porn magazines down, He still loved me. When I lay in the arms of another Saturday-night date, He still loved me. When I continued to ignore him, He chased me desperately, aching to reach me before it was too late and my heart was hardened" (20). Besides the tone-deaf sublimation of a "hardened" heart for the foresworn tumescent penis, what strikes one as novel is not so much the analogy between sexual and spiritual ecstasy but the resurgence of erotic feeling's darker embodiments, in this case sado-masochism, in the midst of sexual suppression. Stoeker's sinful pre-marital sex life is put on hiatus when "the [Holy] Spirit" prevents him from getting an erection during a date. From romantic rival, God the Father turns into controlling Daddy: the Spirit "whispered into my heart, 'By the way, I did that to you. I know it hurt you, but this prac-tice can't be tolerated anymore in your life. You are Christ's now, and He loves you'" (14). *Battle* grounds its sexophobic mandate squarely in scripture: "You are not your own; you have no right [to have sex as you wish]" is anchored to "You are not your own; you were bought at a price. Therefore honor God with your body" from 1 Corinthians (160, 60). In the highly sexualized content of *Every Young Man's Battle*, God's persona as dominating Daddy unites gay and straight sensibili-ties of the capital-D term: Freud meets Plath meets Folsom Street. Rather than make the patently false claim that gay sex and S&M are coextensive, or that sadomasochism forms gay men's exclusive province, I mean simply to convey the queer or nonheteronormative coloring of S&M and how this cognitive dissonance with so-called Christ-built heterosexuality inches *Battle* closer than one would think it wanted to be to homosexuality, how it increases rather than diminishes its pro-pinquity to queerness.

If the engrossing objective of *Battle's* project is "How do I get God to fill this desire in me?" the greatest obstacle to that goal is masturba-tion (131). Given the amount of time Arterburn and Stoeker devote to masturbation—and they devote *a lot* of time to it—a more appropriate title for the book would be *Every Young Man's Battle with His Erection.* It might seem counterproductive to talk so much about the very same activity one is attempting to dissuade one's audience from, but that appears not to concern these authors. Unmarried adult or teenage men should not masturbate, since masturbation and its adjuncts of fantasy and visual stimulation lead one, to judge from the personal stories *Battle* compiles, into an abysmal spiral of addiction, isolation, shame. For single men, purity is defined as abstinence not just from sex with others but even sex with oneself: "When you're sexually pure, it means you're not seeking sexual gratification" (140). One wonders whether desire can be annihilated as thoroughly as intended here. One also has to wonder how a *married* individual is supposed to recuperate, much less reignite, the erotic life he has worked so hard to kill under the tutelage of abstinence culture. In being clear about the gauntlet that they're throwing down before young men ("to live without premarital sex . . . [and] without masturbation"), Arterburn and Stoeker portray masturbation and pornography as so ubiquitous as to be inescapable. "To put it bluntly," they write, "you're living in the era of masturbation. There's more masturbation today and more things to masturbate over than ever before. There are entire industries centered on the practice of masturbation. The porn industry wants you to masturbate compulsively so it can sell you products" (219). The passage is as unwittingly titillating as it is dourly naïve. While it's unlikely that, given the prevalence of internet access, *Battle*'s teen readership is only now learning about the wealth of porn the internet contains, a passage like this manages to render porn's omnipresence and masturbation's ubiquity attractive rather than horrifying. Aside from the expected rehashing of nineteenth-century antimasturbation clichés of guilt, remorse, and addiction, *Battle*'s authors seek to inculcate their audience with assertions about autoeroticism so risibly untenable that one finds it hard to imagine any reader taking any of this seriously, especially a teenager just embarking on the joys of self-stimulation. Arterburn and Stoeker proclaim flat-out that "masturbation . . . is not a real sexual encounter" (124). If readers are thinking "you must doing something wrong, then," the authors' more subtle, though equally bemusing point is that masturbation consists of "*false* intimacy" (120; emphasis added). In their lexicon, real intimacy comprises "sexual gratification . . . only from your wife" (140). And they do mean "*only*": ideally, they say, men should not masturbate before *or* after marriage. Sex with their wives should implicitly meet all their erotic needs, at least those that the authors see as valid.

There's an even more consequential separation supposedly produced by self-pleasuring, however. "Habitual masturbation consistently creates distance from God," whereas a "close relationship with God will make [it] unnecessary" (109, 120). This theory goes further than the swapping of material pleasure for an emotional or intellectual one, a common move for spiritual ascesis. In the culminating chapter of a lengthy section devoted entirely to self-abuse, Arterburn and Stoeker go so far as to contend that the compensatory powers of spirituality are as capable as masturbation of providing tangible satisfaction. Men

> have a baseline sex drive, there's no question. Dr. James Dobson stated in *What Wives Wished Their Husbands Knew About Women* that the human male, because of sperm production and other factors, naturally desires a sexual release every seventy-two hours or so. You're probably wondering what can be done about that. Is there a way to release that stuff [without sin]?
>
> Thankfully, yes. While our body has this natural physical pressure for sexual release, God Himself has provided a built-in "relief valve," something with which you're familiar. Clinically it's called a "nocturnal emission," but long ago, in a dank, smelly football locker room, some kid decided to call it a "wet dream," and that name stuck.
>
> The good news is that nocturnal emissions *can* work for you in your quest for purity. . . . [Y]ou might wonder how such dreams can work toward purity since some of these semiconscious flights of fancy can get pretty hot and heavy! But don't forget that those hot and heavy aspects arise from what you've been feeding your mind. . . . The same pure eyes and mind that keep you from actively seeking release during the day will limit the impurity that your mind can use in your dreams at night. These dreams will be dramatically purer in scope and content than you now realize.
>
> Nocturnal emissions kick in naturally in response to your normal, natural sperm buildup. This means that the fixed part of your sex drive will be more or less taken care of by God's natural relief valve. (130)

Without explicitly invoking John Locke, *Battle*'s authors nonetheless
rely on their own version of the *tabula rasa*. Even though an unquan-
tified baseline level of desire comes as standard equipment with the
male mind (because of sperm production? God-given temptation?),
they contend that anything beyond this comes from the outside. In a
model that gives little credit to the generative faculties of the individual
libido even without external stimuli, sexual fantasy is experienced only
if one allows it inside the mind or actively seeks it out. Impurity in,
impurity out. This scenario also fails to explain how, having joined the
purity brigade, one is to rid oneself of *remembered* fantasies, those that
have already been let in and that, no doubt, have helped one achieve
more than one solo orgasm. It's Arterburn and Stoeker's reliance on
the "relief valve," however, that's most troubling. As a guard against
masturbation, this idea is useless and illogical: refraining from masturbation does not of itself guarantee a wet dream; further, it would
seem difficult to distinguish self-stimulation during a wet dream from
masturbation. Odder still is the notion of relying on an immaterial
being for sexual pleasure. This is the point to which sexualizing purity,
eroticizing abstinence, has led us: nocturnal emission elevated to divine
ministration, a hand job from the Holy Spirit. Even if impossible, the
idea seems calculated to inflict psychological damage, not so much by
its sacrilegious character as by the retrenchment of human desire, the
inhumane curtailment of a significant and natural portion of what it
means to be human. This abridgement—this insistence that, on pain of
damnation, one obtain sexual pleasure from a single, severely restricted
outlet and nowhere else—paints the world as a largely frightening
place. Other human beings, even those committed to purity, present
possible threats and temptations. After years of fearing the corrupting
touch of other people, one wonders how adequately sexuality within the
sanitizing bonds of marriage is going to measure up. Will the pleasure
have grown stale from lying so long fallow? It's disheartening enough
that, as constructed here, the future of a young man who has abstained
from masturbation promises a large dose of dullness in the form of
safe, boring wet dreams that are unstimulated by even the blandest of
fantasies and that relieve "pressure" without bringing much pleasure.
What's worse—and, as the rest of this chapter discusses, what's pointedly burdensome for gay, protogay, and questioning youth—is these
purity authors' treatment of homosexuality. Certainly, Arterburn and
Stoeker deal with homosexuality in far less vitriolic terms than figures

like Fred Phelps or Jerry Falwell. Yet if we're to judge from their insult-
ing, minimal attention to it, their view of homosexuality is that of
something equally beyond the pale of the desirable, the imaginable,
and the human. What may surprise us, however, are the possibilities
purity culture affords for queer exploits *within* its confines, the fissures
it might afford for living under and perhaps *through* its carceral strictures, if not advancing their erasure.

When purity advocates target homosexuality directly (and here
Battle is fairly representative, perhaps even milder than some purity
manuals[10]), homosexuality is alternately baited and pathologized.
Sometimes, however, they end up courting it in spite of their best
efforts, providing an occasional safeguarding recess. Even if these
niches are far from hospitable and do little to undermine the larger
hetero-Christian venture, any foothold capable of sheltering gay teens
buys them time, space, and intimacy—affords them survival if not
growth—even within the homophobic pressures of religious captivity.
Such niches should trouble heteronormative as well as queer notions of
the juncture and noncoincidence of the two identities, suggesting a disparity of ways such identities can be conceived and lived. While *Battle's*
homophobic sorties are sometimes oblique, its authors are not above
some old-fashioned gay baiting. Like most of their ilk, Arterburn and
Stoeker fixate on polarized gender roles harking back to some bygone
era conservatives tend to idealize, contrary to all evidence of memory or history. Without raising the topic of homosexuality directly,
Battle's discussion of "manhood" versus "maleness" implies what they
find wrong with it. *Battle* urges young Christian men to reject mere
maleness in favor of "manhood," which they equate with being "*more
than male*" (65). Manhood initially seems tied to stereotypical Western
masculine traits; achieving sexual purity requires stoic self-control over
one's desires and resistance to temptations. But at least one paradigmatic "manly" trait soon rears its head: obedience. "Acts of obedience
often seem strange," the authors admit, "even illogical." What might
appear a questioning of the commandment to purity turns out to be a
rhetorical feint to make a decree reminiscent of boot camp. Regardless
of whether a purity regimen strikes one as "illogical" by thwarting the
body's natural appetites, one should man up, shut up, and accept the
divine mandate. Those who question or waver are accused of a "lack of
manhood" similar to that of Zedekiah, Arterburn and Stoeker's biblical gay-bashing proof text. Zedekiah, the last king of Judah before

its sixth-century BCE fall to Babylon, is described unblinkingly by *Battle*'s authors as "the greatest sissy in the Bible" (74). The subheading of the section in which this appears reads "Don't Follow This Sissy." Supposedly, the authors are targeting only those young men who are "indecisive and fearful" in obeying God's "standards" as sissies, but the homophobic resonance is about as subtle as a brick wall. While homosexuality's relative invisibility in *Battle*, as well as the solipsism typical of heterosexuality, indicates that *Battle*'s presumed audience consists of *straight* young Christian men, the unacknowledged gay teens among them are sure to receive the message with redoubled strength even though not explicitly addressed.

When Arterburn and Stoeker get around to addressing homosexuality head on, they do so almost as an afterthought, with a brief chapter just before the conclusion. Concomitant with a partiality for gender polarity is their pathologizing approach to nonnormative sexuality. Granted, their pathologizing partakes of a gentler style, free of fire and brimstone and characteristic of Focus on the Family's mitigated approach since 1994.[11] Thus even if *Battle* dresses its discussion of homosexuality in the garb of pastoral care, the advice remains uncompromisingly intolerant:

> We're fairly confident there haven't been many people for you to talk to regarding . . . same-sex attraction. And the fear of being discovered or rejected has no doubt kept you silent.
>
> But the attraction is there. You didn't choose to be attracted to men, but you are. You may have been molested when you were younger, and that started the feelings. . . . There are many theories about why you have the feelings you do. . . . We want to help you understand why you feel [that] way . . . and provide some hope for you. (224)

In short: we understand that you have these feelings. They are not your fault; they are the fault, rather, of someone else who failed you, took advantage of you somehow. (Note the staggering omission of the emotional and physical damage religious inculcation inflicts on its own prey.) But head straight to Exodus, and you can change.

It perhaps goes without saying that within such a narrative the impetus to change one's sexuality—personally felt but responding to ideological and cultural pressures—suspiciously moves in one direction

only: from queer to straight. Regardless of reparative therapists' protestations that they are simply easing their clients' emotional distress
by giving them what they want, the very offer of therapy to eradicate
homosexuality would seem to violate an ethical standard of care. Far
from an impartial course of treatment, reparative therapy, like ex-gay
ministries, is beholden to a distinctly malicious homophobic agenda.
And at base that homophobia is irreducibly religious. The therapy's
very terminology ("reparative," "conversion") implies that homosexuality constitutes some damage or disease that necessitates repair and that
homosexuals should and can be converted to heterosexuality. The latter
notion is somewhat ironic, given the phobic stereotype that homosexuals recruit heterosexuals with unabating predatory fervor. If the
notion of homosexuality's abnormality and destructiveness was not still
validated by religious beliefs, and if religious beliefs were not largely
exempt from criticism and rational debate, then gays and lesbians
would be significantly less likely to see their homosexuality as a source
of distress and view themselves as deviants in need of correction.[12]

Explanations for the origins of homosexuality have changed little
in the United States since the gross psychiatric misapprehension of
Freudian sexual theory following World War II: one is made gay by
being molested by someone of the same sex or having an overbearing
mother or a weak, absent father. No matter how many reputable studies produce findings to the contrary, religious conservatives harp on
the myth that pedophiles are predominantly homosexual and seek to
create more homosexuals by converting heterosexuals through molestation. A mother who is not the biblically prescribed doormat generates
in her sons a "repulsion to women" and makes them "easy target[s] if
they [are] approached by another man" (225, 226). And—contrary,
one suspects, to the experience of any straight man raised by a single
and/or lesbian mother—the boy's yearning for a strong male father
figure somehow morphs into wanting to have sex with another man,
in a misguided attempt to get "a feeling of maleness and connection
to other men" (225). Is *that* what I'm supposed to be getting out of
giving a blow job? It may enrich my sense of my own maleness or my
own sense of gender performance, but I doubt the maleness I experience during this act is the maleness *Battle* depicts young men as ineptly
searching for in the arms of other males. The abstraction of what many
of us might understand or think we understand by "maleness" stands
in tension with *Battle*'s deployment of the term. Without defining it,

Arterburn and Stoeker silently legislate maleness as heterosexual. Like-wise, proceeding as if the only modality of "connection to other men" is a nonsexual one attempts to invalidate the galvanic connection that protogay or experimenting Christian youth might derive from sex with another man. *Battle*'s gay teen readers, or victims, will find their queer sexual experiences at once appropriated and expunged and themselves characterized as "confused and searching men who long to know what's normal and how to experience it" (226). Surely the "change" narra-tive's most damaging lie is that, despite any environmental origins for homosexuality, the blame is laid squarely on one's own shoulders, on a less than manly lack of willpower: "This is where your choices come in, because there's much hope for you, if you choose it" (226). The bottom line is to accept one's same-sex attractions but not to act on them. The choice is celibacy or heterosexuality, with no middle ground allowed.[13]

Reminding gays that they can change—more pointedly, that they must change because it's what God wants—preserves the conserva-tive Christian notion that homosexuals don't really exist. There are no true homosexuals, that is, just ex-gays who haven't been saved yet. It deserves note that the ex-gay gospel is simply another version of what queer theorist Eve Sedgwick calls the "overarching, relatively unchallenged aegis of a culture's desire that gay people *not be*" (43). The message of "change" may be less superficially hateful than out-right condemnation, but this more benevolent version of religious homophobia still seeks to deprive queers of rights enjoyed by their straight compeers. If gays and lesbians change, then they won't exist anymore as a special interest group or a protected class. The bare idea that homosexuals *can* change—which edges, in eugenic fantasy, toward the potentiality of *all* homosexuals changing, no matter how ludicrous the scenario—erodes the rationale of having to argue about something as ridiculous as gay rights or as unsavory as gay sex.

Given the depiction of the purity battle as equally apocalyptic and insurmountable, *Battle* offers incredibly little in the way of concrete advice. Aside from arming oneself with "sword" and "shield" (respec-tively, a key Bible verse or two and a perimeter of purity created by "bouncing the eyes"), their only other substantial recommendation to deter heterosexually inspired lust is the company of other men. To be more exact, they instruct young men to find an "accountability group," a church-based group of like-minded young men committed to purity. Such groups are effective, we're told, only if participants are completely honest. And even though sharing every impulse, every slip, is meant to guard *against* sexual lapses, this kind of "talking cure" seems just as liable to excite as it is to emancipate. Better yet, as if sensing the pitfalls of "a sympathy gathering where each person admits his failure again and again," the authors suggest an alternative that, especially if one is worried about "slips," sounds more worrisome still:

> You may prefer a one-on-one, direct accountability partner, a male friend, someone older and well respected in the church— a person who can encourage you in the heat of battle and ask probing questions like, "What are you feeling when you're most tempted to masturbate?"
>
> . . . Nearly any committed man can be your accountability partner. Let us caution you, however, from enlisting your girlfriend as one. That's a recipe for getting into more trouble. (126)

Because reputedly inept or absent male role models engender homosexuality as well as self-abuse, young men need someone to look up to. Yet it requires little imagination to envision accountability pairings as a recipe for disaster of another, homoerotic kind, the result of grouping together young men who, whether they're straight or gay, are all trying not to have sex or masturbate. Ideally, one would pick an accountability partner who is stronger in his purity than oneself (although, subconsciously, maybe not). Still, isn't *everyone* susceptible to sexual backsliding? Even while struggling to be pure, isn't a male accountability partner as likely as oneself to experience, and possibly yield to, the horniness buffeting the male teenage body, especially under the pressure of "probing" questions about one's masturbation habits? Apparently the danger of succumbing to *heterosexual* temptation, invoked in the caveat against choosing a *female* accountability partner, produces sufficient anxiety to create this rather obvious blind spot. I'm hardly suggesting that accountability groups or pairings will turn young men gay (as salacious as the notion might be; a gay porn film to that effect may already be in production somewhere). Rather, the accountability group exemplifies the claustrophobically homosocial world of abstinence—a *cordon sanitaire* closeted gay teens might find not only oppressive but also titillating. This model raises yet another specter for the abstinence crusade: duplicity. *Battle* acknowledges this threat only in passing, recounting the admission of one young woman that "'our youth group is filled with kids faking their Christian walk. They're actually taking drugs, drinking, partying, having sex. . . . They pressure my values at every turn'" (19). Yet what's more problematic for purity advocates than covert peer pressure is the question of inauthenticity. It's not just a matter of gays hiding out, or straight teens "slipping" sexually. Unless this anecdote reveals an anomaly, abstinence groups may be rife with teens who are indulging a host of sensual impulses and who are using the cover of Christian purity to do so.

It's the *effects* of purity culture on gay teens, however, that concern me from this point, the more obvious effects of enclosure and distress as well as the unexpected effects of sustenance and defilade. This chapter attempts to substantiate some of the ways in which purity and abstinence culture veils, elides, distorts, and often simply erases gay teens' existence. While abstinence culture's exclusion of gay sexuality, except as a source of disease and unhappiness and a subject for conversion, might seem a wholly negative development, gay teen invisibility also provides a potential haven for exploring, off the radar, officially repudiated desires, fragments of selves, even new hybrid identities. Whether or not these impulses and cobbled-together selves prove durable or reliably pleasurable, they show the tenacity of queerness, its ability to find, if only provisionally, some fissure within an unforgiving landscape, its capability of forging an unanticipated, transformative amalgam of Christianity and queerness.

The lyrics of "Daddy's Little Girl," especially the line "You're the end of the rainbow, my pot of gold," can be usefully overlaid on the lives of closeted gay teens. (The position of openly gay Christians, teenage or otherwise, is addressed in chapter 3.) Most revealingly symptomatic of the relative absence of queer teens from abstinence curricula is what the lyrics miss, what they get wrong. The "pot of gold" for pure Christian male teens, in the official narrative of not masturbating, cultivating an anorectic libido and marrying a pure female may turn out to be less the "end of the rainbow" than a beginning of one. One sense in which this might occur stems from the *queerness* of all abstinent Christian young men. Barred from sexual contact with women until marriage, they are queer in the sense of not having gained entry to heterosexuality, to adulthood. Held as they are in a prolonged latency period, their heterosexuality is unachieved and uninhabited until the honeymoon. Quarantine among similarly deprived young men means that their primary world is homosocial, more so even than most male teens. And yet my suggestion is not that sexual frustration must as a matter of course lead nongay teens to turn to their brethren for sexual solace. While possible, and satisfyingly salacious, this is not crucial to my argument. A more intriguing possibility is the muddying of what, for conservative Christians and many gays and lesbians alike, constitute clear, world-informing identitarian boundaries: straight versus gay, Christian versus non-Christian, pure or meaningful versus impure or casual. Even for gays, lesbians, and Christians who understand experience as blurring these rigid categories, the dualism still operates. Even if blurred, the categories stand as unquestioned extremes, as material rudiments or conceptual limit cases.

For gay, questioning, or curious gay Christian teens immured within purity culture, the discourse of abstinence may provide a haven and may do so in a variety of more and less radical ways. To be clear: I mean in no way to make light of the shame and pain such a world inflicts on its inmates. It's undeniable that for many queers raised in and confined to it, this world wields a ubiquitous, punishing logic that condemns their intimate desires, that ruins lives, that crushes spirits, and, as the 2009 film *Prayers for Bobby* illustrates, that kills. This is not to pretend a dangerous naïveté regarding the baleful, deforming, and lethal effects of the closet on queer lives. Nor is it to recommend a credulous confidence about the extent to which secrecy, disclosure, and their respective rewards and punishments are fully within the control of *out* gays and lesbians—in Eve Sedgwick's words, the ways queers' "management of information about" themselves is "vulnerable . . . to . . . a contradictory array of interdictions" toward silence and enunciation (70). Sedgwick eloquently cautions against underestimating "how far authority over [self-definition] has been distanced from the gay subject her- or himself," and that is the last thing I wish to do (79). Nor, in theorizing potential remodelings of identity and relationality by queers captive to conservative Christianity, am I suggesting that any queer should inhabit such a deleterious space longer than he or she has to. My speculative analysis of ex-gays and queer purity-seekers should not be mistaken for an attempt to "glamoriz[e] the closet itself . . . [by] presenting as inevitable or somehow valuable its exactions, its deformations, its disempowerment and sheer pain"—a risk that concerns Sedgwick, a concern that I am hardly the first or last to share (Sedgwick 68). As she rightly points out, queer critical "scrutiny of those who inhabit the closet (however equivocally)" should not obscure attention to "those in the ambient heterosexist culture who enjoin [the closet] and whose intimate representational needs"—naturalizing heterosexuality and othering queerness—"it serves in a way less extortionate to themselves" (69). It's not my intention to obscure but rather to highlight what conservative Christianity gets out of closeted queer adherents, namely, a version of what heterosexual culture derives from its intimate, symbolic relation to homosexuality, a way of masking *its own* definitional instability, incoherence, and lack of the natural, given status to which it pretends. Worse still, perhaps, the presence of closeted Christians in ex-gay ministries might seem to risk endorsing the repulsive narratives of "change" such organizations disseminate, to risk sanctioning homophobic fantasies of "eradicating . . . gay identity" and the perverse interpretations of constructivist models of sexuality on which, along with religious vitriol, such fantasies thrive (Sedgwick 41).

While honoring these concerns, however, it's important not to neglect the less obvious, sometimes counterintuitive avenues that even homophobic, sexophobic environments might potentiate. By their possibility, alternative uses of the Christian closet expand its dimensions, expand it beyond our notions as queers or as conservative, liberal, or moderate Christians of the sorts of experiences that are valid or ethical, that are enjoyable or salutary. Conceivable employments of the purity-cult-as-closet include but should not be limited to fulfilling a number of overlapping functions: providing a hideout, camouflage, or redoubt for protoqueers; allotting asylum or permission for bi-curious experimentation; furnishing latitude for gay revelry in the readiness of pent-up, hormonally engorged peers; affording scope to formulate a future queer self who may or may not be Christian but is not yet prepared for or does not have realistic access to a gay world; and finally, supplying leeway to problematize the categorical opposition at the heart of conservative Christians *and* queer self-understanding. In some if not all of these capacities, the queer Christian operates as a potential double agent, whether willing or suborned, making the most of circumstances he must endure at least for the time being. I would not try to insinuate, for contrarianism's sake, that conservative Christian culture, abstinence education, or purity cults are generous, hospitable havens for young queers. It is certainly not a given that the purity closet is a chrysalis queers are sure to survive and some day escape unscathed, transmogrified into happy gay adults. Some will die, like Bobby. Others will work

for years to stifle their homosexuality for the sake of the Christianity they feel to be their primary, grounding identity. Additionally, my
suggestion is not that horny male teens will turn to gay sex for release
or solace, though this could be an ameliorating or painful side effect
from their point of view. Instead, I'm speculating that purity culture's
claustral enclosure—a system that sexualizes God, spirituality, even
purity itself, thus turning in on itself in a frenzy to avoid its sexually
contaminating Others—to some extent engineers its own queering,
unsettles the clarity of its own operational distinctions. These distinctions are the polestars of more than just conservative Christians. To
purity outsiders, the idea of purity-as-closet presses us to consider how
a gay conservative Christian, self-hating or not, might conjure from the
Christian closet still another capacity: a holdout, not just against the
"change" of becoming straight, but against solidifying oneself in the
positivistic narratives of redemption and consistency that are fetishized
and enforced by most notions of sexual, religious, cultural, and racial
identity. Our own inability, no matter our affiliation, to dodge normativity's most overt, deforming grasp does not preclude opportunities for
nudging sideways the interstices of those and other norms, of discovering provisional apertures and dilating, if not dislodging, its parameters.

TWO

BREEDING FRATERNITIES

Ex-Gay Ministries, Barebacking,
and Alternative Models of Relation

To be sure, Christianity remains overwhelmingly heteronormative despite covert holdouts and deformations by queers within its ranks. Thus queer Christians, whether conservative or otherwise, may find themselves confined to rearguard maneuvers, seeking or crafting religious traditions that are both accepting and acceptable.[1] Recognizing the deep-seated straightness of religion drives my argument in chapter 4 and the conclusion. For the moment, what's noteworthy are the stratagems such as those listed here—stratagems of either insurgence or mere survival, gambits that have been and might be generated on presumptively inhospitable territory, that could adumbrate modes of being that are not hegemonically condoned or perhaps even imagined. One structure capable of hosting one or more of these projects is the peculiar style of kinship already forged in certain ex-gay ministries. By exploring this structure alongside alternative kinship practices from gay sexual culture such as that modeled in barebacking subculture, this chapter theorizes the extent to which the parameters of the purity closet might sustain or foster queerness in addition to attempting to extinguish it. Under religious pressure to "restore" gays to heterosexuality, what models of relation does the purity closet allow? What models of relation *might* it allow, under the opposing pressure of recalcitrant gay desire? Ideally, these alternative models of relation could be inhabited outside the closet, outside Christianity—not that such a move would necessarily impute or unveil a hitherto unrealized liberatory character. We should remain suspect of uncomplicated liberatory claims on either side of the closet *or* the church door, or indeed from any quarter. As we have seen with the strictures of purity/abstinence discourse, the confines of the Christian closet are not always as impermeable and obdurate as one might suppose. The different unorthodox strains of kinship implemented by ex-gays and by barebackers breed modes of fraternity that end up, either intentionally or in spite of themselves, procuring not an escape from identity or visibility altogether but a deferral, a postponement of identification. What I have in mind is more than a deferral of being found out in the expected sense, being outed as gay. The speculative premise of this chapter, rather, is that queer and questioning teens who inhabit and innovate within the Christian closet *put off* being resolved or fixed, that they delay becoming simply one or the other as gays and Christians might equally expect or demand. Most of these teens would likely still claim identities: gay, Christian, or some hybrid of both. They are not repudiating or escaping identity. But they are, in many instances, certainly contesting the lineaments of identity in the positivistic, discrete sense ascribed to by minority-based identity politics.[2] Though none of us can claim to exceed normativity's reach fully or permanently, we may at least strain within its grasp. Regardless of the substantive pain and trauma the queer Christian closet may be witness to, this space may also afford its inhabitants an opportunity to avoid being transfixed. It may extend to its inmates and refugees a way, temporarily at least, to avoid being transfixed; to dodge being codified and moored as rational or fathomable; to elude being installed in a future, whether straight or gay, predicated on having been severed from both past and present actions, from religious as well as sexual desires.

Ex-gay "conversion" is seldom absolute.[3] Periodically, prominent members of the ex-gay movement have been outed or left the movement of their own accord. Love Won Out's leader John Paulk was sighted in 2000 patronizing a Washington, D.C., gay bar; in 2013, Paulk formally renounced reparative therapy as harmful and apologized for his previous, ardent advocacy of it. Some have outed themselves. In 1979, Michael Bussee and Gary Cooper, who helped to organized the first Exodus Summit Conference (out of which the organization Exodus arose), announced to the audience that they were leaving the program because they had fallen in love with each other; furthermore, the two renounced the possibility that homosexuality could be prayed away and repudiated ex-gay therapies. In the case of New Hope ministries—one of the more prominent such organizations, profiled by Tanya Erzen in *Straight to Jesus: Sexual and Christian Conversions in the Ex-Gay Movement*—gay recidivism or "sexual falls" are common. Bussee has continued to critique the ex-gay movement's purported success rates, which because participants are seldom tracked after completing the program, seem inflated. Along with Beyond Ex-Gay founders Christine Bakke and Peterson Toscano, Bussee publicizes the happiness found by ex-gays who have accepted their homosexuality and abandoned the conservative religious frameworks that view homosexuality as a sin incompatible with spirituality. While such stories of failure provide satisfying schadenfreude at the hypocrisy of some and elicit empathy for others' hard-won authenticity, what I find most compelling in terms of this chapter's focus are the tensions exhibited by ex-gays who have not yet resolved their conflict by adopting heterosexual lifestyles, remaining celibate, or living as gay men. Erzen notes that

> most men and women in ex-gay ministries do not experience the clear-cut change that [Exodus president] Alan Chambers advocates. Their lives do not end in marriage but become a continual process of having sexual falls, recommitting to Christ, being celibate, participating in ex-gay ministries, and so on. Their queer conversions attest to the fact that change is a process of sexual and religious conversion and that their identities are constantly in a state of flux. (186)

To some, such failures, whether isolated "falls" or outright rejection of the ex-gay enterprise, might seem to problematize that enterprise's core principles more than Erzen concedes. Gay recidivism appears more the norm, statistically speaking, than cessation of gay desire, development of straight desire, and entry into opposite-sex marriage. Of the eleven men in the "class" of men Erzen followed at New Hope ministries over an eighteen-month period, seven had left after only two months. Of the four who remained to complete the program, two later went on to date men. Though small, Erzen's sample is nonetheless suggestive. Michelle Wolkomir's *Be Not Deceived: The Sacred and Sexual Struggles of Gay and Ex-Gay Christian Men* (2006) records similarly low "success" rates with a somewhat larger sample. Of the thirty men in the ex-gay group she followed, seven got married; four of those seven divorced during the study's two-year duration; the other three remained married but continued to struggle with their desires. Only five of the thirty felt they had achieved significant change. Of course, the term "success" presents some difficulties here: like Erzen, many participants of ex-gay therapy define "success" not as the full cessation of gay sex and desire or the achievement of heterosexual desire but rather as a spiritual commitment to heterosexuality that weathers any instances of backsliding. This intention is the grassroots reality. However, Exodus's publicity efforts foster the public impression that the only true sign of "success" or "change" is abstaining from gay sex permanently. It's striking to note that ex-gay programs (self-servingly, perhaps, lest they lose all their clientele to recidivism) tend to characterize "falls" as neither a sign of failure nor a cause for despair but, on the contrary, as a positive indicator. By "reconstruct[ing] emotional experience," group leaders "show . . . them how to reinterpret a fall, or indeed, any other behavior they considered sinful, so that it [becomes] evidence of continued resistance—an opportunity to reject Satan and accept God, an occasion to rejoice—rather than a failure. . . . [A] fall becomes an example of how to resist and struggle righteously as a good Christian" (Wolkomir 123). While this reading might counterproductively seem to risk eroticizing failure, ex-gay programs turn falls into reinforcements. They do so by reiterating scriptural commands to struggle against sin, by focusing on their *desire* to "'be rid of,' 'resist,' and 'turn away from' the pull of pornography and other men," and by configuring struggle *as* salvation ("as long as we struggle for righteousness we will be in our Savior's hands") (140, 144). Deemphasizing action in favor of desire, if only to build self-esteem, carries the somewhat obvious risk of questioning the entire ex-gay venture and licensing hypocrisy ("I'm still having sex with men, but I *want* to stop, and that's what's important"). Viewing struggle as salvation has long-standing theological precedent in the Puritan doctrine of divine affliction whereby, somewhat confusingly, suffering is a sign not of a sinful nature but of one's divinely favored status. In this scheme punishment is a sign of divine displeasure. Far from being a verdict on one's irredeemability, suffering is intended to chastise, to elicit behavior more befitting to one's chosen status.

Taking a page from queer theory's critique of sexual identity as putatively stable or discrete, Tanya Erzen posits the model of "queer conversion." Distinct from the idea of the "changed" or heterosexual gay man touted by the ex-gay organizations such as Exodus and Love In Action, the term "queer conversion" suggests not that gays can change but that the experiential and identitarian space inhabited by many participants in ex-gay programs is less neatly compartmentalized than one might expect. To the New Hope residents in Erzen's study, homosexual backsliding does not vitiate their claim to want to change, nor does it bode certain failure. At least that's the official narrative embraced by the program: a Christian cycle of sin, repentance, and redemption wherein transgression is a momentary hurdle on the path to ultimate triumph. Viewed from the outside, this narrative strikes Erzen as less compelling than the hybrid identity ex-gays are enacting *on their way to* heterosexuality. Indeed, that may be their only sure identity since they might never arrive at anything beyond it:

> Rather than definitive change, ex-gays undergo a conversion process that has no endpoint, and they acknowledge that change encompasses desires, behaviors, and identities that do not always align neatly or remain fixed. Even the label "ex-gay" represents their sense of being in flux between identities. . . .
>
> . . . [E]x-gay men and women are born again religiously, and as part of that process they consider themselves reconstituted sexually. They grapple with a seemingly irreconcilable conflict between their conservative Christian beliefs and their own same-sex desires. In their worldview, an ex-gay ministry becomes a place where these dual identities are rendered temporarily compatible. Their literal belief that the Bible condemns homosexual practices and identity leads them to measure their success in negotiating their new identities through submission and surrender to Jesus in all things. Even if desire and attractions remain after they have attended an ex-gay ministry . . . their relationship with God and Jesus continues intact. That relationship supersedes any sexual changes, minimizing their frustration and disillusionment when the longed for sexual changes do not occur. (3)

What many of us might judge a rather baroque structure of denial is capable of functioning also as a complication of the hetero-telic arc ex-gay ministries are attempting to set in stone. Contrary to the stark "before-and-after" emphasis of ex-gay success stories like those publicized by Exodus, the experience of the men at New Hope attests to what the snapshot approach omits: the stark gulf that separates "after" from "before." Michelle Wolkomir's account of ex-gay trans-formation underscores just how gutting and disheartening this gulf can be. Whereas gay Christians became "more comfortable with [their homosexuality] in the context of their faith and were able to pursue the lives they wanted," ex-gay Christians

> learned *how* to struggle against sexual temptations and to *value* that struggle; it did not necessarily mean that the men were able to alter their sexuality. . . . [W]hile being an ex-gay Christian could (and sometimes did) mean that an individual had successfully developed heterosexual desires, it often meant that an individual was embroiled in a struggle against homosexuality that could, and perhaps was even likely to, fail. (Wolkomir 147)

The imagined territory in between "gay" and "ex-gay" is uneven; the journey, painful; and arrival and completion, far from certain. This is not to say that, compared to Wolkomir, Erzen is unconcerned with the pain that efforts at ex-gay transformation can inflict on the individual. Rather, Erzen is more hopeful regarding the sustaining properties of "flux" as a model for identity and the chance that such a model might combat, if not denature, the larger identitarian and ideological forces exerted on individuals.

Erzen elaborates on the ramifications of "flux" as a model for iden-tity. Like conservative Christianity, such an identity hinges on unam-biguous oppositions:

> Although men and women in ex-gay ministries do not and cannot envision homosexuality as a positive way to be, their lives also exemplify the instability of the religious and sexual conversion process. Their narratives of testimonial sexuality are performances that, while sincere, point to the instability and changeability of their own identities rather than serve as

a testament to heterosexuality. The ex-gay notion of sexuality as a religious process of transformation may be fraught with sexual falls, indiscretions, and moments of doubt, and ex-gays' notions of change are fluid even if their eventual goal is heterosexuality or celibacy. In its insistence on the influence of cultural, familial, and religious factors on sexuality, the ex-gay mode of religious and sexual conversion unwittingly presents a challenge to a conservative Christian construction that a person can move from homosexuality and to heterosexuality. (14–15)

According to literalist, decontextualized readings of the Bible, homosexuality may be antithetical to Christianity. *Straight to Jesus* allows us to make the case, however, that an ex-gay who is in the midst of finding his way out of homosexuality is, for now, both gay *and* Christian, even though such a creature is not supposed to exist.[4] Naturally, one may be a "fallen" Christian, whose sin has distracted if not separated one from God. But theoretically no sin, not even a monstrous one like gay sex, undoes deeper, spiritual commitments. At once gay and saved, homosexual and born again, ex-gays trouble conservative Christianity's static, absolutist ideas about not only sexuality but also a putatively immutable opposition between religion and homosexuality. From a slightly different perspective, most ex-gays aim not to become heterosexual (such programs emphasize dating women and marriage less than one would think) but to refrain from gay sex. Aware that same-sex attraction may never disappear entirely, their goal is to refrain from acting on such desires. Yet simply because ex-gays manage to stop *acting* gay, manage to forgo gay sex, gay socializing, camping, or appearing nelly, this does not mean they have ceased *being* gay. For if they were not still gay in some key, substantive way, if homosexuality, as such programs contend, inhered *altogether* in a set of *actions*, then there would seem little reason for these men to feel conflicted. Chapter 3 addresses another possibility—namely, that the Christian Right *needs* them to feel conflicted, that conflicted ex-gays are a necessary human casualty in the New Right's ideological battle for cultural and political power. For the present discussion, the hybrid or fluid character of these "queer conversions" remains elusive, but we can attempt a provisional definition. For one, queer conversions are not so much conversions as they are durations. Instead of transformations in the conventional sense, they entail a queer process of becoming—becoming without conclusion, though. They amount to a state of suspended animation with special emphasis on animation, a protracted ambition that bends toward the erotically unappealing but prescribed objective of heterosexuality while still desiring, and plangently missing, what a converted queer has or will have left behind. Hybridity on this order appears to exceed the anti-identitarian model proffered by queer theory,[5] inclining toward a state that is both troubling and troubled. Queer Christian "flux" can be viewed as a state of unwanting, a reluctance to become completely either of its root components yet also determined *not* to be both.

In this unsettled, unsettling landscape where traditional bets are held off, fraternity surfaces as an accessible amalgam, a model of survival in more than one sense. The fraternity of ex-gay residential programs for men serves not only the officially sanctioned end, rehabilitation, but also purposes beyond, askew, or in direct defiance of that end. Relevant questions pertain to the ways ex-gay rehabilitation relies on notions and structures of fraternity, what kinds of relations ex-gay fraternity entails, and the extent to which ex-gay brotherhood might be progressive in spite of itself, shielding queers rather than rooting them out. Homosocial dormitory-style settings like those at New Hope and other ex-gay residential programs contain a likely pitfall, especially when the men living and sleeping in close proximity are sexually attracted to other men. Grouping together men with a shared problem makes practical sense and, therapeutically speaking, mirrors 12-step-based models for in-patient treatment of drug and alcohol addiction. But when the single-sex group living in close quarters is trying to stop wanting and having gay sex, the approach might seem more fundamentally problematic. One can hardly accuse directors of ex-gay residential programs of being naïve: New Hope has a rule that men in early phases of their residency cannot be alone in groupings of fewer than three—"safety in threes," it's called (qtd. in Erzen 99). Ostensibly, if a third man is present, none of them will be tempted to act out on his same-sex erotic impulses. In accountability groups, a structure shared with purity groups, the idea is that the residents will monitor each other—a variation on Foucault's panopticon. Another assumption seems to be that, in any group of three men, at any given moment one of them will possess the fortitude to resist temptation: "When a person cannot be alone with another person, he is less likely to have a sexual fall" (99). This safeguard has at least two glaring flaws. Presumably, all three men in such a grouping have gay sexual desires, either slumbering or wakened. And as savvy as the rule may be, it betrays a significant blind spot: have those in charge, many of whom are former homosexuals, never heard of a three-way? This failure of imagination speaks, perhaps, to the intrusion of heteronormativity's fetish for monogamy: the presumptive valuation of sex within a couple as more meaningful or valuable than sex in other contexts or among other combinations of people.

With a nod to a ludicrous strain of pop psychology almost universally cited within conservative Christian ex-gay and abstinence culture, the supposition of the single-sex therapeutic model is that among all-male company one can repair "unmet emotional or psychological [childhood] needs" for nonsexual male bonding *without* confusing such bonding with erotic attraction to other men (Wolkomir 33).[6] It seems impossible to miss a striking parallel with the perverse sexual logic of the purity ball: ex-gay therapy adjures men to fulfill the unmet needs that they have supposedly misconstrued as desire for gay sex by reenacting moments of emotional neglect from their childhood and adolescence. Reenacting such moments in the company of men suffering from similar emotional deprivation and sexual confusion positions these men as surrogate fathers for one another. Purity balls and ex-gay therapies, then, operate along the same unstable vectors, equating fathers with lovers, using father figures to redirect and sublimate sexual urges. What renders ex-gay therapy more problematic is that participants are asked to substitute nonerotic attraction for sexual urges in relation not to their actual fathers but to other men whom they might well experience desire for—potential sexual partners, were they not engaged in fighting their urges.[7] The fact that the nonerotic activities encouraged in such therapy tend to be infantilizing (hugs, cradling) does not make them any less physically proximate and therefore problematic. It seems wholly counterintuitive that the first step in a process whose goal is the overcoming of one's attraction to men and the assumption of a heterosexual or, minimally, nongay lifestyle is to cohabit, establish intimacy, and form close bonds with other same-sex-attracted men. As Erzen puts it, "the problem with the homosocial model is that one heals homosexuality through relationships with people to whom one could potentially be attracted" (91):

> At the same time they speak of belonging, members of the
> ex-gay movement perpetuate the idea that the "gay lifestyle" is
> inherently harmful, empty, promiscuous, and dangerous, and
> many men in the program assimilate these ideas. The idea of
> a residential group is to build a site of belonging in opposition
> to the notion of a gay community while idealizing hetero-
> sexual dating and marriage. Yet while the leaders of the ex-gay
> movement state that heterosexuality and marriage are eventual
> goals, the men and women in the program contradict this idea.
> As part of their queer conversion, they take on an unstable
> identity—ex-gay—that resists a binary heterosexual or homo-
> sexual definition. Contrary to the Christian Right notion of
> family values, the men and women affiliated with New Hope
> forge extended ex-gay networks and accountable relationships
> with other ex-gays, eschewing a privatized notion of marriage
> and family. Long after they have exited the program, many of
> their primary relationships are with other ex-gays. (89)

Like the larger evangelical culture, ex-gay ideology is heterosexually
vectored toward marriage and family, or at minimum a gay-abstinent
life. But the entire operation is homosocially centered—an odd seques-
tration of male participants *away* from the women they are theoretically meant to develop social if not also romantic relationships with
and confinement *among* the population they are trying to curb their
sexual attraction to. Not only do the staff tend to be all male with
few exceptions, such as Anita, the wife of New Hope's founder Frank
Worthen. During activities such as Straight Man Night, heterosexual
men who are not ex-gays—that is, "real" straight men—visit the residents at New Hope to "answer questions about what it means to be
heterosexual and masculine" and thus show residents "that they have
common ground with heterosexual men" (Erzen 107). By exploring
"points for identification"—such as whether authentically straight men
have ever felt homosexual urges or experimented with gay sex—the
implication seems to be that ex-gays will discover that *they too* are actually straight men, if more confused than their non-ex-gay counterparts
(108). The point is that a program intent on fostering a "family atmosphere" attempts to do so by way of an exclusively male environment—
the definition of working at cross-purposes, one might say (90). What
interests me is the possibility that a claustral, almost claustrophobically

fraternal setting involving erotic or nonsexual intimacy at close quarters could not just foster gay attraction but also nurture queer feelings,
gay affiliation, and could breed a queer(ed) fraternity.

Even when gently couched in terms of support and love, the ex-
gay movement's core commitment is eugenic in nature. It desires, to
return to Eve Sedgwick's words, "that gay people *not be*" (43). More
intractable obstacles may exist, however. For instance, to the majority
of ex-gays who remain in the program as counselors or manage to
abstain from gay sex after the program, fraternity and homosexuality
stand as irreconcilable opposites. Erzen observes that

> [t]o many men in the program, the gay community is static
> and bounded, a place where promiscuity, drug use, and gen-
> eral hedonism are rampant. In their conception, only marriage
> offers an alternative to their loneliness or unhappiness.
>
> Most men at New Hope were never part of a gay commu-
> nity, and most never even self-identified as gay. Their experi-
> ences with homosexuality consisted of sexual behavior rather
> than a cultural, political, or identity affiliation with other gay
> people. Coming mainly from rural backgrounds and small
> towns, many had never lived in places where there were large
> numbers of gay people. Others lived a fairly closeted exis-
> tence, even though they were in relationships with other men.
> The lack of connection to a gay community or gay identity
> was almost universal among the men at New Hope, and it
> explained why their sense of religious belonging at New Hope
> was so important and profound.[8] (110)

The small towns to which many but not all of these men's lives tend
to have been confined are exactly the sorts of places where, as queers,
they are likely to feel more isolated, to see no future in coming out
since they have available to them no community except the omni-
present straight one. Although small-town and rural settings hardly
have a monopoly on feeling disaffected with or disconnected from gay
communities and institutions, urban environments frequently supply
cultural and subcultural infrastructures that provide the opportunity
not to feel so. Urbanized gay areas offer multiple opportunities for
affiliation, erotic knowledge, and divergent ways of being queer, of
inhabiting sexual, ethnic, and cultural identities. Though urban areas

can be homogeneous in a number of ways, there's a higher chance that small-town, rural, and, for that matter, suburban locales will contain a higher degree of heteronormative uniformity and greater homogenizing pressures—even if those pressures are not explicitly homophobic. To put it as neutrally as possible: although there may be a gay bar or a gay social network in small-town or rural settings, it's nevertheless likely that straight culture in such contexts will *appear*, oppressively and deterringly, the only game in town.

Regardless of their geographic origins, however, it might seem unlikely that the sense of fraternity these men find among fellow ex-gays is one that nourishes gayness, much less a broader queerness. Yet the company in which they are thrown together enforces a degree of brotherhood that holds homosexuality in a queer sort of suspension in therapeutic settings. Held in adjournment yet constantly in danger of reemergence, homosexuality for ex-gays is not to be cast off or escaped but eluded, refrained from. The special sense of fraternity they experience is that of identity with other functionally gay men whose homosexuality unites them as the common ground they have sworn in common to abolish from their lives. No wonder ex-gays' most enduring bonds are with their ex-gay brothers, a bond that sustains them at the same time it continues to distance them from, and to buffer them from assimilation into, straight society and culture. Even if some of them manage to date or marry women, they will always be set apart from "real" heterosexuals; *having been* gay remains the core of their identity. Those who manage to abstain from gay sex (as opposed to gay desire) face an even slimmer margin separating them from homosexuality. They may, in their own view, no longer be gay, but it's not certain precisely what or where they now are. What remains unclear from an outsider's perspective is whether the perverse bonding among ex-gays—bonding over that which they wish to escape from, to subdue—is too perverse to form an innovative substrate for fraternity, a basis for fraternizing with those who, by virtue of being gay, may tempt them. After all, the combination of platonic support and erotic tension renders them simultaneously allies and enemies.

As chapter 3 will explore in the context of broader conservative and liberal Christian ideology, the inhospitable can be surprisingly *hospitable* to forbidden desires, making unexpected provisions for impulses and actions it has sworn its contempt for. The hopeful note within the threnody of ex-gay life is the carving out of a foothold, the working out of a modality for surviving and, in small, nonalgorithmic ways, a means of queering life in the Christian closet—ameliorating slightly the confines of purity, abstinence, or ex-gay subculture, making it more tolerable but also denaturing the master narratives that captive queer and protoqueer audiences are compelled to serve.[9] What is *less* hopeful, by contrast, and what chapter 3 goes on to argue, are the long-exercised hostilities of religious institutions and religious beliefs toward homosexuality; indeed, toward nonnormativity in any form. Rather than bad habits that may be blamed on fallible individuals, folk ignorance, or institutional inertia, it might be time to face the apparently discouraging but actually quite liberating possibility that religion's animus toward homosexuality is a genetic component of religious faith itself. Religious moderates consider themselves to have found a solution to their faiths' histories of violence and intolerance. However, as skeptics like Christopher Hitchens and Sam Harris have pointed out, in doing so they merely delude themselves and wreak further damage by exempting belief from criticism or culpability, by muzzling objective, reasoned argument, and thus actually endorsing the hate and violence that extremists—let off the hook as merely voicing or acting in accordance with the beliefs they "have a right to"—direct at anyone who differs from or disagrees with them.

———

An alternative and perhaps less hampering template for breeding fraternity within the confines of the gay closet originates in the world of barebacking as analyzed by queer psychoanalytic theorist Tim Dean. In *Unlimited Intimacy*, Dean investigates the erotic and ideological motivation of barebackers. Dean accepts the fact that to many gay and straight people, barebacking is an unthinkable behavior, a reckless response to newer medications that have transformed HIV from a death sentence into a manageable condition or the result of "conflicting messages that bombard gay men, as if we were essentially victims of a homophobic culture" (3). Refraining from a knee-jerk "'othering' [of] bareback sex as deviant or pathological," Dean proposes that "bareback subculture actually signals profound changes in the social organization of kinship and relationality": "sharing viruses has come to be understood as a mechanism of alliance, a way of forming consanguinity with strangers and friends. Through HIV, gay men have discovered they can

'breed' without women. . . . For some of its participants, barebacking
sex concerns different forms of life, reproduction, and kinship" (4, 6).
Most immediately useful to my argument is Dean's exploration—in
ways that advance beyond our customary, normative, and often blinkered purviews—of bareback subculture's modeling of intimacy, kinship,
and familiarity versus otherness.

"Breeding," barebackers' favored term for unprotected anal sex that
sometimes concludes with insemination, might appear to resonate too
closely with heterosexuality's rhetoric of impregnation for it to be useful in radical or gay causes. Few corners of the landscape are free from
heterosexuality's enshrinement of pregnancy and reproduction as concrete and symbolic vehicles of genetic, capital, and cultural transmission. Yet the parallel is quite to the point; the straight cultural baggage,
played to the hilt. Barebackers see themselves not just as passing on a
virus but also as transmitting a cultural legacy, cementing community
in what to many is the most radical way imaginable. Given barebacking's transgressive import, it's worth emphasizing that its participants
are not laboring to mimic straight relations but, rather, performing in
an alternative relational system. This system represents just the latest
iteration of novel relationality that queers—who typically grow up in
isolation from their kind, stranded among heterosexuals whose familial
ties endow the latter with context, lineage, and a sense of communal
belonging—have long learned to build for themselves. By necessity,
queers have long proven themselves bricoleurs through made families
and extemporized communities. "Breeding," for barebackers, is not just
about infection or liberation from normativizing categories of health
and life versus illness and death. It's a way, in Dean's words, for "gay
cultural membership" to "become irrevocable in a way that neither
national nor religious cultural membership is" (83–84). Bareback sex
certainly "reinscrib[es] same-sex eroticism within the sphere of transgression" just as mainstream discussions of gay marriage and adoption,
although not producing universal acceptance of homosexuality, moved
it out of the social margins it inhabited in the 1980s and before (85).
Still more transgressive than barebacking's association with promiscuity and "outlaw" status is its renovation, its forceful and profound reor-
ganization, of heteronormative structures of alliance and affinity (85).
Given the legal and cultural battles over marriage, civil unions, and
domestic partner benefits, marriage might seem the obvious target of
barebacking's parody and transgression. Dean suggests, however, that

a better analogy than marriage is that of conceiving and bearing children. As the quotation from a bareback Web site . . .
indicates, much of the rhetoric around bareback sex concerns
breeding ("Breed, get seed and get on your knees to feed").
One of the earliest and most notorious bareback-porn mov-
ies . . . is titled *Breed Me* (dir. Paul Morris, Treasure Island
Media, 1999). Breeding the virus in other men's bodies creates simultaneously lateral and vertical kin relations: the man
whom one infects with HIV becomes his sibling in the "bug
brotherhood" at the same time that one becomes his parent or
"Daddy," having fathered his virus. If this man also happens
to be one's partner or lover, then by "breeding" him one has
transformed what anthropologists call a relational affine into
a consanguine; one's "husband" has become one's "brother" via
a shared bodily substance. (85–86)

Barebacking forges what Dean calls "consanguineous communities" out
of friends, lovers, and strangers (88). Although daddy/boy and father/
son rhetoric is also employed by gay subcultures including leathermen, bears, and S&M adepts, the dizzying sequence of metaphor and
action by which one's lover becomes one's "Daddy" and by which one's
"brother" becomes one's "son" holds an added pungency of meaning for
gay barebackers. The incestuous tenor of barebacking rhetoric seems
very much to the point, for it's that shocking act of equivalence and the
frisson it evokes that warp the conventions of kinship in experimental,
visionary ways:

> bareback subculture has the distinction of not conforming
> to any established kinship model. By transforming relational
> affines (lovers) into consanguines (siblings) and by confusing
> relations of consanguinity with relations of descent, bareback
> "breeding" irrevocably contaminates the elementary categories
> of kinship, even as it appeals to them for a measure of its pro-
> vocative power.
>   Understood in terms of kinship, bareback subculture
> changes what kinship means. Obviously the form of kinship
> is not heterosexual; instead, it involves homosexual or mono-
> sexual breeding. To the extent that it entails erotic relations
> between persons understood as brothers, bareback kinship is

eminently incestuous. Barebackers transform other men into
fraternal relatives in order to keep having sex with them, and
they do so by means of a virus. Thus bareback kinship is homosexual and incestuous differently from what those terms usually signify. In Western cultures the incest taboo distinguishes a
comparatively small number of persons as sexually prohibited;
through HIV barebackers have discovered a means for making sex with any number of strangers tantamount to incest.
In this way, the "unlimited intimacy" desired by subcultural
participants undermines the basic classifications and typologies
through which anthropologists differentiate relations. From a
conventional perspective, the viral mixing performed by barebackers hardly qualifies as kinship at all. (92–93)

It's not merely a queer confrontational spirit that leads barebackers to
subvert one of heterosexuality's deepest taboos: incest. Although people
often manage to craft alternatives outside or within normative heterosexuality, we all grow up within heterosexual culture, even if raised by
gay or lesbian parents. Its customs form our first classroom; its sacred
cows, our early, if later rejected, totems. Inasmuch as they are not actually related by blood, barebackers, who may be straight or bisexual
as well as gay, thwart the taboo against incest. By invoking—indeed,
by embracing—discourses of blood-relatedness, barebackers parody
heterosexual familial relations, showing how liable those relations and
the transmitted values are to being violated and destabilized. They
show how constructed those discourses are; how vulnerable they are,
if not to being shaken off, to being questioned, parodied, and queerly
recoded; and the extent to which their so-called naturalness can be
seen through, read against the grain and highlighted as inauthentic,
consciously performed roles. Furthermore, by relating to one another
through blood and semen, barebackers' version of "breeding" shows
how *labile* vehicles and systems of relation can be, how they may be put
to other than routine, prescribed purposes. It registers those systems'
ability to give pleasure, to transmit pain, and, most eye-openingly, to
serve other ends than biological, ideological, and capitalist propaga-
tion, rote replication of babies, workers, and shoppers. It shatters, for
its participants, the unconscious iteration of roles and norms.

Although many gays and straights will find barebackers' methods controversial, their commitment is undeniable. Such reactions

notwithstanding, Dean persuasively argues that bareback subculture commits not merely to "creating viral consanguinity" but to "conver[ting] ... strangers into relatives" (91). The reconstitution of kinship enacted by barebackers recommends itself as an unlikely but galvanizing analog for gay brothers in Christ, those teens and men within ex-gay or purity subculture embarked on queering the closet, queering purity, and—battling desire for their peers—queering kinship. Dean's eloquent elaboration of the extent to which "queer experiments with kinship alter what kinship is" refers most immediately to barebacking, but this is also a nod to gay and lesbian subculture's distinctive practice of deforming and re-forming given, heterosexual structures into more amicable, usable forms. In suggesting earlier that "the viral mixing performed by barebackers" and thus the system of affiliation they are crafting "hardly qualifies as kinship at all," Dean is hardly imputing a dearth of meaning to their nonce form of sociality (95). Rather, he is seeking a better term to evoke the resonance of barebackers' "relational experiments" less with "marriage, family, or community than [with] tribes or gangs." The term he settles on is "biosociality," another anthropological term, one that connotes the extent to which "subcultural participants express commitment to intimacy *beyond the couple*," investing "more in *group membership* than in privatized union with another individual" (95; emphases added). The import seems enormous—not merely for gays and lesbians who find themselves nudged toward normalcy by the same-sex marriage debate with its emphasis on coupled monogamy, social responsibility, and property rights but also for those gays who find themselves invested or interred in purity cults and Christianized abstinence education. To the extent that barebacking constitutes an experiment in "deregulating intimacy" beyond the couple form, it yields a *model* for embracing or inhabiting a counterintuitive positionality, for developing and innovating other ambivalent patterns of communal belonging (Dean 96). It affords not a literal behavioral template but, rather, the potential for finding *within* that ambivalence pleasures that might be sexual and transgressive but might also supply a vehicle for resisting the crystallizing, normalizing effects of identity—gay, Christian, or otherwise.

The target of Dean's critique is not identity politics per se but what he calls "*identification* politics" (21; emphasis added). This refers specifically to "struggle[s] over images and identification . . . [over questions like] 'Is this movie conveying a positive image of gays?' . . .

[as they] constrain . . . politics to the imaginary domain" (21). "[T]
he time has come," he urges, "to dispel this constraint on our political
thinking," to critique and to resist "any politics grounded in recognition, namely, the politics of the ideal image" (21). The problem with
identification as a model for politics or relationality is that it prevents
necessary and *potentially* productive alliances with those with whom
one finds it difficult to empathize or identify, such as barebackers, ex-
gays, closeted gay purity teens. A "subculture [that] seems foreign to
everything one knows and believes," whether this applies to nonreligious gay men trying to understand gay conservative Christians or
conservative Christians seeking to annihilate or cultivate some part
of their own identities, "demands [a different] ethical approach" (25).
Instead of a "cogent demystification in the name of politics," or the
explaining away of aberrance in order to preserve operative, recognized
identity categories or to exert political leverage in accustomed ways,
Dean recommends an "ethics of alterity" (25), an openness to that
which is strange, foreign to one's experience and beliefs, even to one's
sense of what counts *as* an ideal, as an inhabitable, sensible identity,
as personhood. Even though Dean says his critique is directed less at
identity politics than identification politics, it's the latter that critically
impinges on identity politics, that drives and, from his point of view,
confines gay identity politics to its current, substantively unproductive
form. He contends:

> identities of whatever sort remain incompatible with openness
> to alterity, and thus identity may be understood as not merely
> illusory but also, in this sense, as unethical. Contrary to the
> Christian ethic of viewing the other as a neighbor and loving
> him or her "as thyself," the psychoanalytic ethic insists that
> the other's strangeness be preserved rather than annihilated
> through identification. (212)

In line with the strains that homosexuality exerts within purity/absti-
nence culture and ex-gay programs, the torsions it produces when
sequestered in the Christian closet, Dean hails barebackers' active
undoing of positivist understandings of identity that are shared by
queers and straights alike. Still, identity as commonly conceived—the
ethnic/identity-politics model foundational to the post-Stonewall gay
and lesbian movement—is limiting in definable ways that might yet be

productively circumvented. It may not be fully possible here to adju-
dicate cause and effect: whether it's the case that barebacking brings
about the diffusion of identity and "openness to alterity" or whether
understanding identity as fundamentally "illusory" precedes and facili-
tates "relational experiments" in bareback subculture or the Christian
closet. Even so, the enriching interpenetration of unlikely means and
unexpected ends should not be overlooked. Instead, it should be enter-
tained if not roundly endorsed. To be clear, I am not suggesting that
barebacking is the best or sole route to modes of relationality capable
of dodging the *full* grip of normativity. Nor am I proposing that gay
Christians bareback their way out of their conflicted mindset or that
anyone else do so to slip the harness of cultural norms. Rather, I am
recommending that the Christian closet in the various incarnations
discussed here might hold strains of alterity, might be amicable to
modes of affinity that summon new uses or employments for identities, for ideological positions such as gay and Christian that together
or separately have ended in cul-de-sacs for many of their adherents.
The need for alternative modes of affinity is made more urgent by
the extent to which practitioners of dead-end, deadening identities
and ideologies feel themselves drained by the seesaw of relentless legal
battles and petitions for so-called suitable media visibility, enervated by
physical and rhetorical violence, by commercial and political discourse.

   Dean's advocacy for the pursuit of alterity invites comparison to
the energy that Arterburn and Stoeker enjoin their young male readers to husband. Equating conserved semen with greater spiritual force,
Battle's authors counsel that refraining from masturbation supplies one
with more spiritual energy to "expend . . . on God's kingdom" (118).
While the latter would appear to imply something as mundane as religious devotion, the very next sentence suggests that a quasi-Aryan
dedication to purity prepares one to serve in a more literal, mundane
Christian kingdom: "The world hasn't yet seen what God can do with
an army of young men free of sexual fevers" (118). What this chapter
and the previous one have explored is, of course, a distinctly different
"fever," a desire unaddressed by *Battle*, or at least not taken seriously,
but one that tangibly courses through the purity, abstinence, and ex-gay
movements. The fever of being a Christian in the closet, whether one is
seeking to exterminate his homosexuality and/or to indulge and enact
it, bears instructive similarities to the fever of "unlimited intimacy"
that concerns Dean: a febrile, heightened state—call it queered purity,

queered Christianity—by which abstinence and ex-gay participants might vet, explore, and repurpose the tools of their vexed, hateful, sustaining proclivities, if not also, in small ways, the larger political objectives and cultural repercussions of their chosen or enforced identities.

There are important resemblances between the behavior of ex-gay Christians and that of the barebackers studied by Dean, yet these resemblances also contain instructive differences. Both identities embody hybridity. Ex-gays are both gay and Christian; barebackers inhabit the roles of lover, on the one hand, and father/son/brother, on the other. A salient difference between the two groups is the relative priority each gives to desire versus action. Ex-gay subculture emphasizes desire over action: one may always *feel* gay desire but should refrain from acting on it. By comparison, among barebackers action takes precedence over desire; one might even argue that here the two are inextricably intertwined—but even if this is the case, it is still a point of stark difference from ex-gays.

Other parallels, at least initially, include the two groups' engagement with biosociality: that is, with any act or mode of relation in which "subcultural participants express commitment to intimacy beyond the couple" by investing "more in group membership than in privatized union with another individual" (Dean 95). For ex-gays, the biosociality upon which they base their shared identity is highly unstable. It's not concretized like the relations between Dean's barebackers, who are constructing a tightly knit brotherhood of incestuous, consanguineous relations. To the extent that ex-gays *can* construct a form of kinship, as small, limited, and circumscribed as it may be, *their* brotherhood only stands to get smaller under the constant threat of one of their "brothers" either becoming straight and leaving the group or becoming irrecuperably gay and having to leave for that reason. Those who manage to remain are brothers only by negation of the dormant queerness that brought them together in the first place. The sense of brotherhood permitted to ex-gays is antithetical to their gay sexual desires, hostile to any nonheterosexual expression of brotherhood, and cemented by their own annulment. Befitting the imagery of barebacking culture, the only thing that ex-gay brothers are giving birth to is their own erasure. Brothers in barebacking are midwifing a *positive* kinship in both the literal and symbolic senses. They are connecting their sexual desires and acts to a form of sociability and communal belonging, yet one that destabilizes known structures of kinship, monogamy, and reproduction—the linchpins of heteronormativity. If ex-gay kinship is contingent on the erasure of gayness, barebackers' style of kinship *embraces* gayness, if in an extreme, somewhat controversial form. Gayness is something to be shared among them as much as the possibly present virus; indeed, in the post-AIDS world, HIV is the most condensed, intense, and embodied shorthand for the pressing civil rights issues confronting queers. And this seems true not only or necessarily in a pejorative sense. HIV, as well as the mere possibility of receiving the virus, might represent all the threats queers have to live with, all they have to combat from without. The intimacy and brute intensity of unprotected sex embody, even court, the risks of all that is at once vital and moribund in (gay) human nature.

Though unquestionably distinct, their modes of relation share one characteristic. In both instances, members breed new fraternities in environments hostile to their project. They invoke spaces in which unexpected kinship gives rise to new, oppositional identities within the larger community to which they belong. Chapters 1 and 2 have roughed out some of the ways in which the Christian closet and ex-gay subculture may subvert heteronormative, homophobic objectives by improvising patterns of relation conducive to covert gay pleasure, by carving out niches—as impromptu and fragile as they may be—in which homosexuality may find refuge instead of marginality, erasure, and extinction. I've chosen to use barebacking subculture as a model not to dictate or limit the configurations of queer communal belonging, ritual, and identity. Rather, I've intended for barebacking to function as a theoretical rather than literal pattern for developing styles of biosociality that are equally or more innovative and stimulating. Heading into the next chapter, which explores queer efforts to rehabilitate religion and their ultimately reactionary or insufficiently transformative character, it's only fair to admit the possibility that even covertly innovative modes of relationality, such as the purity closet or ex-gay ministries, may not be sufficient. They may not be enough to hold up, especially within an institution with a centuries-long commitment to demonizing and eradicating homosexuals. Even if such a model *can* work, it can't do so within the physical or ideological reach of a church. Thus, a form of kinship resembling that of barebackers, even if not practiced in the same material fashion, emerges as the *better* hope of the two communities for a vigorous, or at least nonsuffocating, queer future.

One final distinction lies in the extent to which a claimed sub-cultural identity embraces or redacts the characteristics of its members. Gays who join a barebacking community are still gay; they're just barebackers as well. Yet conservative Christians aren't supposed to be gay. The official line is that ex-gays are not really, authentically gay, that homosexual behavior can be refrained from, and that gay desire has been inflicted on them by others through molestation or defective parenting. Therefore, ex-gays have no community except one to which admission is conditional (as it is not with barebackers). Admission to the conservative religious fold is conditional on the repression of what for many ex-gays are their strongest sexual desires, a core element of their humanity.

It's likely that some readers, gay as well as straight, may strongly object to the discussion of barebacking subculture as a model of rela-tionality that others might profit from by imitating or adapting, even if only symbolically. Others might object to *any* discussion of bareback-ing, as irresponsibly encouraging risky, destructive behavior. Bareback-ing poses admitted health risks, to be sure, especially for those who lack adequate health insurance or access to the drug treatments that have converted what was once a death sentence into a manageable condition.[10] Looking ahead to the next chapter, my reasoned response would be that seeking to inhabit the church is *also* risky behavior for queers. I would suggest that in attempting to salvage faith traditions that are at best indifferent but more frequently hostile to their interests and lives, queers are risking not just their psychological, emotional and sometimes physical health, or their social or political inclusion. They are putting at risk their cultural vitality, the very shape and promise of a queer life.

THREE

JESUS NEEDS GAYS, YES HE DOES

Gay Religion, Queer Spirituality, and the Recalcitrance of Ideology

What remains in need of clarifying from the previous chapter is the difference—and the relation—Tim Dean makes between identity and identification, and whether or not this difference informs, limits, or amplifies our attempt to understand the motives and conflicts of gay conservative Christians, in terms of average individuals, leaders, and the movement as a whole. As I speculated in chapter 2, identity may not be a fully or an always intractable obstacle, at least not in the particular subculture I'm investigating. Queers who have joined the purity or ex-gay movements, whether willingly or under compulsion, may find occasional footholds in these movements' glaring rhetorical and ideological interstices. By doing so, queers in the Christian closet may find ways of improvising shelters for their own queer erotic pleasures, means of rendering the confines of those spaces slightly more livable, strategies for rendering their impulsions and strictures temporarily less crushing. But the question remains as to whether such moments of relief, pleasure, or evasion have the power to abrade ideological muscle beyond individual experience, to wear away at or reverse the wider rhetorical, political, and cultural entrenchment of religiously

endorsed homophobia. The remaining chapters seek to answer this
question, as well as the corollary question it suggests. What if we widen
the focus to not just conflicted queer teens in purity culture or ex-gay
ministries but to queer Christians in general? What about gays and
lesbians who are seeking not to subdue their sexuality to conservative
Christian homophobic mandates but rather to *reconcile* queerness with
Christianity, to locate or fashion a gay-positive form of institutionalized religion or deinstitutionalized spirituality? How intractable are gay
Christian, religious, and spiritual identities? Along what axes do they
yield, and where, despite momentary evasions of brutality and discov-
eries of pleasures, are they not likely to? It's my contention, particularly in the remaining chapters, that the resistance and intransigence of
such belief structures seem to outweigh their potential for gay-positive
reform, that, *in spite of* liberalized theology and tolerant leaders and
congregants, they remain fundamentally heteronormative and incompatible with the breadth of queer pleasures, individuals, and modes of
communal belonging. My conclusion, which is the motive force of the
book as a whole, is that the most pragmatic, self-preserving response is
for queers to abandon religion and spirituality altogether—and not just
because religion has historically been, and to a great extent remains, a
heteronormative and homophobic enterprise. More importantly, continuing to seek the sheltering acceptance of any religion, conservative,
mainstream, or liberal, fails to repudiate the presence of religious belief
as a legitimate participant in civil rights discourse and thus ends up
condoning the toxic exercise of religious rhetoric's more homophobic
strains and the emotional, physical, political, and cultural damage it
inflicts on queer Americans.

To begin answering these questions, I need to return momen-
tarily to the point with which I opened this chapter. What difference, if any, does Dean's identity/identification distinction make for
parsing the extent to which conservative Christian queer identity is
not merely survivable, on occasion, but transformable as opposed to
intransigent? There's certainly one specific sense in which the contrast Dean draws between identity and identification seems applicable
to the plight of conservative Christian queers struggling to subjugate
their homosexuality. For Dean, identification politics is any "politics
of the ideal image" that restricts our ability to empathize or identify with those other people whom identity politics, especially queer
identity politics, would encourage us to consider our allies and fellow

travelers (21). Identification discourages the "capacity to imagine [our-selves] in [an]other's place" and thus deters us from making common cause with anyone who, despite sharing a broad identity marker like GLBT, seems *too* much unlike us in terms of finer distinctions (they may seem too promiscuous or too prudish, too effeminate or too mas-culine) (21). Thus defined, identification would be one way to name the force that imprisons those in the conservative Christian closet, what attracts them to ex-gay ministries, as well as what keeps many of them there. Having identified with conservative Christian theology and cultural values more profoundly than with their own sexual desires, the ex-gays of New Hope could thus be seen as making an error of identification politics when they should be accepting the otherness of their desire, its conflict with their religious beliefs. This reading feels right—unless that tension is the point, that it is as much transforma-tive as it is imprisoning and enervating. If the conflict between being gay and being evangelical strikes some of us as having but one sensible solution (to value gay desire over religion's demands), might we be overlooking the possibility that such individuals might view being gay, being evangelical, or even both, as unchosen conditions, states of being that cause them pain but that they find sustaining in other compensa-tory ways? Might we be tendentiously imposing our own norms by expecting denizens of the Christian closet to sensibly accept what *we* see as the healthier or correct relation of identity, identification, and the unconscious? Even if we end up retracting this imposition, or decide it is not an imposition but an ethically sound intervention, it's worth puzzling through what Christianity and homosexuality productively get out of their fraught interrelationship. It might provide some clue as to why, despite toxic as well as productive results, they seem unable to slacken their reciprocal grip.

As chapters 1 and 2 have explored, the conservative Christian movement's commitment to eradicating, or at least sanitizing itself of, homosexuality is undercut by an ideological *dependence* on homosexu-ality, a compulsion to preserve the source of so much of its rhetori-cal fuel. That conflicted commitment is what queers the conservative Christian movement in distinct ways, as previously outlined. If the effects of this queering fail to incapacitate the movement, compromise its ideological persuasiveness, or sap its political and cultural muscle, these queer moments might be felt to be transformative or sustaining, in isolated or more systemic ways, by some of the movement's queer adherents. Queer conservative Christians, even while being told they must abstain from gay sex, may find their queerness shielded as much as targeted. Or they may find their religion unexpectedly queered and interrogated. This perverse commitment potentially energizes what to many outsiders could only be a punitive, untenable, purely damaging position.

By contrast, from Tim Dean's point of view, gays who demonize barebackers as being irredeemably outside reasonable models of queer community are failing to identify not just with the transgressive actions and ethics of others (barebackers) but with the transgressive, antisocial content of their own unconscious: those antiheteronormative desires that even "good" queers harbor but that, to remain in good social or cultural standing *as* "good" queers, they feel impelled to condemn and disown. For the queer movement as a whole, then, identification constitutes an error because of its tendency to enforce homogeneity, to idealize certain politically expedient images, values, and persons (affluent, white, suburban, monogamous gays and lesbians with children) over others (drag queens, barebackers, dykes on bikes). This is not to say that the polarities never overlap, that suburbs house no drag queens, dykes on bikes with children, or forms of nonmonogamy. These are idealized images, however, and their ideal character depends greatly on a putative polarity.

At first blush, it would seem fair to apply Dean's critique to purity cults, abstinence education, ex-gay programs, and evangelical Christianity in general, in order to underscore their blinkered, telic drive toward homogeneity and polarization. Even though Dean says his critique is directed less at identity politics—because that's "been done plenty of times already"—elsewhere he concedes that his beef *is* as much with identity as it is with identification (21). His objection is that identity as practiced under the aegis of present-day identity politics depends on and tends to foster identification with an ideal image, ignoring politically inexpedient or embarrassing elements, desires, and individuals.[1] Even if a conservative Christian identifies with an idealized image that demands the suppression or elimination of his homosexuality (heterosexual Christianity), he must also identify with that which is inherently, doctrinally *other* to him (homosexuality), if only in an attempt to quash it. If he were not at least potentially gay, there would be no conflict, no call for the Herculean effort to maintain purity or achieve heterosexuality. Although homosexuality is certainly the target of repression by ex-gays as well as straight conservative Christians—in fact, *because* it is so—it makes little sense to view homosexuality as an *unconscious* desire on their part. These groups may view homosexuality as "other," but they nonetheless identify *with* it—perversely, constitutively. Thus, although the conservative Christian position is structured around an *opposition to* alterity in the form of non-Christians, homosexuals, and feminists, there's a certain truth to the notion that conservative Christians *are* "open . . . to alterity" (212): straight or seeking to become so, much of their identity rests on homosexuality as an ideological linchpin, rhetorical propellant, and emotional nucleus. On the one hand, then, Dean's astute critique of identification politics is invaluable in illustrating the potential of certain alterity-based models of communal belonging such as barebacking or ex-gay ministries for facilitating kinship and relationality, their capacity to parody, question, and unsettle heteronormativity's strictures and thus improvise what Eric Clarke calls "other possibilities for imagining queer existence" (20). In terms, however, of fully understanding the peculiar dynamics of queer evangelical identification, as well as of those straight conservative Christians who identify being evangelical with actively combating homosexuality, we may have to search elsewhere.

If one concedes the potential of some ex-gay Christians to partially resist identity's reifying demands, this resistance contrasts nicely with, and perhaps serves as counterweight to, conservative Christianity's obligation to keep homosexuality alive in all its aberrant glory. It's this commitment that contradicts its own stated goals of dissolving all things gay. Whether this declared intent is cast in hostile or loving terms depends on the gloss of the particular messenger. But the goal is the same: gay erasure. My point is that not only do conservative Christians seem incapable of effectively shutting out homosexuality, as we see in *Every Young Man's Battle* or *Straight to Jesus*. Rather, they *cannot* escape it in a more profound sense: without homosexuality, they have lost their main totem besides abortion and premarital sex. Although they themselves might use the term "taboo" to describe their relationship to homosexuality, "totem" captures the true nature of that relationship, which is constitutive rather than imaginary. They might even be said to *worship* gay sex despite—or, more accurately, *through*—their deprecations of it. Surely, one can be said to worship that around which a significant portion of one's ritual, theology, and social and cultural policy is centered, toward which its most febrile energies are directed. Of course, the fixation on homosexuality among a panoply of other nonprocreative, nonmonogamous kinds of sex is not unique to conservative Christians but in fact characterizes any number of institutions deriving their terms and values from the Enlightenment model of the citizen and Western sexual humanism.[2] Yet my focus is the *religiously* couched ideology that, thanks to its increased political and cultural prominence, admittedly impacts, and in turn is impacted by, current understandings and realities of public sphere participation. More specifically still, I've limited myself to the workings of that ideology as a ground for sexual and religious life, action, and identity and the possible spaces offered for distension and noncompliance by the confluence of, and conflict between, "gay" and "Christian."

This focus connects my project to a larger debate regarding the ideological rigidity of identity. Specifically, that debate concerns whether substantive transformation—the development of counterpublics, as Michael Warner dubs them—requires escaping an irredeemably calcified and recalcitrant system or whether—as those like Robert McRuer and Eric Clarke argue—transformational possibility resides in developing and sustaining a critical consciousness of one's compromised, conflicted loyalties. For instance, a capitalist subject could be invested in leftist principles. Though to differing degrees, McRuer and Clarke argue not merely for jettisoning toxic or calcified systems of relation and normative ideological strictures but also for rethinking our relation to various interpellating institutions, reenvisioning the ways the terms and strategies of those institutions relate to and operate upon one another.[3] Eric Clarke's *Virtuous Vice* offers an especially useful intervention in this regard. Reevaluating the work of Kant, Marx, Foucault, and Habermas in relation to public sphere theory, value, and visibility politics, Clarke's *Virtuous Vice* (2000) investigates the "open question [of] how far the inclusive mechanisms of the public sphere can go in overcoming their historical [bourgeois, heteronormative] limitations and admitting excluded groups [such as gays and lesbians], particularly when the very nature of such groups challenges the proprietary codes that (inappropriately) shape publicity practices." An "even more urgent question" for Clarke is the "future of queer self-definition and its relation to the social" (5). That is, "what *effects* [does] inclusion"—when it can be attained—have "in translating oppressed and/or minoritized concerns into issues of public interest"? Clarke's response is that, "[w]hile the inclusion of previously excluded groups seems to validate publicity's capacity to self-correct, it also leaves intact—because it can legitimately dissimulate—the normalizing calculus operative within inclusive procedures" (14). This chapter seeks to do due diligence to this line of thinking in regard to queers and religion. Religion is a delimited system of belief and a narrow way of thinking. As McRuer and Clarke argue in respect to able-bodiedness and liberal pluralism, it's my contention that religion, whether institutionalized or deinstitutionalized, blocks the discovery of possibilities for erotic and communal belonging beyond its own deep-seated heteronormative priorities. Religion deforms civil debate and harms the emotional and cultural well-being of queers even if it ultimately proves unable to block their access to legal parity.[4] It must be set aside. Certainly, the general fabric of heterosexual culture is ingrained with normative valuations privileging certain forms of sexual intimacy, affect, and relationality over others—valorizations that disparage anyone *questioning* heteronorms (like reproduction, monogamy, and bourgeois morality) as unhealthy, perverse, antisocial, or otherwise nonnormative. Yet religion is either the source or the fuel of many, though hardly all, of those queer-punitive and queer-exclusive norms. However, religion's antiqueer animus is attributable not merely to specific theological tenets but also to the fact that religions tend for the most part to have been heterosexual in origin and thus geared to serve heteronormative interests over queer ones. And unfortunately they often do so, specifically by slandering or persecuting queer interests.

This line of thinking seeks to do right by Eve Sedgwick's insight in *Epistemology of the Closet*: identity's effects are not always, or not always fully, in our control, not always recuperable or reformable, an insight relevant whether the focus is queer identity, religious identity, or both. Admittedly, of course, heteronormative demands on queerness, homophobic punishments, and erasures of queerness, whether disclosed or hidden, go well beyond religion. This is why it seems important for gay Christians to come out of religion, why in my view we must all exit out of religion with its dangerously self-authorizing moral investment, its tendentious, invidious narratives of change, and its intransigence toward reason and ethical objectivity. Religion is one closet we *can* exit, one structure we *can* manage our disengagement from. We owe it not only to ourselves but to the closeted gay Christians who may not always have a choice. Jettisoning religion will hardly, of itself, automatically dissolve the apparatuses that divest queer subjects of full control over self-definition, disclosure, or play. But it's a significant step in the right direction, a step toward cultural parity, toward authentic realization, toward individual and social dignity. It is a place—a crucial one, one within our power—to begin.

This chapter looks at the ways in which projects of gay religion and queer spirituality often retain, even despite their best liberal intentions, a heteronormative aversion to embracing certain elements of gay affect or queer experience. These elements are resisted, in part, because they threaten to subvert or question the moralizing hierarchies and priorities endemic to heterosexual culture and religion, to call conscious attention to the cultural performance and prescription of roles whose *apparently* pervasive, natural, inevitable character—their indispensability to (heterosexual) life itself—depends on their being unquestioningly, *un*consciously performed. My aim is to examine some of the *limits* on transformation, confines faced not simply by those seeking to transform their homosexuality, in order to accommodate their religious beliefs, but also by those attempting the superficially more tolerant project of rehabilitating religious institutions and beliefs to accommodate, to accept and embrace, one's homosexuality. Corollary aims of this exploration are (1) to expose bounds on our notion of what the transformation of beliefs and desires, of individuals or of larger institutions, can or should entail, and (2) to honestly assess what effects such transformation, whether homophobically or antihomophobically conceived, can actually produce.

Attempts to derive a form of religion that is amicable rather than inimical to homosexuality fall into one of two categories. The first category involves projects of gay religion such as the Metropolitan Community Church (MCC). The second entails projects of queer spirituality of the kind exemplified by Toby Johnson's *Gay Spirituality* and Marcella Althaus-Reid's *The Queer God*. My fundamental objection to both options is that, in spite of their attempts to avoid many of institutionalized religion's mistakes (commitments to biases and traditions inhospitable to queers and unsympathetic to their cause), liberal and deinstitutionalized religious ventures end up repeating these mistakes or committing other heteronormative retrenchments. These failures to move beyond unconscious heteronormative valuations, or the resistance of those commitments, limit the extent to which religion or spirituality can host, much less nourish, gay-positive forms of communal belonging and difference. Gay Christians such as those who attend MCC services tend, much like ex-gays, to credit religion with effecting changes in their lives that might more accurately be attributed to other, more concrete causes or be simply viewed as coincidence. Although gay Christians refute homophobic interpretations of the Bible, their failure to more broadly question divine or theological authority betrays an incomplete commitment to institutional transformation, a hedging move that, despite liberalizing intentions, leaves unquestioned other heteronormative religious and social values (such as a binary opposition between sacralized monogamy and casual intimacy/promiscuity). This move is simply another version of the compromise attempted by many *ex*-ex-gays, those ex-gays who renounce the attempt at overcoming homosexuality. These individuals make peace with their gayness. In criticizing religious homophobia, however, they often hold out hope for redeeming religion and spirituality from the homophobic crusade in which they view it as a coerced as opposed to an inevitable instrument.

By comparison with experiments in gay religion, enterprises of queer spirituality—a terminology that implies a more thoroughgoing effort to break free of normativity's contours—still display corresponding complications. In *Gay Spirituality*, Toby Johnson's Jungian reliance on nonreligious or pre-Christian archetypes results in a blunt, unproductively essentialist view of homosexuality. Displaying an unwarranted confidence in the inevitability of progressive, liberalizing trends in religion, Johnson also banks too heavily on vanguardism and a somewhat jejune notion of transgression. In addition to sharing the latter two flaws, Althaus-Reid's *The Queer God* presumes that, rather than needing to be introduced into theology, queerness is endemic to it. Thus Althaus-Reid gives little thought to the more basic question of queerness's capacity to weather the normative, homophobic pressures of religious and heterosocial orthodoxy. Althaus-Reid and Johnson likewise overestimate the potential of decentering efforts, of queering, to weaken religion's normative hold not just on theology but on the plethora of political and cultural attitudes affecting the lives of queer Americans. In both cases, the quest for enlightenment outside the strictures of conventional religion ends up meaning little more than a bid to rehabilitate religion itself. What's most disappointing is that, considering religion's unremitting, poisonous influence on debates over queer civil rights, none of these well-intentioned individuals or organizations seem willing to wash one's hand of religion as not useful to queer existence, as unreformable or, quite simply, as not worth reforming.

———

Any conscientious theorizing of generative possibilities for a space like the Christian closet must concede its punitive, even murderous attributes. It would be unconscionable to suggest that anyone endure such an environment a moment longer than he had to. There are inarguably safer and more sustaining places from which to actualize queerness. I am only speculating on the extent to which one might make the queer best of such a situation, were one held captive or unable to imagine a life without it. I would hardly suggest that the attempt to denature religious homophobia or sexual repression is best attempted from such a hostile hideout as the Christian closet, even if that was the best or the sole pressure point for such an endeavor. Even were the battle against antiqueer ignorance and hatred winnable from that vantage point—and this book argues that it is not—it would be an unthinkable sacrifice of emotional integrity or physical health to ask of any queer.

Together, the closet and religion have proven a deadly combination for more than one gay person experiencing denial or self-loathing. I'm referring not merely to the more glaring examples of the Christian closet's crippling weight: the successful and attempted suicides; the tales of physical, psychological duress and depression; the relief and joy of many gays who leave the church, or at least the conservative church or faith of their upbringing; and the continued emotional conflict felt by others who, like ex-gays, remain either unwilling or unable to fully accept their sexuality. And rank-and-file queers are not the only ones affected by the pressures and instabilities of the Christian closet; it frequently disgorges influential ministers and political operatives who, far from being confessed gays wanting to change, have been living as heterosexuals, stridently advocating antiqueer religious intolerance and social policy and leading secret gay sex lives. Beyond the heightened drama of being outed as hypocrites *as well as* homosexuals, these high-profile outings express how volatile the powerful mixture of religion and homophobia can be: a volatile compound likely to blow up in the face of those who brandish it.

Antigay figures outed as gay themselves do not necessarily have to be as prominent or influential on the national level as Ted Haggard or George Rekers for their exposures to be instructive of conservative religion's symbiotic yet ambivalent relationship to homosexuality.[5] Minnesota Lutheran Evangelical pastor Tom Brock made headlines for claiming that the unpredicted tornado that struck Minneapolis in August 2009 was an expression of divine wrath against the Evangelical Lutheran Church of America (ECLA), that denomination's more progressive branch. The ECLA was holding its national conference at the Minneapolis Convention Center to debate, among other issues, "whether [openly] gay and lesbian clergy in committed relationships would be ordained as pastors" (Townsend par. 11).[6] Among other structures, the tornado destroyed "part of the roof at the . . . Convention Center . . . as well as the cross on the roof of Central Lutheran Church, the conference host, across the street" (par. 11). Despite the tornado's so-called message from above, the ECLA approved the measure by a margin of 559 to 451. Now, an intrasectarian battle over homosexuality, gay clergy, or same-sex marriage is hardly newsworthy in and of itself. In June 2010, however, Brock himself was outed as gay by an undercover reporter for *Lavender* magazine who had been attending local meetings of Faith in Action, a group affiliated with ex-gay Catholic organization Courage. During these meetings Brock had admitted to "falling into temptation" and to having gay sex while on a church-sponsored "preaching mission" to Slovakia (par. 35). He blamed his weakened resolve partly on what he described as Slovakia's "'weird, demonic energy. I just got weak, and I had been so good for a long time. . . . [But] there's a lot of gypsies there'" (par. 36). Brock's church put him on a two-week suspension but gave no immediate indication that he would be dismissed. As one might expect, the *Lavender* exposé prompted debate over journalistic ethics and whether outing someone based on information shared confidentially violates those ethics. I have no interest in that debate, at least in cases like Brock's (or, for that matter, Haggard's or Rekers's). To my mind, publicly advancing homophobic policies, especially from a position of authority, categorically nullifies one's claims to privacy or confidentiality. The actively homophobic, closeted queer is opportunistic, disingenuous, and simply unethical. My immediate interest in Brock and his ilk, by contrast, lies elsewhere, in the disheartening lesson of their outings. Exposures of sexual transgression and hypocrisy occasion embarrassment, disgrace, and sometimes, though not always, loss of position. On the whole, however, revelations that antigay crusaders are themselves gay appear to do little to undermine the antigay stance of individual religious leaders and churches or of the religious Right in general. These exposures may provide a diverting fillip of schadenfreude to some of us, yet the antigay faithful seem perennially nonflummoxed and unenlightened by such revelations. Ideology has an answer for everything. The individual has faltered, not the institution. The outed party may be shunned, forgiven, even defended. The overriding agenda, which includes but is hardly limited to a commitment to curing gays, seems in no danger of being called into question or reevaluated. Chalking up failure to *individual* shortcomings leaves ideological architectures standing tall, unshaken.

There's undeniably a negative side to the Christian closet. The accounts of those, like ex-ex-gays, who have made it out of that closet not unscarred attest to the damage that the firebrands and everyday practitioners of evangelical and fundamentalist Christianity have inflicted not just on queers in the abstract but also on the individual gays and lesbians who are the friends or relatives of homophobic Christians, whom they have claimed to love but have actually hated, disowned, and abused. A story like Brock's divulges the toxic implication that gay Christians will be forgiven only if they renounce their homosexuality; the second, ancillary implication is that, given evangelical Christianity's definition of homosexuality as antithetical to spiritual salvation and mundane civilization, those who embrace their homosexuality will be rejected and vilified. As *willing* homosexuals, they cannot also be authentic Christians. Notwithstanding this defining antithesis, it's objectively true that without homosexuals in their midst the conservative Christian movement risks losing the reactor core that, along with abortion, has fueled its rise to mainstream awareness and political influence since the 1970s. In a sense, gay conservative Christians cannot be allowed by their straight counterparts to exit the closet and, through it, the movement. It's not so much that conservative Christianity is loath to relinquish homosexuality as its *bête noire* as that it *cannot* give it up, that it *could not* even if it sincerely wished to do so. Given the virulence of that necessary partnership, which ends up harming queer evangelicals more than it undermines the conservative Christian movement, it's unsurprising that some queers have sought to reconcile their homosexuality with their commitment to a religion that has historically condemned it. This truce, between the homophobic religious values by which they were raised and the more liberal religious, political, and sexual values they possess equal, if not deeper, allegiance to, has been attempted through two distinct avenues: gay religion and queer spirituality. By "gay religion," I refer to any attempt to rehabilitate traditional Western religious institutions; by "queer spirituality" I mean projects to construct a spiritual system outside traditional, institutionalized religious configurations.[7] It's my conviction that in both cases the compromise ultimately turns out to be a ruse, a false solution that diverts us from the actual problem: the intolerance seemingly ingrained in Western social formations and religious systems in general. Religions tend to be reactionary, heterocentric, and, despite localized areas of liberal revision, ultimately recalcitrant.[8] Chapter 4 builds on this line of argument to contend that recent defenses of atheism by Christopher Hitchens and Sam Harris should have compounded force for queer audiences. Religion, perhaps even spirituality, may carry too debilitating a cost for gays and lesbians who have survived on, and would do well not to forget, the best critical insights of their own forged communities on the corrosive, bullying tendencies of any dogma claimed to be natural, incontrovertible, and unassailable.

In *Be Not Deceived*, Michelle Wolkomir examines the motives and experiences of both ex-gay and gay Christian men as they seek, with very different objectives, to reconcile their homosexuality with their religious beliefs. According to Wolkomir, their respective decisions to accommodate their sexuality to their religion or their religion to their sexuality depend on which part of themselves they experience as their prior or more central identity. If, for ex-gays, being an authentic Christian takes primacy over being authentically gay, those who join gay Christian groups prioritize their homosexuality as the core identity, as that with which *religion* needs to be reconciled.[9] For my purposes, what's most enlightening in Wolkomir's subtle analysis of the intellectual and emotional exercises involved in both ex-gay ministries and gay Christian reeducation are the parallel methods of these diametrically opposed groups. Although the groups disagree on one key point—the (in)compatibility of homosexuality with Christian life and belief—their approaches possess surprising and instructive similarities in tone, strategy, and objective. For the purposes of brevity and clarity, I will employ Wolkomir's respective umbrella terms for ex-gay and gay Christian organizations: "Expell," which includes groups such as Exodus International and its predecessor Love in Action, and "Accept," which covers the MCC as well as gay-positive groups sponsored or allied with some Christian, Catholic, and Jewish congregations or denominations.[10] As one might expect, the shared tactics involve identity reconstruction: identifying with a new group, reframing the self with different ideas, and separating the old, supposedly false self from the new, true (and in this case) restored self. The commonalities most relevant to my argument, however, are the reliance on strategies of "emotion management" and "ideological maneuvering" (130). Emotion management, a common therapeutic tool, involves coaching individuals to overcome negative feelings, to generate positive new ones, and to label and monitor the (re)appearance of dangerous impulses. In Expell groups, those impulses would be fantasies about gay sex; in Accept, they would be feelings of shame regarding such fantasies. Feeling authentic as a gay man or an ex-gay Christian depends on a match between feelings and expectations and on how naturally one feels the "right," meaning therapeutically valued, emotion. Wolkomir pinpoints the flaw in such a model of authenticity for both types of groups:

> Ironically . . . the feelings that the men learned as markers of authenticity—those that arose *naturally*—had to be *learned*. This paradox, that the men had to learn how to feel if they were to experience their true selves, was invisible to the men, and they instead perceived that the changes in how they felt resulted from healing and thereby getting close to being the person God intended. Initially, though, group members had to be shown how to do this kind of interpretive work. (142)

Thus, the quest for authenticity, gay or ex-gay, problematically relies on emotional signals that can be faked—or, as the last sentence hints, misinterpreted. Motives for finally pursuing either gay or ex-gay identity stem, Wolkomir asserts, from a variety of factors. These factors range from idiosyncratic biographical factors such as developing one identity before the other to the satisfaction of various emotional needs, including feelings of greater belonging, safety, or worthiness as a Christian or a gay man. Regardless of such variations, the common catalyst for choosing one over the other appears to require three ingredients: a period of distress, addiction, or depression; a moment of bargaining during that period to give up whichever identity is felt to have led to the distress; and improved circumstances occurring *after* their association with a gay or ex-gay Christian group. Rationalization, read as God's plan, appears central to many of these men's experiences: in composing the narratives of their own transformations, they tend to correlate recovering from drug or alcohol abuse, experiencing emotional upturn, or ending an abusive relationship with their coming into contact with Expell or Accept. In what Wolkomir calls a "post hoc interpretation of contingent events," the men read their lives' improving during contact with religion not as a matter of chance but as the *result* of that contact—in fact, the result of divine intervention (64). Because such correlations depend on chance occurrence as well as acts of their own volition, Expell and Accept's shared reliance on the manipulable tactic of wish-fulfillment undercuts the claim of either approach to be uniquely "right," compassionate, or ethical. While that claim may appear obviously false in the case of Expell-type groups, it's only fair to admit that, based on the strategy of emotion management, the pro-gay Christian argument, though more humane than the ex-gay one, stands on equally weak logical ground.

As for ideological maneuvering, both Expell and Accept resist the stigma imposed on homosexuality to different degrees. Expell groups teach that homosexuality is a sin but not an "especially damning" one, encouraging their members to "shift the blame for their intense shame and self-doubt from themselves to a culture that unfairly castigated or oppressed them" (103). Through "guided reexamination of biblical passages," individuals in Expell are coached to see themselves as victims—not merely of neglectful, emotionally unavailable parents, as already discussed, but also of the "*human* bias" of Christians who misinterpreted the Bible by singling out homosexuality as worse than any other "ordinary sin" (101, 103). By comparison, Accept-type groups view *judgment* of homosexuality rather than homosexuality itself as the sin. Like Expell, Accept attributes homophobic readings of biblical passages to human prejudice, but progay Accept also faults human errors such as mistranslation and erroneous interpretation. They reverse antigay readings of biblical passages containing the word "sodomite" by arguing that "'sodomite,' translated from the Hebrew word 'qadesh,' was a poor translation and should refer [only] to male temple prostitutes" (99–100). By antihomophobically locating flaws in existing antigay *readings* of the Bible rather than in gays or in the Bible itself,

Accept seeks to develop a "new theology that is gay positive" (14).[11] Yet the question remains: how new does this gay-positive theology tend to be? Even as it questions certain homophobic assertions, what heteronormative assumptions does it leave in place? As with Expell, the strategy of biblical reinterpretation relocates disapproval of gayness from the sacred realm to the secular. Accept groups shift blame for unhappiness experienced by gays and lesbians regarding their sexuality from "an inferior self (e.g. not in obedience to God's will) to an oppressive society" (100). As gay positive as this might seem, under closer scrutiny it is not: queers are once again cast as victims. The intention is quite different than it is with Expell, but it's still—perhaps more—troublesome when Accept does it. One of Wolkomir's most compelling observations for my own argument is that neither ex-gay nor gay Christian organizations question divine/theological authority in their approach to scriptural interpretation; in fact, they go to sometimes gymnastic lengths to avoid it. The objective to integrate homosexuality within the Christian church is superseded by, and subordinated to, the priority of *not* disturbing any ideas other than the sinfulness of homosexuality.

Furthermore, the emphasis on portraying gays as victims underlines another shared failure of ex-gay and gay Christian endeavors: the failure to question, much less trouble, religion's heteronormativity. Even though Accept seems infinitely less judgmental of queers than Expell, the unexamined heteronormativity of Accept still pathologizes gays and lesbians, even if it does so less overtly. Gay Christians remain the unfortunate, mistreated minority to whom tolerance needs to be extended. While this would seem to many to be the point of queer inclusion, in religion or the culture at large, Wendy Brown compellingly argues that tolerance is always extended, like noblesse oblige, from a position of superiority by those who belong to outsiders who definitionally do not.[12] Distinctions between normal and abnormal endure even if explicitly questioned. In studying biblical passages to discover that, despite antigay messages previously heard from religious figures, "condemnation" of homosexuality was in fact "missing" from the passages themselves, gay men in Accept are encouraged to distinguish "loving, monogamous homosexual relationship[s]," which they are told the Bible does not actually condemn, from gay sexual encounters and relationships that are promiscuous, casual, and implicitly devoid of intimacy, affection, or fulfillment. Even—and especially—for an ostensibly gay-positive project, valuing a narrow range of gay pleasure and intimacy (committed monogamy) while, and indeed *by*, denigrating anything else as hollow and vacant seems particularly problematic. To say the least, such a move is callowly unaware of the way such normative valuations have for so long been used, and clearly still are used, to belittle or vilify queers themselves. Dismissing a whole range of sexual relations, or bracketing them as not worthwhile, marks the progay project of Accept groups as basically conservative and consequently more quietly homophobic than Expell, but homophobic nevertheless.

MCC offers a case in point of the subtler blockages to overcoming broader, ultimately intolerant, ideologies that can characterize even gay-positive religious entities. As a historic leader among religious communities on the issue of gay positivity, MCC has the reputation of being one of the most liberal denominations of Christianity aside from Unitarianism (although Unitarianism relinquishes liturgical elements retained by MCC). Individual MCC congregations can differ widely, however, and in ways less common within other Protestant sects. Content of services varies by individual congregation, ranging from liberal practices including Reiki and other New Age exercises to conservative phenomena such as evangelical "healings" or speaking in tongues. The wide berth MCC gives to religious individualism and to the primacy of individual agency partly explains this diversity. Yet as Melissa Wilcox notes in her study of specific MCC congregations, *Coming Out in Christianity: Religion, Identity, and Community* (2003), the more complete explanation lies in the church's roots, which, like its present-day character, are "*both* radical and conservative" (Wilcox 167). Founded in Los Angeles by the Reverend Troy Perry in 1968, MCC is likely popular with congregants of varied backgrounds because of its successful combination of essentialism, evangelical Protestantism, Pentecostal theology, and liberation theology (Wilcox 14; see also Wolkomir 19–28). Essentialism in this context refers to the contention that sexual identity is inborn, not chosen; MCC's liberal credentials stem in part from its subscription to this idea. Yet MCC's theology, driven by Perry's own upbringing, derives from a fairly "conservative, evangelical Protestant" strain, "emphasiz[ing] the importance of conversion (rebirth)," "sharing the faith (evangelizing)," and asserting that "there is one triune God, that the Bible is the divinely inspired Word of God, that Christ is the route to salvation, and that the Holy Spirit indwells in the believer" (Wolkomir 22, 21). Conversely, the liberal character of MCC's "gay-affirming doctrine" stems as much from Perry's Pentecostal leanings as from his attraction to liberation theology: Pentecostalism's emphasis on grace and "the experience of God's love" led Perry in founding the church to highlight "Jesus['] exemp[tion of] Christians from the Levitical rules in the Old Testament, including those that condemned homosexuality" (Wolkomir 23). Liberation theology, popularized by many liberal American clergy during the 1960s civil rights battle, views sin as the "structural oppression of others, not simply individual wrongdoing," and construes salvation "not as a reward in the afterlife but as the construction of a just society in this life" (23). It's this sort of dedication to social justice and consciousness of cultural and political discrimination that naturally led Perry, who founded MCC not as a specifically gay church but as a church of inclusion, to welcome gays and lesbians among his congregants and to speak out against their social exclusion and oppression.

MCC's admixture of conservative and liberal theology no doubt attracts many GLBT persons as well as heterosexuals seeking an alternative to other sects' religious extremism and/or homophobia. Unfortunately, the church's "centris[m]" also renders its message too moderate, on balance, to adequately counter the shrill volume and Grand Guignol rhetoric of the far Right, perhaps too mild even to unveil the quieter homophobia of some mainstream sects. As Wilcox notes,

> although [MCC] leaders are often on the forefront of social activism, the denomination in general is not radical in this way. ... While [some congregants] wish to affirm LGBT difference rather than pressing for assimilation into heterosexual society, the difference they affirm is not a radical one in the strict definition of the word. No one spoke to me about destabilizing the mating-pair model of love relationships or about developing new social and domestic arrangements—both of which are important themes in the more radical areas of LGBT/queer activism. Instead, they spoke of difference in terms of creativity or spiritual gifts, a different perspective on the world, or simply the obvious difference in sexual or gender identity. *These are differences that do not threaten radical social change.* (167–168; emphasis added)

Given this "hybrid nature," perhaps it's unsurprising that, its advocacy of tolerance aside, MCC's combination of liberal and conservative influences ends up confining its allegiances to the mainstream. The version of homosexuality that MCC tolerates—at least, the one it puts front and center in its pleas for tolerance—is a rather idealized, blinkered one, characterized by coupledom and monogamy. Needless to say, this portrait excludes the actual, often sustaining experiences of straights as well as queers. If, as I've previously suggested, conservative Christianity requires homosexuality at its core to animate its defense of heteronormativity, it appears, too, that even a more liberal Christian denomination relies on, or fails to question, its reliance on a normative version of homosexuality. Even if MCC's view of homosexuality is admittedly more palatable than one finds in rhetoric of the religious Right, it is a caricature nonetheless. Many MCC services, it's interesting to note, are not as overtly GLBT-themed as one might expect. Wilcox characterizes the church's assimilative tendencies as aiming for an "atmosphere of normalcy": "'Protesting too much' [that is, emphasizing the GLBT investment of congregants] would suggest that LGBT Christian identity is in question; people come to MCC seeking a haven from such challenges, and MCC's atmosphere of normalcy helps to provide it" (145). The rationale given by some of Wilcox's respondents for espousing sameness while embracing diversity is unconvincing: "Overemphasizing the assertion that LGBT identity and Christian identity can be reconciled would draw attention to counterarguments that they cannot" (138). As a strategy, this seems counterproductive and unhelpful, to put it mildly. If queer differences must be unspoken or deemphasized in an environment ostensibly friendly to them, part of what sets MCC apart from conservative Christianity turns out to be a matter of degree—albeit an appreciable one—in heteronormative commitment. Finally, although MCC views GLBT persons as victims of social oppression, of others' unjust treatment, the cultivation of gays as victims retains a troubling pathological resonance. Victims are to be accepted and helped but also, it seems, implicitly pitied. And that acceptance and pity come from a position of heterosexual privilege.

That ex-gay and gay Christian organizations share certain tactics and assumptions is not to suggest that either group is at all insincere. And here I am making an external, objective assessment. From an *internal* perspective, Wolkomir keenly observes, each side vehemently regards the other as its antithesis, insincere and dedicated to distinct, wrongheaded tactics. The parallels between progay and ex-gay Christian approaches are instead symptomatic of a larger shared dereliction. They indicate a failure to question larger theological and cultural constructs, including heterosexual privilege; they evoke the inequality embedded in the concept of tolerance; and they divulge the persistent heteronormative valorizing of certain models of sex, relationships, and community at the cost of other stigmatized ones. Although one might well expect *ex-gay* organizations to fall short on this score, it may come as a greater disappointment from gay Christian groups. After all, the latter seem to turn out happier graduates than their ex-gay counterparts, and the gay Christian approach to change, targeting cultural prejudices rather than human sexuality, is less damaging and potentially more productive on both individual and social levels. But while Wolkomir concedes that gay Christians and ex-gay Christians alike are carving out "new cultural niches," the transformations enacted by *both* these groups fail to "threaten the integrity of the doctrine as a whole," whether that doctrine is conservative or moderate Christianity (146, 184). Borrowing from sociologists James Scott and Michael Schwalbe (who are in turn indebted to Michel Foucault and Louis Althusser), Wolkomir concludes that both Expell- and Accept-type groups are attempting to forge new subcultural spaces, and that such efforts *can* result in the "achievement of resistance," an "expan[sion of] our cultural terrain, chiseling new identity niches out of old cultural materials to make room for new selves" (185). Nonetheless, in the case of both groups

> [t]hese niches remained linked to dominant ideology and power, thereby constraining the degree to which cultural changes could be made and limiting the challenge that could be leveled against hegemonic notions of sexuality. At the same time that group members *felt* freed and empowered by ideological revisions, they were also *performing* activities that reasserted the superiority of traditional notions of gender, sexuality, and family. In doing so, they were reproducing to some extent (more in Expell, less in Accept), the very secular ideologies and religious theologies that initially oppressed them. How was it possible that group members, in trying to resist oppression,

actually recreated it and found the experience of doing so to be empowering? (186)

Even when subordinated groups are resisting certain norms that constrict their rights or dignity, they can also end up "recreating their own oppression" (184). Seeking to revise *some* concepts, such as the sinfulness of homosexuality, they have left the "fundamental dominant structure . . . intact" (185). Attempts to construct "new cultural niches" by groups like Exodus International or MCC fall flat due to their incomplete innovation. Their "failure to transform" results from willfully or unthinkingly failing to buck more sweeping cultural and theological biases that inhibit material or symbolic changes in the treatment of queers, as opposed to merely occasional rhetorical adjustments in the way gays and lesbians are personally addressed.

By "moderniz[ing] heterosexism" through their recuperation of gays and lesbians, both ex-gay and Christian gay projects end up largely "reassert[ing] the primacy of heterosexuality" (Wolkomir 188, 192). As Wolkomir explains:

> Group solutions to members' dilemmas, while helpful to some individuals, revised beliefs and subsequent behaviors in ways that sustained, at least partially, the dominant heterosexist ideologies that members struggled against initially. Further, each group's theological revisions and theories about homosexuality also could function to "modernize" heterosexism; that is, these revisions functioned in some ways to mask old prejudicial ideas with a new façade of therapeutic or social justice rhetoric, making them more palatable (and even moral) in contemporary society. In doing so, they sustained ideas about what constitutes appropriate sexual practices and, correspondingly, who is worthy and good and who is not. In this way, these groups helped to maintain the social inequalities surrounding sexuality. (188)

Whereas Expell attempts to "make traditional patriarchy more appealing" through its machinations, Accept's "calls for inclusion are structured in ways that create the *potential* for heterosexism to be reasserted in the guise of tolerance" (190). If ex-gays fail to beat homosexuality, their failure is cast as their own; they have, in a sense, *chosen* failure. As Wolkomir observes, "We see here how coercion can get camouflaged as choice" (191). Acceptance and support is only for those who make the "right" choice. Further, their therapeutic language focuses on the individual, "discouraging any examination of the social conditions that gave rise to these difficulties" (194). If Expell makes "the endorsement of heterosexual privilege seem like helping behavior, not discrimination," Accept-type groups such as MCC are likewise guilty of "camouflaging reassertions of heterosexual privilege and superiority" (192, 190). Accept lifts the stigma from homosexuality but *only* in ways consistent with dominant theology. Consequently, their "dependence on existing power structures . . . leaves open the possibility of reproducing the stigma attached to homosexuality and of reasserting the central and privileged position of heterosexuality in our culture" (194). MCC's argument for gay rights, for example, rests on a refusal of the homosexuality-as-choice fallacy. What's problematic here is not so much the ground of their argument; most secular arguments for gay rights depend on a similar refutation of sexuality as chosen, modeled on the civil rights notion that depriving rights on the basis of inborn characteristic is unjust. The problem rests with the form in which MCC's antichoice bid for gay rights is expressed: "it's not their fault" (195). The rhetoric of fault might insinuate, even unintentionally, that "it's not [gays and lesbians'] fault" that they're different, that they're less than heterosexual, less than normal. The shortcomings of ex-gay and gay Christian endeavors suggest that tolerance is inherently "exclusionary," "recreat[ing] the very hierarchies it [seeks] to dismantle" and "enabling the oppressors to feel virtuous" (196).

Despite sincere antihomophobic efforts and intentions among individual members, then, "no group entirely challenged these cultural norms" on the denominational or organizational level—that is, with anything approaching critical mass (198). If this reading comes across as an unfairly pessimistic version of Foucault, the fair response is that for Foucault resistance requires the employment of "reverse discourse," the counterhegemonic employment of dominant terms and ideas. The "group solutions" of Exodus or MCC may have

> made members feel liberated from past oppression and empowered to choose to act in ways that allowed them to redefine themselves as moral and good Christians. This sense of power,

however, was, to some degree, illusory; group solutions were inadvertently structured such that the only right choice, the only choice a moral Christian could make, was to act in ways that reconstructed dominant ideologies. (197)

Relatively speaking, there's no doubt that gay Christians go further than ex-gays toward questioning predominant notions of sexuality, gender, relationships, and family. They just don't go far enough. The major, reactionary terms of Christianity and heteronormativity—and their rightness, their patent value—remain uninterrogated. I'm not proposing to set a benchmark for ideological resistance: problematize this much, or your project is a failure. For that is a litmus test faced by all discursive and activist projects. My point is simply that some ideologies, particularly religious ones, when coupled with insufficient self-scrutiny, are more invulnerable to transformation, more inimical to queer sustenance and health, than others.

———

Efforts at gay religion endeavor to render institutional structures and theology more amenable to queerness. By contrast, projects of queer spirituality attempt to sidestep the ideological brambles particular to Christianity, if not to religion in general. In doing so, they strive to shed the burden of institutionalized religion's cultural baggage when it comes to homosexuality. As an examination of two such projects will illustrate, however, similar obstacles confront their evasive maneuvers, obstacles that result from conceptual fuzziness, equivocal intentions, or the ambivalence of religious discourse itself.

Gay Spirituality: Gay Identity and the Transformation of Human Consciousness (2000) is one of several books on queer spirituality by Toby Johnson, former Catholic monk and current psychotherapist and activist. Inspired by the work of Carl Jung and Joseph Campbell, Johnson presents a vision of homosexuality as the ideal modality for countering and transforming the strictures not just on queer sexuality and spirituality but on human nature in general. Gay vanguardism, which is the core of what Johnson is offering, has much to recommend it to a queer audience: it's flattering; it constitutes a noble, under-standable retort to homophobic repression; and it has precedent in a strain of gay separatist thought largely bypassed by current mainstream

GLBT movements, whose allegiance tends toward integrative, transitive models of sexual identity and political activism.[13] The problem is the entanglement of Johnson's efforts with a brand of essentialism that fails to be incisive or useful in an activist or disruptive way.

Gay vanguardism has its attractions. Despite Johnson's statement that "we do not claim superiority over heterosexuals," *Gay Spirituality* brims with moments where he does exactly that (259). The assertion that "[h]omosexuality retards aging" may be only mildly overblown in reference to gay men's ability to "maintain . . . youthfulness" by not parenting children or, for those who do have children, by "resist[ing] the tendency [in straight parents] to drop sexual identity and refocus on fatherhood" (144). Although one might quibble with the latter idea, Johnson lands a valid point regarding the conservative animus that parenting exaggerates, if not also generates. Still, Johnson's Jungian background inspires him to take his paean to gay authenticity further than some readers may be willing to follow. Gays' tendency toward the unconventional and the adventurous comes, he contends, from their embodiment of "*puer aeternus*," Jung's archetype for "gay boyishness" (143):

> Gay youthfulness has only partly to do with maintaining physical beauty, though because we are concerned about our attractiveness we likely use moisturizers and skin creams. It is more about how we feel in our bodies. Gay men stay playful. We cuddle kitty cats. We sit on the floor, like children, not adults. We skip down the path in the park.
>
> But there are achievements that come from not shifting self-image from youth to parent. . . . The eternal boy saves the day . . . by being kind and truthful and concerned. We save the day by being good guys. (144)

Whether or not one is a Jungian, it's hard not to find a passage like this a bit absurd. Even so, the intent is understandable. By turning to myths and archetypes external and antecedent to Christianity, the objective is to transcend the latter's heteronormative legacy by connecting it to a symbolic framework less saturated by Western religion and its attendant homophobia. While this makes for a flattering account of gay identity and a welcome riposte to over a century of homophobia, the result is too flattering to be effective as counterdiscourse, much less reverse discourse. Overdone and reductive, this vision of gayness merely turns heteronormativity on its head, replacing one essentializing, vilified term with another. Gay becomes wholly good; straight, its soulless antithesis.[14] And while turning the tables no doubt makes a welcome change for gay readers, trading heteronormativity for homonormativity, in addition to being a numbing illusion, preserves normativity's hegemonic structure even as the majority and minority terms change places. In fact, one might argue from a Foucauldian standpoint that reversal only reinforces *hetero*normativity's weight and fails to effect any change whatsoever. As if anticipating this objection, Johnson makes a nominal concession: "Of course, not all gay men are good and not all good guys are gay. . . . We challenge the macho stereotype that men are hard and competitive, ill-tempered, crude, and arrogant" (145–146). On balance, though, a fulsome, mawkish brand of vanguardism carries the day: "Gay men glow. There is a sweetness and light that surrounds us. . . . There is a cultural stereotype of the gay man as a loving and unexpected saint" (195). Reverse aggrandizement is bound to be soothing for any historically demonized group. Whether it's an effective tool for cultural, political, or even personal advancement is another question entirely. Feminist and queer theorists understandably tend to favor constructionist accounts of sexuality, especially the kind popularized by Foucault's *History of Sexuality*, both for their intellectual truth and for their power to refute unequal allocations of symbolic and material power. As Diana Fuss argued in the late 1980s, though, one does well not to dismiss essentialism, which has invaluable pragmatic applications of its own, especially when grounded in descriptions of lived queer experience or leveraged as political weight in arguments for civil equality. But the sort of cartoonish essentialism we encounter in *Gay Spirituality* lacks tactical bite, the groundedness in complex, practical realities of queer experience that essentialism's strategic deployment requires. An overexaggerated outline lacking subtlety and contradiction, Johnson's reductively essentialist version of gayness pits a playful straw man in a losing contest against a culture whose homophobia is deadly serious.

My intent is hardly to deny the serious goal of vanguardism in *Gay Spirituality* or in queer spiritual endeavors as a whole. As a form of flattery, it's obviously alluring. When Johnson calls "being gay . . . a blessing, a higher incarnation, a better way to be" or when he describes gay men as "blessed—and sometimes cursed—with this vanguard vision," I admit to being sympathetic with the profounder aim behind his assertions of gay superiority (259, xi). Vanguardism has a legitimate, if sometimes forgotten, antecedent in modern gay history. As Eve Sedgwick reminds us, Benedict Friedländer, "co-founder (in 1902) of the Community of the Special, concluded that 'homosexuality was the highest, most perfect evolutionary stage of gender differentiation.' . . . 'The true *typus inversus* . . . as distinct from the effeminate homosexual, was seen as the founder of patriarchal society and ranked above the heterosexual in terms of his capacity for leadership and heroism'" (88–89).[15] This was the origin of the separatist position that eventually lost out to the assimilationist, continuum model as the lodestar of post-Stonewall, mainstream gay and lesbian activism; the latter model derived from the work of Magnus Hirschfeld, Friedländer's better-known German contemporary. It's possible, and preferable, to make a similar argument without Friedländer's troubling anti-effeminate bias, and to his credit Johnson does so. Take, for instance, an early comment by Johnson on gay sex:

> The culture supports heterosexuals with a steady explanation of what sex is for, though usually relegating it to a simply biological, reproductive role. As gay people, we have to create our own explanations, our own myths, our visions of why "God" created us and what it means to be homosexual. . . . What forces a theory—or a theology—to expand and rise to a higher perspective are not the findings that fit the theory, but those that do not. (27–28)

The exclusion of gays as sexually and culturally anathematic, while unjust, forces them into a more enriching, expansive outlook. Oppression and discrimination, like the conflict between religion and sexual desire, grants gays an outsider perspective, a tendency to question the accepted narratives and values, presented as "givens," that sustain heteronormative culture and fortify it by unconscious performance.

Gays' status as tradition-breakers extends their transformative potential beyond the limits of a gay or queer world: "We have changed our myth. . . . We are freed from the momentary appearance of things . . . . We transform our interior worlds and the world at large" (68). That transformation stems in part from a rejection of heterosexualized models such as family and the monogamous couple: "We do not see mommy and daddy . . . as the models for the life we wish to live" (15). For Johnson this rejection has literal as well as symbolic weight: "Many gay men can rightly be thought of as eunuchs for the kingdom because we have responded to [the] irresistible vocation [of pleasure, enlightenment] and turned our lives away from normalcy for something more wonderful, more innocent, and more immediate" (145). Forming the subtext here is the contentious but intriguing proposal that homosexuality serves an evolutionary shift in response to heterosexual overpopulation.[16] Whether one credits this sort of speculation or not, the guiding thesis—that queer experience is capable of conferring a healthy critical engagement with (hetero)normativity that the latter's beneficiaries have little reason to question—is not unique to Johnson's work. And up to this point I don't disagree with him. But this notion has little to do, necessarily, with spirituality. It's *there*, in regarding spirituality as the necessary, perhaps exclusive gateway to queer critical insight, that *Gay Spirituality* treads on more uncertain and less useful ground.

Gay Spirituality's wider contention is that gays, naturally or by virtue of their marginalization, are endowed with a vantage on spiritual enlightenment that escapes the limitations and divisiveness of religion—in Johnson's words, a "higher perspective from which to understand the wisdom hidden behind the religious myths" (xiii). At least in this incarnation, the reputed aim of queer spirituality, enlightenment outside the confines of institutional religion, amounts to little more than institutional religion's rehabilitation.[17] Seeing "beyond religion" means striving for this broader spiritual vantage point. To preserve the necessity of religious belief of *some* sort, however, is to confine oneself to a limited set of options at the outset. Johnson contends that only spirituality can "offer a vision of hope and meaning in a world that sometimes appears to be a hopeless miasma of pain and suffering" (xiii–xiv). One might pause to ask: might not a consciousness of pain and suffering, alone or in balance with pleasure and enlightenment, be a more honest vision? Or might hope be derived from a nonspiritual (i.e., humanist, secularist) framework? Dismissing these objections out of hand, as Johnson seems to do, means that he fails to question the idea that religion has an exclusive corner on truth. He thus fails to meet two of gay spirituality's chief vaunted objectives: being "evolutionary" (in the sense of evolving) and "insight-provoking" (xvi). Pledging one's troth, without hesitation or deliberation, to spirituality—and, as already noted, for Johnson this implies a pledge to some rehabilitated form of institutionalized religion—is to deny oneself the possibility that positive change and insight might just possibly lie elsewhere, might be derived from sources subject to reason, challenge, and debate.

In Johnson's view, gay spirituality is not only the best outcome of a gay "reevaluation of religion" in the face of religious homophobia (xiii). Via gay Jungian psychotherapy, it ascribes

> most of the problems homosexuals experience . . . [to] "internalized homophobia." Transforming how we think about our homosexuality allows us to discover that the guilt and shame we feel is a shadow that belongs to mainstream society. It allows us to see that homosexuals are the scapegoats for the culture's shame and secret sins. Discovering that we are fundamentally innocent allows us to let go of character-deforming, self-afflicting, wrong-making attitudes that generate many of our personal problems. This allows the healthy and adaptive gay personality to shine through. (xiv–xv)

Gay spirituality elucidates the way in which gay men, as "straight culture's 'shadow,'" are "blamed for their fears and their sexual feelings" (96). The appraisal of hetero culture's scapegoating of *queer* sex and culture as exclusively hedonistic and destructive, a danger to straight civilization if not also straight lives, resembles Lee Edelman's analysis in *No Future: Queer Theory and the Death Drive.* By projecting solely onto queers the pursuit of pleasure without the redemption of procreation and its attendant fiction, futurity, heterosexuality cements its normative standing by positing homosexuality as not just extrasocial but *anti*social. Yet leaving this similarity aside, Johnson's concept of internalized homophobia, along with his dependence on it as the pivot of his argument, is much more one-dimensional. While many gays and lesbians might feel guilty about or ashamed of their own homosexuality at some point in their lives, internalized homophobia is not *sui generis.* It is inculcated in young gays and lesbians through messages about their difference, abnormality, or sin; messages that pelt queers in overt and subtle ways from all manner of cultural signals, from religious, political, educational, familial, and social vectors. Johnson hardly denies that causal link, yet he proposes that internal, psychological adjustment is capable of changing not just one's own outlook, but the world around one. "This is not a book about the monumental problems that face the gay community," Johnson writes. "This is a book about the positive spiritual experience of homosexuality, about an attitude, a way of looking at the world that would resolve many of the problems before they ever got started" (xiv). Elsewhere this implicit proposal is more explicit: "Embracing our innocence, relaxing our fears and unrealistic demands might go a long way toward solving *practical* difficulties that beset the gay community" (147; emphasis added). While chapter 4 examines in more detail the objections that lead me to dissent from such an assertion, suffice it to say for now that granting spirituality a degree and breadth of efficacy such as this strikes me as overly optimistic and impractical. And to do so exclusive of more concrete, practical measures like legal action, political organizing, and social clamor, or even as *the* best hope for change on a social and individual level, borders on the fatalistic. It seems callous, moreover, to say that the "problems that face the gay community," such as gay bashing, teen suicide, or legal discrimination, are ours to solve, because that's awfully close to insinuating, if unintentionally, that we are partly to blame for those problems. Viewing queers as the shadow of heterosexuality induces a certain gratifying payback for endured violence and discrimination. As Edelman has persuasively argued and as Johnson alludes to, the formulation has acute accuracy as a verdict on queers' material and symbolic lives. Undeniably, queers are blamed for a multitude of problems more accurately laid at the feet of straights, as well as problems that may be the fault of no one in particular. Yet even a shadow self can have—can cast or shape—its own shadow. Queer egos cannot be uniquely exempt from projection, whether onto straights or other queers. Another way of approaching the same point is to note *Gay Spirituality*'s ambivalence. In light of the fact that nondualistic thinking numbers among gay spirituality's chief positive traits ("To be able to rise above polarity and contradiction is a great ability. It is the only way to achieve peace" [25]), heavy reliance on a dualism-prone system like Jungian psychology would appear problematically incongruous.

Johnson's prediction of a gay-driven spiritual/religious revolution seems, finally, misguided and troublingly yoked to reactionary models. In the chapter on spiritual evolution, he contends that religion, saddled with an "inadequate notion of right and wrong," has been outpaced by history and "failed to keep up with cultural change," meaning, one assumes, liberalizing trends in politics, education, science, and culture

(39, 84). Religion has failed to adapt on the whole; indeed, conservatives would count this a virtue. A proposal that religion *can* evolve, under the guidance of gay insight, toward bona fide tolerance and ethical enlightenment on matters like sexuality must also tackle religion's constitutive rigidity, as well as find some means of offsetting it. Yet against the still unflagging onslaught of religious homophobia, Johnson relies solely on queer spiritual, psychological growth: "In the long run, the know-nothing stance of the Fundamentalists regarding homosexuality will further isolate the churches and temples from mainstream reality. This will hopefully foment the necessary reformation in religion" (48). While antigay legislation passed during the last couple of decades has been reversed in some areas and shows significant promise of reversal in others, a thoroughgoing positive final outcome is not necessarily inevitable. What's more, the cultural heteronorms and religious "values" that drive and legitimate those laws, commitments running deeper than any referendum can reach, will remain. It would seem that Johnson's generous, if ill-judged, confidence stems from the observation of liberalizing trends in social attitudes toward difference and from a Whiggish faith in humankind's innate tendency toward progress and equality. On this count, Johnson's project fails because of two significant observational and interpretive errors. First, while it's true that attitudes about homosexuality have gradually become more tolerant over the last century, this development occurred only in the last three decades and, until the 1990s, slowly and begrudgingly at that. Such an assessment fails also to explain the persistence, and even growth, of an *anti*gay voices and organizations during that same period of increased tolerance. Second, it's true that the past few decades have witnessed increased tolerance for sexual diversity, but this has occurred no thanks to religion. If anything, religious belief can be credited with generating much of the antagonism toward progressive views on homosexuality and liberalized attitudes toward gay rights. Since the late 1970s, and most palpably in the form of the religious Right but extending across the religious spectrum, religion has been singularly responsible for agitating antipathy and hatred toward gays and lesbians. And this occurred not just via the religious rhetoric of evangelical leaders but through religiously led national and grassroots political campaigns for antigay initiatives and candidates, as well as participation in political lobbying organizations and think tanks such as the Family Research

Council, Concerned Women for America, and the American Family Association.

As the continued fervency of religious homophobia suggests, the transformation not just of conservative Christianity but of religion's general resistance to queer inclusion is not so assured as Johnson wishes to believe. Even if a gay-positive transformation of religion is possible or forthcoming, it seems apparent that more is required than simply waiting for homophobes' intolerance to render them politically irrelevant and culturally moribund. The progressive transformation of religion predicted by Johnson hardly seems inevitable or fast-approaching. *Gay Spirituality* is also unhelpfully vague about the process by which religious traditions would evolve beyond homophobia. Perhaps Johnson doesn't feel the need to speculate more concretely since, by his account, the homophobia and other loathings endemic to religion must wither of their own accord: "As we will see, traditional Christian religion will inevitably fade away, and a scientifically sound and psychologically sophisticated worldview—based in Buddhistic moral and mystical notions, stripped of Orientalisms, liberated from traditional anti-sex bias, and enriched with the social teachings of Jesus, stripped of their supernaturalisms—will replace it" (60). Even were a crunchy revolution of this magnitude ineluctable, much less possible, my question would be "How long are queers willing to wait, as they remain rhetorically pilloried, politically dismissed, physical assailed? When it comes to execration, what is the queer breaking point?" I admittedly lack Johnson's faith in the inexorability of progress. Disagreements about the efficacy of faith aside, when he confidently declares that a "major lesson from the history of science is that it is hubris to think you have all the answers" (86), I feel compelled to observe that religion *thrives* on precisely that purblind order of calcified certitude. A more plausible alternative, as I argue, would be the search for principles of sociability and ethics *un*warped by religion's commitment to blind trust in authority, its allegiance to reactionary norms of behavior, its hostility to rational inquiry and independent thought, its antipathy toward the challenges to and revisions of principles inhibitive of progress.

In *The Queer God* (2003), Marcella Althaus-Reid proposes a queer permutation of liberation theology meant to advance beyond the latter's foundational, political focus. By "dismantl[ing] the sexual ideology of theology"—the normative heterosexual grid to which it has been reified and reduced—she hopes to facilitate the "coming out of the closet of God by a process of theological queering" (2). In relation to "colonialism, divine transcendence, bisexuality . . . and popular spiritualities" of Latin American and European cultures and literatures, Althaus-Reid attempts a "heavy sexual theology outside the normal conventions" of both heteronormativity and "T-Theology," or traditional theology (3, 29). Her strategies for queering theology include not only reading *back into* institutional religious ritual, scripture, and discourse the queerness that has been redacted *out of* them but also radicalizing Christianity by interposing native and/or non-Christian traditions. By recuperating "visible centers which have been rendered invisible," we may "recover the memory of the scandal in theology, and with a vengeance" (33). As laudable as such a project is, one may be forgiven for lodging certain objections; at least, *my own* argument impels me to do so. For instance, blithely reading gayness and straightness in the Old Testament ahistorically transposes a relatively modern model of sexual identity onto ancient traditions. While such a reading conforms to an essentialist understanding of sexuality subscribed to by many practitioners of gay religion and spirituality, it problematically conflicts with the constructionist view of sexuality central to most adherents of queer theory, among whom Althaus-Reid counts herself. In addition, she presumes that "scandal," whose privilege and shock she uniquely arrogates to queerness, resides in theology, elemental and autochthonous. As the following analysis lays out, it's incumbent that one ask not merely whether queerness is native to theology but whether, found or interjected there, it can *survive* there. Can queerness survive the ideological pressures of religion, a habitat characteristically hostile to unorthodoxy? And if it survives, how well can it effect transformation from there? These questions seem more than fair in light of, for example, the Catholic Church's success in subsuming native practices, incorporating them in superficial and neutralized states like festivals and saints, or suppressing them when they cannot be productively conscripted or voided.

My disagreement with Althaus-Reid is not meant to disparage her broader endeavor, which laudably locates alternative models of queer community "outside the restrictiveness of the heterosexual parental [procreative, queer-phobic] imaginary" (3). I take no issue with this principle. Althaus-Reid's efforts are clearly in sync with the impulses of queer theory as well as with Stonewall-era gay liberation politics.

The destabilizing, anti-identitarian projects to which these currents of gay and lesbian thought have given rise include memorable, worthwhile political and theoretical endeavors that, more than once over the past few decades, have shown intellectual and material promise for the realization of queer community, rights, and authenticity.[18] My dispute with *The Queer God* stems, rather, from its inability to resolve theoretical and practical impasses attendant on both the jettisoning of strategically essentialist applications of identity and the more general project of religious recuperation. To be sure, these are serious impasses that may not be capable of resolution. No one is to be faulted for trying or failing to resolve these hard conceptual and practical obstacles. But to be unconcerned at their persistence in the face of bodily, legal, and cultural aggression toward queers, and at the failure of "queering" work to offset or substantially address those obstacles and vectors of aggression, is to be negligent in some vital way. My concern is not so much that queer theory may be incapable of forging sustaining modalities of desire and community; I leave that much larger debate for others to pursue. Rather, my concern is that its best decentering efforts may be insufficient to loosen religion's grip on political and cultural policy, to stave off the continued inequity and accelerating harassment of queer life in America.

Even as Althaus-Reid draws frankly on the counterhegemonic register of queer theory, she fails to address legitimate fears one might have regarding religion's historical and, perhaps, intrinsic ideological recalcitrance and antiqueer animosity. To be fair, Althaus-Reid anticipates this concern and provides what she regards as ample reassurance and ammunition. As a self-professed queer theologian, Althaus-Reid privileges, among other states of affairs, contingency, instability, "disauthorisation," "disaffiliation," and "de-essentialisation" (25, 43, 54). Typical of these concerns is her view that "queering theologies" is a sure means of combating, even revitalizing, hegemonic faith traditions:

[Q]ueering theologies . . . gives space for new, even if sometimes contingent, formations. . . . Queer theologies do not disregard church traditions. . . . Most of the work done around queering church traditions has been related to re-positioning the Queer, Indecent subject in theology and to do that by giving testimonies of other traditions (or the traditions of the Other) concerning love and sexuality. . . . [T]he real Queer traditions of the church . . . are characterized by processes of disruption in Christianity, and not by its continuity. Disruption is our diaspora. (8–9)

Instrumental to overcoming the rigidity of "reif[ied]" sexual and religious ideologies are the tactics of ambivalence, contingency, and subversion—staples from the poststructuralist armory on which queer theory, among other critical traditions, draws. Althaus-Reid states, for example:

> Theology (and theologians) may be hiding in the shadow of their hetero-orthodoxy, but there are ambivalences or subversive aspects to be rescued and encouraged even in heterosexual systematic theologies . . . .
>   Any theological praxis which seeks to save us from fixity, the obsession with coinciding with the eternal sexual ideology and the limited choice of angles, may be inspired by that. (42)

On the one hand, "limited choice of angles" describes the "troubling," narrow "dyadic constructions" to which normative heterosexuality confines expressions of desire, the limited pairings through which it mandates the channeling of legitimate sexuality (14). On the other hand, the phrase also pertains to those couplings to which Christianity traditionally restricts the expression of *religious* desire: believer/God, confessor/confessant. The chief "theological praxis" Althaus-Reid relies on for ungluing fixity is a "critical bisexual" stance: "it is only critical bisexuality which displaces and causes tension [within] the established heterosexual dyad implicit in the theologian's identity and task" (15). Bisexuality's inherent radicalness—the question of its ability to exceed the reductive duality of heterosexuality—has been much touted, and often eloquently.[19] Yet it's fair to suggest, as I have done elsewhere, that the character and extent of that radicalness remain up for debate. Far from impugning bisexuality as a valid identity or state of desire for individuals, the debate centers around questions as to whether, as a construct, bisexuality remains to some extent dualistic or dyadic. That is, might bisexuality be construed as homosexuality merely annexed to heterosexuality? Do same-sex pairings trouble, or on the contrary risk being obscured by, the historically privileged opposite-sex template that is part of bisexuality? Does bisexuality's inclusion of the male-female axis adequately trump the oppositionality that, according to bisexual theorists, undermines the transgressive, transformative power of both homosexuality and heterosexuality?

Although Althaus-Reid presumes an affirmative answer to the last question,[20] it's instructive to note that she proceeds to further supplement the position of critical bisexuality—a move some might take to insinuate that bisexuality by itself is insufficiently radical. Playing off the "encounter of the third" in the theological notion of Trinity, she calls for a turn to "triadic" thinking (16). Whether this constitutes a turning away from bisexual thinking is debatable; it certainly muddies the waters. Althaus-Reid offers triadic thinking as a strategy for "providing a location of non-rigid exchanges amongst people's actions and reflections" (16):

> Critical bisexual thinking may be closer to the way of thinking which could *leave behind* the complicity (and, we will add, the secretiveness) of *rigid dyads*. . . . A triadic Bisexual Theology has a third, undisclosed sexual component in the confessor/confessant model then. As a process, this may almost be represented as a body of knowledge, the body of the Queer Other in transit from closets while relating with other bodies in their own transits. Triads are more than three only if this flux exists. . . . The Queer Theologian develops a Bisexual Theology by understanding this fluidity of thinking and by permanently introducing "unsuitable" new partners in theology, which makes it difficult to fix. (17; emphasis added)

If bisexuality seems too dyadic to escape the clutches of binaristic essentialism, it's striking that even a triad—the Trinity as a spiritual collocation or as a physical three-way—is insufficiently transformative. In spite of assurances to the contrary, moving beyond dyads or binary pairs seems not an entirely sure bet. Otherwise, why insist that a third must be "*more* than three," must contain "flux," if not for the implication, or lingering fear, that even extra-dyadic formations risk falling back into oppositional, essentializing patterns such as hetero/homo? While not quite verging on infinite regress, such a maneuver begs the question of how many times this move outward, this leap at transcendence, can be attempted before one doubts its feasibility. For Althaus-Reid, a reliance on queer theory's anti-essentialism supposedly quells any such doubts. From her point of view, the more confining normative formations grow, queering work just pushes that much harder, that much farther afield from the well-worn rut of convention. When multiplicity starts to collapse into reductive channels, when instability begins to steady itself, when flux gives signs of calming (so this line of argument goes), one simply returns to the well to renew queering work's extravagant, norm-eluding force. Yet for *my* money, an appreciation for the insights yielded by queer theory does not entirely erase concerns about the resiliency, dynamism, and material efficacy of counterhegemonic discourse under mortal, hostilely adverse conditions. Heteronormativity's ossifying, hegemonic power is as much to be feared, if not more so, than that of queerness. Definitionally as well as practically, it's the spokespersons for hegemony, for heteronormativity, who call the shots in practical, binding ways. Persistent antigay violence and discrimination, funded by the inexhaustible reservoir of religion's confidence and incontestability, renders the extent to which we can "leave behind the complicity . . . of rigid dyads" an increasingly less acute concern, if not a moot question.

As with its debts to queer theory, *The Queer God*'s parallels to Stonewall-era gay liberation rhetoric shed light both on the ambitions of queer theology and its shortcomings as a praxis for combating social and legal outrages like the religiously justified second-class citizenship of queers. These were the sorts of conditions that gay liberationists, including Carl Wittman, were attempting to tackle in the early 1970s. One of gay liberation's central goals, of which queer theory's passion for destabilization is a later, more realistic incarnation, was the attrition of all gender roles and sexual identities. Given the long, wearying history of inequity and biased behavior that had accreted around these roles and identities—inequities that identities were themselves accused of generating—the logical solution seemed to be to scrap identities, roles, and labels altogether. In "Refugees from Amerika: A Gay Manifesto" (1970), Wittman asserted that the endgame of this dismantling project would be the discovery, or rather *recovery*, of a polymorphous pansexuality that was more authentic than the partitioned identities of straight, gay, and lesbian, and therefore, though the causal connection was unclear, less generative of bias and discrimination. Wittman informed his gay and lesbian audience that

[t]he reason so few of us are bisexual is because society has made such a big stink about homosexuality that we got forced into seeing ourselves as either straight or nonstraight. Also, many men got turned off to the way men are supposed to relate to women and vice-versa, which is pretty fucked up. Gays will begin to get turned on to women when 1) it's something we do because we want to, and not because we should; 2) when women's liberation has changed the nature of heterosexual relationships.

We continue to call ourselves homosexual, rather than bisexual, even if we do make it with the opposite sex also, because saying "Oh, I'm Bi" is a cop out for a gay. We get told it's okay to sleep with women, too, and that's still putting homosexuality down. We'll be gay until everyone has forgotten that it's an issue. Then we'll begin to be complete people. (159)

As in *The Queer God*, bisexuality denotes a more authentic, less essentializing state of sexuality, supposedly anterior to homosexuality and heterosexuality. Both equate bisexuality, without exception, with polymorphous, putatively nondyadic relations. Being "complete people" requires the demolition of discrete identitarian positions such as "gay," "lesbian," and "straight." In both Wittman's and Althaus-Reid's utopian sequences, the trajectory theoretically aims at the erasure of *all* demarcations of sexual identity. It's true, Wittman seems to value homosexuality at first, holding it apart from subsumption in bisexuality; yet in the very next sentence, gay is only an anterior stage of development, and therefore a developmentally *inferior* one, in the process of becoming a "complete person." So although the intent may be to combat homophobia, seeing both gay and straight as less "complete" than bisexuality is only partly less antiqueer than seeing only gayness as incomplete. Also like Althaus-Reid, Wittman has a fuzzy sense of agency, viewing sexual "liberation" as simultaneously the cause *and* the effect of political change.

Martha Shelley, a contemporary of Wittman, paints the bisexual or sexually polymorphous future in nearly the same terms. Addressing straight readers, she declares:

We want to reach the homosexual entombed in you, to liberate our brothers and our sisters, locked in the prisons of your skulls. We want you to understand what it is to be our kind of outcast—but also to understand our kind of love, to hunger for your own sex.

Because unless you understand this, you will continue to look at us with uncomprehending eyes, fake liberal smiles; you will be incapable of loving us. We will never go straight until you go gay. (34)

The sequence encountered in Wittman's "Gay Manifesto" appears reversed in Shelley's version of erotic life after liberation: heterosexuality dissolves once straights relinquish it by an apparent act of will, and that in turn brings about the dissolution of homosexuality. It's striking that even though the intent is the mutual demolition of discrete sexualities, the way Shelley phrases that last sentence has the rhetorical effect of suggesting that straight and gay positionalities are only exchanging places, which would appear to scotch the dismantling objective. The other notion at work here—that homosexuality is a differential construct that, aside from other effects, props ups the contrasting, ostensibly superior identity of heterosexuality—is one that makes a good deal of intellectual sense, and queer theory has focused a great deal of energy elucidating the texture and implications of its constructionist view of sexuality.

The parallels between Wittman, Shelley, and Althaus-Reid are marked and instructive. For instance, Althaus-Reid frames sexual and theological liberation as an act of excavation: "In theology, the libertine is amongst us and is buried in us" (26). And again: "To disengage ourselves theologically from binarism, there are more options than simply lesbian and gay theology. Queer Theology is a broader category whose permanent intent is instability" (27). As with much writing by gay and lesbian liberationists, the tendency is to idealize those paths that lie *outside* ideological control—an understandable gesture amid the countercultural weather of the late 1960s. Like Wittman and Shelley, Althaus-Reid predicts the possibility of a sharp, conceptual rift with the present, a "new theological epistemological break," and targets habituated identitarian and ideological constructs as the chief barrier to that advancement: "main roads, unfortunately, cannot depart from their goals. The main road of T-Theology sooner or later always leads us to the same (forced) agreements" (33). Further reminiscent of these earlier manifestos is her hard stand against *any* construction of sexuality:

a continuous attempt to understand sexual identities as a process consisting of the movement of emptiness not only of heterosexuality and heterosexual constructions, but of *any other
constructions of sexuality*. . . . What is at stake here is . . . God
devolving itself . . . in the Trinity, and in the Trinity understood
as an orgy, that is, a festival of the encounter of the intemperate
in two key elements. The first is the theological presentation of
God as an immoderate, polyamorous God, whose self is composed in relation to multiple embraces and sexual indefinitions
beyond oneness, and beyond dual models of loving relationships. The second is the commitment of an omnisexual kenosis
to destabilise sexual constructions of heterosexual readings of
heterosexuality itself, bisexuality, gay and lesbian sexual identities, and transvestite identities.

. . . [Queer] Trinitarians do not need to have heterosexual
relations, nor so-called "same-sex relations" since no same-sex
relations in reality ever exist. The invention of the concept of
"same-sex" relationship is heterosexual, since it is based on the
notion of a limited number of sexualities and also their equiva-
lences. The fact that two women may have a sexual relationship does not imply that they belong to the "same-sex" at all .
. . . (57, 59; emphasis added)

The double qualification in the phrase "so-called 'same-sex' relations"
is of a piece with the liberationist impulse, whether in 1970s America
or present-day Latin American liberation theology. But it's an impulse
that doesn't feel particularly useful as a way to come to grips with those
pundits and parties who vilify queers, those moralizers and legislators who seek to maintain queer citizens' exclusion, their separate but
*un*equal status. To proclaim, in the face of anti-queer brutality and
denigration, that "no same-sex relations in reality ever exist" seems
callously ineffectual. It's also frustrating to those, myself included, who
find the deployment and habitation of essentialism strategically useful
and descriptively satisfying. Jettisoning what is limiting or rigid about
homo and hetero identity has been a touchstone of bisexual theorists,
from Wittman and Shelley to, more recently, Althaus-Reid and Donald
E. Hall. In pushing *beyond* identity, however, one risks jettisoning what
can be nurturing, protective, and pleasurable, what is politically and
culturally tactical, about sexual identities. As happens with Johnson's

reductive panegyric to gay sex, this embracing of bisexuality leaves untroubled certain heteronormative strictures like gender dimorphism. What's more, Althaus-Reid dismisses couple-based forms of intimacy as intrinsically limiting, and thus antithetical to political or social innovation, even though for many gay men the couple is not uniformly complicit with the heterosexual ideal of monogamy.

The further implication of liberation theology and gay liberation, that we can abandon these identities by fiat or sheer will, may be comforting. But in addition to opting out of acute material questions of justice and survival, a utopian absconding from the trappings of constructed identity seems honestly nonviable. As David Halperin concedes in *One Hundred Years of Homosexuality*, the intellectual sense made by the constructionist understanding of homosexuality, the view that grounds his own critical work, fails to diminish constructionism's emotional and psychological dissonance with the lived experience of many gays and lesbians:

> To say that homosexuality and heterosexuality are culturally constructed . . . is not to say that they are unreal, that they are mere figments of the imagination of certain sexual actors. . . . Homosexuality and heterosexuality are not fictions, inasmuch as there really are, nowadays, homosexual and heterosexual people, individuals whose own desires are organized or structured according to the patterned named by those opposing and contrasting terms.
>
> . . . Just because my sexuality is an artifact of cultural processes doesn't mean I'm not stuck with it. Particular cultures are contingent, but the personal identities and forms of erotic life that take shape within the horizons of those cultures are not. To say that sexuality is learned is not to say that it can be unlearned—any more than to say that culture changes is to say that it is malleable.
>
> . . . I would be very untrue to the position I've been arguing if I didn't acknowledge squarely and forthrightly the cognitive dissonance it involves. I don't think that there's any way that I, or anyone else who grew up in bourgeois America when I did, could ever believe in [a constructionist reading of sexuality] with the same degree of conviction, with which I believe, despite everything I've said, in the categories of heterosexuality

and homosexuality. Those categories aren't merely categories of thought, at least in my case; they're also categories of erotic response, and they therefore have a claim on my belief that's stronger than intellectual allegiance. That, after all, is what it means to be acculturated into a sexual system: the conventions of the system acquire the self-confirming inner-truth of "nature." If one could simply think oneself out of one's acculturation, it wouldn't be acculturation in the first place. (43, 51–52, 53)

This argument can naturally be extended for quite some distance on both sides. For my immediate purposes, the point is this: the gay liberationist strategy of dismantling accreted sexual identities entails conceptual as well as practical difficulties not unlike those raised by critical bisexual theology, and, in similar fashion, it fails to resolve them satisfactorily. It's worrying to dismiss outright forms of identity that make emotional, experiential sense to many gays and lesbians—not to mention, the emotional sense that heterosexual identity, for all its constructedness, makes to many straights. The fact that these identities make sense because, as Halperin argues, they are the concepts through which we have been acculturated to think about and experience sexuality, makes little difference. That they're the result of acculturation speaks to their tenacity and renders questions of their logic largely academic. As Diana Fuss puts it, "Fictions of identity are no less powerful for being fictions" (qtd. in Hall 104). A further cause of attachment to discrete sexual identity positions, for gays and lesbians certainly, is their practical use. While it's arguable that identity politics have not been so effective in the argument for queer rights as to settle the matter, gay and lesbian identities have proven productive concepts for establishing radical as well as mainstream communities, for aiding subcultural and political innovation, and for problematizing, if not altogether dismantling, homophobic cultural narratives.

Some tactics seem ineffective because of their simplistic nature. Take queer theology's dependency on transgression in queering work: "The exchange of power and the habitat of affection can be surprisingly transformative. To say do not worship God's male attire leads on to exchanging it for fishnets and high heels. It is to ask for a radical destabilisation of the gender and sexual performances of God as community" (75–76). Verging at times toward the puerile, Althaus-Reid's appeal to the efficacy of transgression descends at other times into the fatuous. She asks, for instance:

> Are these [queer] bodies to be compared to nomadic theolo-
> gians permanently searching for the warm lips of the Other, as
> voyaging vaginas stretching themselves into strange and loving
> borderlands? . . . The nomadic condition of our bodies is there-
> fore the starting point of Queer theologians . . . searching for
> God's nipples and soft lips and trying to bite them in oblique
> ways in order to achieve some oblique transcendence in their
> lives. (49)

What gives me pause is not some prudish outrage at the sexualizing of divinity or the scandal of sacrilege. What I find worrying is the frivolity and essential toothlessness of verbal japes such as these, their lack of substantive, practical impact on matters of antigay policy and proclamations. Althaus-Reid, perhaps anticipating such a response, insists that, to the contrary, queer(ing) theology demands more than garden-variety kink:

> The objective is to transgress whilst remaining Queer and not
> just kinky, that is, to have . . . a suspicion about what also quali-
> fies as transgression. For transgression to be truly transgressive
> it must carry tactical elements sufficient to be transformative of
> our lives, or to be "acted up." Transgression is about agency. . . .
> [T]here is a need to queer God both outside and inside that
> particular structure or combination of patriarchal oppression.
> Our re-reading needs to be one that retains the moment of
> unveiling God's clandestinity of sexuality, poverty and violence
> while respecting God's determination to remain in the streets
> and the alleys of theology. (99)

Regarding the wishful, somewhat paradoxical notion of queer theol-
ogy being at once hegemonic *and* counterhegemonic, it would seem, as in Johnson's case, that transgression of this sort merely produces a reversal of terms. And that begs the question of what advance one makes by turning traditional theology inside out. This idealization, if not reification, of subversion extends back to *The Queer God*'s lead-ing concept: "critical bisexuality." "The bisexual theologian . . . thinks

critically bi- or polyamorously" and thus achieves a "unique position" in "the relation to the closet" and "the way of transcendence via the instability of God, sexual identity, and humanity" (15). The fuzzy distinction made between polyamory and bisexuality seems indicative of queer theology's imprecision and, by extension, queer spirituality's tactical ineptness. The exhortation to "introduc[e] non-monogamous and sexually unstable structures of loving relationships for a change" conjures a titillating but not terribly substantial image of queering God by having three-ways or orgies (37). If sexual transgression were capable of transforming religion symbolically or practically, one would think some effect would be apparent by now—from the efforts of gay Christians or even ex-gays. If nothing else, one would certainly expect Catholicism to have been negatively transformed, its reach disfigured and its power weakened by the sexual abuse of children it has so long sheltered within its collective robes.

If one's intent is to locate a workable praxis for queer vocality, advocacy, and survival, or at least to clear away those gambits that ill-serve or even obstruct such efforts, then another valid concern is queer theology's rather easy equivalence between excess and escape. Althaus-Reid regards "showing through excess how totalitarian interpellations . . . can be subverted by that same excess. [And that] may be the . . . role of irony in Queer Theology, as an excess of dis-authorisation in T-Theology" (25). In answer to the question "how [do] Queer lovers do theology"? she replies that

> they wander into each other's spaces, digress at points of desire, position and reposition themselves amongst themselves and amongst others and, eventually, participate in some creation of new (partial) conceptualisations of love and God. . . . Queer theologies are a refusal to normalization, to the recycling of old borders and limits of any theological praxis, while resisting current practices of historical formation . . . (50)

Aside from an unfortunate but fashionable vagueness that characterizes some work in queer theory as well as queer spirituality, this passage offers a puzzling contradiction. It's not that contradictions are unwelcome; for inhabitants of the Christian closet, for straight, homophobic Christians, and for queers generally, contradictions can be sheltering, even sustaining. They are not inherently counterproductive. Yet the contradiction in this case appears impracticable. If one refuses to heed or repeat "old borders and limits," it's unclear how one is to surpass or denature those perimeters without acknowledging their location and disputed propriety. *The Queer God*'s core defect is a fundamental misjudging of the damaging force exerted by ideologies in queers' everyday lives and of Derridean poststructural play's potential to advocate a parity of dignity, to secure personal safety and civil privilege on a more than temporary basis.

The inadequacy of transgression as imagined by *The Queer God* and *Gay Spirituality* stems from another shared strategy, the privileged status abrogated to vanguardism. For the transformative aspirations of both volumes, the underlying problem with vanguardism and subversion by excess appears to be twofold. First, if that method did work, it would fashion a queer-positive space so tolerant, so nonnormative, as to no longer resemble the world as experienced by most queers, even those lucky enough to live and work amid a decent degree of tolerance. For proponents of utopian thinking, this disparity would be the point: an objective toward which to gear one's activism and praxis. My perspective, by contrast, strives to be not just practically but also critically minded. After all, vanguardism proposes to lead a constituency such as queers toward a predesignated end that not all its members may find desirable. Speaking for myself (and, I hope, others), a world without differential sexualities of gay, lesbian, straight, and bisexual not only seems unrecognizable—an objection that may be written off to conceptual limitations—but also impracticable. Even if gay identity is a construct, it's one from which many queers derive pleasure, nourishment, and ambivalence. Even if that construct betrays a limited perspective, it's a perspective shared by others. It partakes of a shared cultural discourse about personhood that, *because* it is shared, permits me to negotiate the shared field of discourse in advocating for the equity, dignity, and pleasures that accrue to me as a gay man, and to highlight the artifice of norms that lobby for the heterosexist status quo. How does one broker for legal rights accruing to an identity position, or argue against violence and discrimination toward those occupying such a position if the position doesn't really exist? The other possible outcome of succeeding by excess is the creation of a hospitable corner within religious ideology, typically among religious moderates, tolerant enough to accommodate queerness. At the same time, however, that ability to accommodate, that hospitableness and moderation, renders such an ideological sector *too* tolerant to success-fully question, much less battle, its more phobic incarnations. It's also important here to differentiate the sort of transgression idealized by Johnson and Althaus-Reid from that explored by Tim Dean in *Unlimited Intimacy*. For Dean, what's innovative and potentially progressive about the modes of relation inhabited by barebackers is the extent to which such relations contest the authority of normative relations, confound heterosexual channels of kinship, and supply an invigorating alternative for community. In *The Queer God* and *Gay Spirituality*, local acts of transgression are not enough because they may not trouble those overarching institutions and ideas (religion, spirituality, heteronormativity) that are inherently inimical to queer interests or that offer declarations of tolerance and paeans to flux. What would be more useful, as queers routinely face assault, harassment, and discrimination by religious as well as secular authorities and individuals, are more concrete tactics of defense, advocacy, and engagement.

For those who prefer the warrant of a theoretical diagnosis, *The Queer God*'s exegesis of queer theology seems oddly innocent of Foucault's problematization of discursive production in volume 1 of *The History of Sexuality*. Althaus-Reid's allusions to Foucault's *Discipline and Punish* and *The Birth of the Clinic* render such an omission stranger. In *The History of Sexuality*, Foucault analyzes the growth, dispersion, and impact, from the eighteenth century onward, of discourse "around sex"—by which he means not only discourse *about* sex but "a whole network of varying, specific, and coercive transpositions [of sex] *into* discourse" (34; emphasis added). Far from being hidden or silenced, sexuality was incited more and more to speak itself, to unveil the truth of one's identity, a truth to which sexuality supposedly held unique and profound access. Furthermore, far from being hidden or unspoken, the perversions or "new" sexualities that Victorian sexologists claimed to discover (which included any nonconjugal, nonheterosexual, and sometimes even nonprocreative kind of eroticism) were likewise incited to reveal themselves. "Pervers[e]" sexualities were not dispersed but "implant[ed]" in types of individuals, distinguished from normative heterosexuality while held in the same discursive network (37).[21] For Foucault and the many queer theorists he influenced, sex came to be viewed less "as a natural given which power tries to hold in check, or as an obscure domain which knowledge tries gradually to uncover" but, instead, "a historical construct . . . a great surface network in which the stimulation of bodies, the intensification of pleasures, the incitement to discourse, the formation of special knowledges, the strengthening of controls and resistances, are linked to one another, in accordance with a few major strategies of knowledge and power" (105–106).

Equally relevant for considering *The Queer God*'s campaign of transcendence by excess is Foucault's declaration that the "oft-stated theme, that sex is outside of discourse and that only the removing of an obstacle . . . can clear the way leading to it, is precisely what needs to be examined" (34). At its core, *The History of Sexuality, Volume 1* questions and rebuts such a notion. Instead, discourse surrounds and enmeshes—in fact, is said in a sense to *produce*—desires and bodies, whether those desires and bodies are labeled as perverse or normal, obedient or miscreant. Discourse does not simply reflect desire but actively shapes it—and in turn is also shaped by it, as the phrase "controls *and* resistances" reminds us. To say that "one is always 'inside' power, [that] there is no escaping it" is to "misunderstand the strictly relational character of power relationships," which "depend . . . on a multiplicity of points of resistance" (95). Resistance in the form of counterdiscourse is possible, but such counterefforts exist in the same overall system as discourse and control; counterhegemonic effort would have little meaning or effect without the confining pressure of hegemony and normativity, the machinery of secular legal force and the weight of cultural and religious disapprobation that accompanies and gives life to it. In light of my objections to Johnson and Althaus-Reid, I want to distinguish here between, on the one hand, the ineffectuality of rhetoric that characterizes their projects—rhetorical sleights of hand that are unattended by equally innovative ethical insights or that fail to question religion's reactionary core imperatives—and, on the other hand, discursive practices that truly dispute normative discourse and, through what Foucault called reverse discourse, sometimes effect its transformation. Foucault's primary example of reverse discourse is the conscription of homosexuality, initially a pejorative medical classification, by gays and lesbians who created a positive sense of self-identity and community around it, even as the terms continued to accrue negative connotations.

Foucault's argument problematizes some of Althaus-Reid's more assured claims in ways she fails to acknowledge. For example, she asserts: "Queer theologians . . . introduced the body into theology, bodies in love, bodies entangled in ethics of passions—and transgressive

bodies at that. These bodies are not the usual ones: they are libertine bodies" (48). Foucault's seminal theory of discursive production
prompts one to suggest that those bodies, even "libertine" ones, were
there before queer theologians got around to them. Whether disci-
plined or resistant, whether complying or mounting a counterdiscourse,
libertine and queer bodies, like others, already existed within and were
to a certain extent shaped by discourse. So how can a libertine or queer
body transgress *outside* the potential reach of discursive, normative categories? At one point, Althaus-Reid seems to concede this point ("Disruption then, fulfils the law" [78]). But the concession is momentary,
outweighed by the number of her declarations to the contrary (that is,
that bodies may escape the orbit of discourse).

At times, *The Queer God*'s intent is plainly non- or anti-institu-
tional. Its author seeks an "understanding" "outside the system of the
sacralisation of the ideology of heterosexuality" (63).[22] "[L]iberationist
and Feminist theologies," she recounts, "have striven to redefine power
from the margins" (56). Stranger still, given the valorization of transcendence through excess and implied escape from the reach of normative discourse, is the frequently displayed longing to stand both inside
and outside heteronormativity. Althaus-Reid describes queer bodies as
"nomadic," as "excitable and incorrigible," "stretching themselves inside
and outside the constraints of totality and hegemony" (25). The text
is rife with passages combining an aspiration to be at once outside
the system, to escape, and to be also inside it, grounding theology in
bodiedness:

> Queer hermeneutics is [a matter] of transcendence. Can we
> displace transcendental heterosexual ways of reading the Scrip-
> tures by sexually disconcerting the bodily logic of positioning
> the reader in the Scriptures? (3)

> Church committee decisions and organisation are contained
> in a closed circuit of signifiers. . . . . However, the powerful
> theological praxis of transformation usually comes from the
> direction of aliens working through these systems. (30)

Moments such as these lead one to question the value, so often asserted,
of transcendence. More puzzling to note, given the negative associa-
tions of institutionality and "T-Theology," is an emergent fantasy not

of avoiding centrality but of *achieving* it: "queering the Trinity . . . means that in reality it is the Queer at the margins who is entering into a dialogical healing of the Trinity" (69). For Althaus-Reid

> the most interesting insight . . . may be the displacement of sexual theological knowledge, in the sense that the heterosexually disemboweled Trinitarians can embody lesbianism, while lesbians at the gate can embody the knowledge of bisexuals or transgendered people. This would mean that all these suppressed, displaced embodiments of knowledge could feel at home in the Trinity, just as the Trinity should feel at home in gay bars and S/M scenes, displacing temporary hegemonies and allowing a real plurality of religious experiences and theological practices by giving hospitality to strangers, in the most radical way.
> . . . [T]he strategy should be relatively simple: undress the father of power and glory and leave God sitting in the cold while the Queer community occupies the Trinity. (75)

In addition to a perceptible hankering after centrality, after a long-denied hegemonic status, the simple reversal of queer and straight fails, as it does in *Gay Spirituality*, to clearly revise the systemic dynamic of privilege and authority. What's more, difference—the difference between gay and straight but also gay and lesbian, or between fetish play and transvestism—is evacuated altogether.

In a redeeming moment, Althaus-Reid admits that queer strategies can be unstable in debilitating as well as empowering ways and that they are routinely liable to cultural subsumption and conscription. Contrasted with *The Queer God*'s tendency toward heady utopianism, this delineation of queers' systemic theological exclusion and political erasure is soberingly welcome:

> In practice . . . our beliefs in a gospel of justice may be welcome as long as we (as people, or as the strangers of theology) are excluded. Our ideals of peace and justice as rooted in the gospel may be treated well and offered a chair in a meeting, but meanwhile we, as people, are forced to take our Queer identities outside and die. . . . The reading for oppression (even in the name of just causes) has thus been successful in eliminating

us in the process even if we are still there. The original has displaced us. (80)

What undermines the clarity and focus of such moments is the text's refusal not necessarily to submit to but at least to confront the difficulty of "avoid[ing] assimilationist trends in biblical interpretation" or queer spirituality generally (80). It's not that Althaus-Reid doesn't ask the question. She does: "How can we reflect . . . in an unfilial theological way, that is, in a grace not indebted to historical subjugation processes and without criminalisaton?" (46). But her solution—the introduction of "turbulent," "unrestricted bodies"—seems inadequate to the size and scope of the task (47). It's hard to be convinced that the tactics she offers in the way of subversion ("to find . . . God sitting amongst us, at any time, in any gay bar or in the home of a camp friend who decorates her living room as a chapel and doesn't leave her rosary at home when going to a salsa bar" [4]) are subversive enough. It's unclear, also, how sufficiently contrary deployments of identity and desire can avoid becoming oppositional, binaristic, or themselves hegemonic—a state queer theology has sworn to elude. Can religion be queered, as Johnson and Althaus-Reid assure us it can? Or do religion and spirituality overwhelm, co-opt, and frustrate our attempts to recuperate, even fantasize, some authentic, more tolerant version of them? Are repression or exclusion written into religion's DNA?

This impasse, repeatedly grappled with by theorists such as Althusser and Foucault, was best encapsulated by Audre Lorde as the dilemma of "the master's tools." In her 1979 speech "The Master's Tools Will Never Dismantle the Master's House," Lorde laid out the paradox confronting marginalized inhabitants of normative discourses who wish to mount resistance or effect transformation. Though the immediate object of her critique is second-wave feminism (or "white american feminist theory"), she speaks to all those "forged in the crucibles of difference," including queers:

> Those of us who stand outside the circle of this society's definition of acceptable women; those of us who have been forged in the crucibles of difference—those of us who are poor, who are lesbians, who are Black, who are older—know that survival is not an academic skill. It is learning how to stand alone, unpopular and sometimes reviled, and how to make common

cause with those others identified as outside the structures in
order to define and seek a world in which we can all flour-
ish. It is learning how to take our differences and make them
strengths. For the master's tools will never dismantle the master's house. They may allow us temporarily to beat him at his
own game, but they will never enable us to bring about genuine
change. And this fact is only threatening to those women who
still define the master's house as their only source of support.
(112)

The master's house might as easily refer to religion as it does to patriarchy, for the concept includes all aspects of normativity in American
culture, the axes by which the heteronormative, masculine, white, and
religious are valorized over the queer, the feminine, the nonwhite, and
the freethinking. Althaus-Reid at times offers a similar assessment:
"we struggle for our sexual theological identity, while using phallocratic
language to speak of God and ourselves" (108). But when confronted
with hegemonic complicity, her customary response is withdrawal. She
asks, for example, "Are we allowed to fight sexually with the gram-
mar of T-Theology using the same hermeneutical tools which include
binary oppositional thought, sexual stability premises and the legitimi-
sation of a sexual epistemology to the detriment of others?" (89). Her
answer is "obviously no," and yet the means by which one can opt out
of oppositional thought are less transparent: "the permanent attempt
to work on a Random Theology . . . to redefine our location of doing
theology" (89).
    The crux of my objection to a project of queering religion like this
one is that, as a strategy of material survival and advocacy, the pref-
erence for "neighbourhoods of unclear demarcations" is unobligingly
inchoate:

    The dungeon . . . [of] Binary Theology . . . tr[ies] to make us
    straighten out our theological praxis by an alliance amongst
    the false memories of heterosexual traditions and systems of
    thought. Are we Christian enough? Are we becoming too
    Queer? Can theology or God exist without a prescriptive sex-
    ual centre around which we should gather as a community to
    celebrate our struggles for justice and peace in our lives? (90)

Yet if there is really no such thing as "straight" or "queer," if identities don't really exist, then how can heterosexuals force us to straighten out? More to the point, "*can* theology exist without a prescriptive center"? Althaus-Reid clearly intends this as a rhetorical question to which her answer is "yes." It's neither my purpose to deflate hopes for transformation nor to convince anyone that the answer to this rhetorical question ought to, and can only, be "no." I simply ask that we be practically *as well as* theoretically minded about these matters. It's not that religion can't be altered, queered, made livable. But for American queers at least, at this point in our history, this is an uphill battle, and, on balance, an unwinnable one. Even if it *were* winnable, it would likely be a pyrrhic victory. As ideologies go, religion is innately, perhaps congenitally, intractable. The pursuit of a rehabilitated religion or a refreshing spirituality—unwarped by superstition and prejudice, unsullied by wanton authority and a will to dominance over others—seems, at worst, a waste of time; at best, a diminishing return. To some, quests for queer religion and spirituality may yield therapeutic, personal dividends. To queers at large, however, such missions are more responsibly viewed as a misapplication of energies profitably spent elsewhere, on other methods of queer support, other paths to queer justice, safety, indulgence, and security.

Despite, then, the best of gay-positive intentions, the normative force of religion seems to reassert itself. Quite possibly, this is the result of a group psychology or heteronormative predisposition endemic to, or deeply acculturated in, humankind—a normalizing impulse that will remain even without religion. That's not to say it's an impulse we must give in to; it simply requires a more thorough challenge. Admittedly, some projects of queer spirituality attempt not to sidestep institutionalized religion but to rehabilitate it, not to evade its grasp but to tame and queer its force. A question facing such endeavors, of course—a question posed but unresolved by Foucault and Althusser, among others—is the extent to which the force of hegemonic discourse can be ameliorated by counterdiscourse or reverse discourse. To what degree can its objectives be hijacked, refashioned in a genuinely subversive way, one that exceeds bounds and disrupts the labor of broader discursive norms? My point is hardly that normativity should be capitulated to without a struggle, an attempt to abrade and problematize its putative naturalness. Yet it's worth facing the *remote* likelihood of efficacious, transformative resistance from *certain* angles of discursive approach, especially when, like religion, those discourses have a long, still pulsing history of aggressive apathy, of ferocious opposition, to one's very being.

If this cuts across my own speculations in chapter 2 about the potential for identitarian revision within the Christian closet, that's precisely to be noted. It not only draws attention to a much-debated point within queer studies; in my own argument—under the pressure of real-world disparagement, violence, and despair directed at and felt by queer Americans—it also marks a breaking point within *Slouching towards Gaytheism*. It represents an adherence to and faith in theoretical, provisional play only where it sustains, where it aids survivals, innovation, or substantive inversion. That sort of faith turns to ambivalence when such play fails to forestall queer destruction—not symbolic erasure but the brutal, palpable erasure of violence and repudiation. My faith in speculative, parodic play falters when it fails to equip or defend against rhetorics, initiatives, and laws that prostrate queer pleasures, enfeeble queer rights, and subjugate queer lives. While various junctures of Christian and queer identity (gay or ex-gay; closeted or out; conservatively Christian, moderate, or spiritual) hold potential for agitating and denaturing the familiar confines of identity, it may be only that: potential. Transformation may not be forthcoming, or it may be stunted. It may turn out not to be conducive to queer survival. The Christian closet, like other identity positions, ranging from conservative Christian to radical queer, may prove bafflingly mucilaginous, adhesive in negative as well as positive ways. Furthermore, the transformative potential of gay, ex-gay, or closeted Christianity may be of use only to those queers and protoqueers presently confined within conservative religious environments. Those individuals living under duress or in chosen hiding may denature their confines enough to be able to hide out, to find furtive or guilty pleasures, even to resist full subsumption. I am willing to speculate on the capability for resistance that might be mined from within the Christian closet, the resistance or transformation that might be possible, if only within a painfully limited range of impact. Practically speaking, though, I have doubts about the uses of such speculation. Ethical realities are more pressing; speculation may be a luxury we can't afford. There is enough evidence of religious discourse's murderous, punitive power to convince me that it cannot house long-term sustenance for queers. Even if it can, the costs seem to outweigh any substantive payoff. As much as I sympathize with and appreciate arguments for the queering of—the destabilizing and transformation of—identity beyond conventional, reductive, and binaristic normative bounds, this is a theoretical argument that queers not currently stranded or held captive in the Christian closet cannot safely await the practical realization of. Queer survival and the cultivation of more rewarding modes of relation are best sought elsewhere. Gay religion and spirituality's demonstrated inability to overcome the intellectual strictures and ethical blind spots of institutionalized religion and normative sexuality argue resolutely for leaving religion behind. It's possible that unconventional modalities of relation such as those Tim Dean outlines within barebacking subculture may offer analogical, inverted models for alternative ways of belonging. The longevity of such alternatives, as well as their plasticity, rewards, and practicality as tactics for contests over discrimination and equality, remain to be determined. Regardless of their ultimate usefulness, the point is that models of community and ethics that are sustaining rather than injurious to queer survival are not to be found under the auspices of religion.

The time has come to give up trying to reform religion to be queer-friendly. Instead of wasting time and breath commanding the restless waters of religious homophobia to be still, and reasoning with irrational propositions, the time has come to jump ship. This is not to say that ideology trumps any attempt to revise or combat it. But at some point we must evaluate whether our energy is being expended on a worthwhile venture. We are not going to win the argument with religious homophobia because religion does not countenance argument. For queers especially, in the present historical moment, to hold onto religion suggests that *without* religion there is less or little value in being human, that queer principles and community are not enough, are not capable by themselves of ethical and fulfilling behavior. And that strikes me as a terribly poor prospect.

FOUR

SLOUCHING TOWARDS GAYTHEISM

Gay Suicide, "It Gets Better," and
Religion's Stranglehold on Queer Survival

Statistics regarding the exact size of the American GLBT population, as well as the higher suicide risk for queer youth, have been
repeatedly cited, debated, contested, and recalibrated over the past
few decades—by mainstream GLBT organizations such as HRC and
Lambda Legal arguing for legal and political parity, and by youth-
focused groups such as the Gay, Lesbian and Straight Education
Network (GLSEN) working to advocate for the safety and dignified
treatment of GLBT middle and high school students by peers, teachers, and parents. It's often stated by GLBT organizations, for instance,
that queer teens are three to four times more likely to attempt suicide
than their straight peers. Finding accurately representative numbers for
these demographics becomes critical in the face of efforts by antigay
groups such as the Family Research Council. Citing its own studies,
widely agreed to be dubious, the FRC portrays gays and lesbians as a
much smaller minority than claimed by GLBT advocates in order to
undercut queer demands for legal protection and equality. Moreover,
the FRC also relies on these dubious studies in order to foster the
impression that queers are even *more* prone to depression and suicide

than claimed by GLBT organizations and thus promulgate stereotypes equating homosexuality with disease, abnormality, and death. Queer advocacy groups claim that 10 to 14 percent of the U.S. population is gay, whereas antigay sources, as well as some neutral ones, contest this as an inflated figure based on estimates by Alfred Kinsey in the 1940s and cite, instead, recent polls placing the figure between 1 and 3 percent. Debates over the validity of the sources from which these various statistics have been derived, the math involved in different calculations, and disagreements about underreporting and overestimating will no doubt persist for quite some time.[1] In September and October of 2010, though, wrangling over which estimate was the most accurate came to seem less important, if not callously academic, as a succession of gay teen suicides captured national attention. Friends and parents attested to the anguish and depression suffered by the now-dead teens as a result of persistent online and face-to-face antigay bullying and harassment by peers.

A partial list of these pained individuals seems at once hollow and sensationalistic, but neither assessment is fair. Details, concrete and unpleasant, make the case for the current potency of homophobia in American schools and beyond. In July 2010 Justin Aaberg, a fifteen-year-old Minnesota high school student, hanged himself after being bullied at school and breaking up with his boyfriend. His death did not capture mainstream media attention at first, however, and was reported by gay online sources only in September when, in a single month, at least five other gay teens committed suicide: Billy Lucas, fifteen, in Greensburg, Indiana, by hanging; Asher Brown, thirteen, in Houston, Texas, by self-inflicted gunshot; Seth Walsh, thirteen, in Tehachapi, California, by hanging; Raymond Chase, a nineteen-year-old sophomore at Johnson and Wales University in Rhode Island, by hanging; and perhaps most well known, eighteen-year-old Tyler Clementi, by jumping off the George Washington Bridge after his Rutgers University roommate had "secretly recorded him [on webcam] having sex with another man and broadcast it over the internet" (Associated Press, "US Student Tyler Clementi" par. 1).[2]

Soon after Clementi's death, gay columnist and radio host Dan Savage made a short video in which he and his partner Terry Miller discussed their own experiences of antigay harassment as teens and their later, positive experiences as openly gay adults. By posting the video on YouTube and asking others to make similar videos addressing queer teens, Savage quickly sparked a campaign, soon known as the "It Gets Better" Project, in which numerous celebrities, politicians, and everyday individuals shared their own experiences of harassment as queer teens or expressed their support as straight allies. My aim is not to disparage the intentions of Savage or anyone else who has made such a video, but I do want to address the rhetorical and possibly quite material impact of the "It Gets Better" campaign. By its impact, I mean two things: the effect of Savage's initial video (which fails to address queer teens who might disidentify with or fail to connect to the narrow vision of gay adult experience embodied by his life with his partner) as well as the broader resonance of the campaign as a slogan and a media trend (its unhelpful recommendation of stoic endurance and passivity in the face of harassment and discrimination). The bullying faced by queer kids is not just personal and physical. True, the harassment they most painfully and directly feel may occur at the hands of their peers. But that behavior is sanctioned, even in this palpably tolerant age; messages that gays are deviant and have questionable worth assault them from across the culture, in disputes over matters as theoretically distant from their lives as same-sex marriage and military service, or as close to them as battles over organizing a gay-straight alliance at a school that allows meetings of religious clubs. I would argue that, as a mantra and strategy, "it gets better" is unhelpful in addressing, much less combating, the besieged status of American queer teens and is ultimately injurious to those teens' ability to engage with, much less challenge, the assaults and exclusions that await them as queer adults.

It's by way of discussing the "It Gets Better" videos—and the acute questions of how to counsel harassed gay teens and combat antigay bullying—that I mean to approach the interrelated topics of this chapter and the conclusion: (1) the continued, detrimental consequences of religious beliefs, (2) the unnecessary, noxious, yet commonly accepted equivalence between the intolerant habits of religion and rationally vetted ethical principles, and finally, (3) the weight those beliefs exert, in American public discourse, on queer life and survival. In the current climate, it's not just queer rights but queer lives that are at stake: not just teens but the queer adults they will become, as well as the queer adults they see now whose adult lives, though not always less buffeted by violence, remain subject to debate as to their worth as citizens and humans. It's my conviction that, on either count, it's vitally important that queers no longer look to religious tolerance and, by extension, religion itself as vehicles for securing their rights or their lives. Religion cannot effectually advance the cause of queers. It cannot protect their lives. After analyzing the origins of and reactions to the "It Gets Better" campaign, as well as its practical and ideological pitfalls, this chapter reviews arguments for atheism by Christopher Hitchens and Sam Harris that should have particular weight for gay and lesbian Americans, since they are the ones who continue to suffer not just religious hatred and the forms of violence it generates but also the politics and civil policies it either drives or impedes. Relinquishing institutional and even deinstitutionalized religion offers queers a path to a brighter political, emotional, and cultural future. Finally, this chapter reviews more recent successes on the gay equality front, such as the DADT repeal and legal challenges to DOMA, *in balance with* the continued homophobic animus directed at gay interests and lives in American culture through the twin conduits of heteronormativity and religious discourse as parameters for political discourse and civil policy. What I conclude from such a review is that, despite the historic erasure of certain barriers to equality, religiously fueled homophobia endures in molding public perceptions and the treatment of queer people. Gaytheism offers a way out of this rhetorical and often practical impasse. It enables one to retain—or at least it refuses to cloud—a clear focus on the norms and dicta that inflict violence and intimidation on queer teens and that bully and buffet queers of all ages from multiple directions in our shared heteronormative culture. Bullying and gay-bashing are only the most blatant, physical manifestation of the social, cultural, and emotional coercion that daily inveigles queer affect, requisitions queer life, and dismisses queer desire.

Before enumerating the shortcomings of the first "It Gets Better" video phenomenon and my qualms about its consequences, it's only fair to present some of Savage and Miller's representative statements in it:

[Miller:] Honestly, things got better the day I left high school. I didn't see the bullies every day. I didn't see the people who harassed me every day. I didn't have to see the school administrators who would do nothing about it every day. Life instantly got better.

[Savage:] However bad it is now, it gets better. And it *can* get great. It can get awesome. Your life can be amazing. But you have to tough this period of it out, and you have to live your life so that you're around for it to get amazing. And it can. And it will.

[Miller:] Those moments [referring to time spent with his and Savage's adopted son] make it so worth sticking out the bullying and the pain and the despair of high school. And if you can just do that, you have moments like that and so many more ahead of you.

[Savage:] One day you will have friends who love and support you, you will find love, you will find a community. . . . [L]ife gets better. And . . . the bigots don't win. . . . And once I got out of high school, they couldn't touch me anymore. ("It Gets Better: Dan and Terry")

To be even-handed, Savage has spoken strongly, both before starting the "It Gets Better" project and since, against the contextual factors influencing the bullies of these dead gay teenagers, the day-to-day antigay comments by ministers, teachers, politicians, and parents that inflame homophobia in large and small ways across the culture. On October 14, 2010, Savage responded in his syndicated sex-advice column to email criticizing his "comments [in an interview about the project] regarding people of faith and their perpetuation of bullying" (qtd. in Savage par. 1). Savage outlined the homophobic imperatives that the peers of queer kids absorb daily, directly and indirectly, with the sort of frankness that characterizes most of his public statements: "Gay kids are dying. So . . . *Fuck your feelings*" (par. 7). My point is that as a campaign and a slogan "It Gets Better" not only elides this more substantive discussion, but it also sidesteps the fact that "it"— meaning, culturally pervasive homophobia—in many palpable respects has *not* gotten better. Is the project's message fulsome or somehow incomplete? What if, at least sometimes, it doesn't get better? What if Savage's hasty declaration that "once [you get] out of high school, they [can't] touch [you] anymore" turns out not to be true in all instances? What if, for some queers (if not queers in general), it's gotten better in some ways yet stayed the same, or even gotten worse, in others? Is the message being conveyed, even unintentionally, that homophobic harassment is okay for now or at least an unavoidable evil that has to be endured? Is what "gets better" simply—and dishearteningly—queers' ability to deal with bullying, to endure it, and not the eruptions of homophobia themselves?

At minimum, the ambiguity of the pronoun reference is instructive of a confused or not fully articulated intent. What exactly is the "it" that gets better? Does "it" refer to cultural homophobia, implying the debatable proposition that it lessens over time? Or does "it" refer to one's ability to *endure* harassment, discrimination, and exclusion, which would seem likely to increase over time by either empowerment or induration? Or a third possibility: is the "it" one's ability to confront and combat homophobia, to engage with it articulately and productively? Many of the videos posted by Savage and those who followed seem to emphasize the second interpretation: one gets older, gets out of high school, goes to college, and, after finding supportive friends, lovers, and mentors, gets better at weathering or removing oneself from the brunt of the worst assaults. The assertion that non–high school environments are inevitably safer is contentious at best. At worst—although this might vary by experience, location, wealth, and other factors—it's demonstrably untrue. What's more, the existence of "It Gets Better" videos underscores the reality that in the present "it" has *not* gotten better. If, to take but one example, we interpret "it" as referring to not simply the bullying of queer teens but the homophobic resonance of Prop 8 and the lead-up to the 2010 midterm elections, then for queer teens, children, and adults "it" has *not* gotten better. Culturally rampant, religiously sanctioned, "it" has remained vibrant, has perhaps amplified, even if there are more supportive voices in response to homophobic baiting. As with the muscular potency of the Christian closet, and the intransigence of religious discourse in barring sensible debate on questions of ethical treatment and civil rights, it's safe to say that the "it" of cultural homophobia does not get better of its own accord. It especially fails to get better when those who defend queer rights do so on the ideologically compromised grounds supplied by religion and spirituality in conservative as well as moderate to liberal forms. Louder voices on both sides are not inherently comforting. Vehement antigay religious rhetoric, particularly in its right-wing forms, may be more strident than ever, more deranged, irrational, and, one would think, harder to take seriously. But that doesn't make it less disturbing to queers or less poisonous, potentially, to straight cultural attitudes toward queers.

Without impugning the good intentions of Dan Savage or the many other queer men and women who have made similar videos, it's possible to engage critically with the assumptions that most iterations of the project seem to make, the ideas invoked about being gay and the lack of a realistic view of the political and cultural climate as it currently and palpably exists. *Atlantic Wire* columnist Alex Eichler and bloggers Femmephane and MSJacks each posted attentive critiques of the original video. With a few exceptions, their comments were fair and objective, part of a productive dialogue the GLBT community and Americans in general might have about combating antigay harassment and advocating for queer youth. What I found disturbing was the knee-jerk response to any criticism of "It Gets Better," as on Joe Jervis's blog, *Joe. My. God.* Although Jervis's response was measured compared to the flood of vitriolic reactions from a discussion thread on Jervis's Facebook page attacking Femmephane, I was disappointed to see Jervis writing off what seemed to me a measured, thoughtful analysis as a "navel-gazing, over-intellectualizing queer theor[y]" tirade (Jervis, "Predictable"). Such a response is premature, anti-intellectual, and counterproductive—a pronouncement that certain statements are exempt from critique, that certain topics are simply not open to discussion. I concur with Femmephane in saying that to critique a project like "It Gets Better" is not to discourage anyone from addressing queer youth. It might not be comforting for a desperate queer youth to hear that it doesn't always get better or that it's better but not all of time, in every area of one's adult life, yet that would constitute a more honest account. Much of my ambivalence toward the campaign stems from the inevitable but unfortunate reductiveness of slogan-driven rhetoric. True, many who made later "It Gets Better" videos advocated material support strategies for queer youth such as the Trevor Project—although some queer teens either do not have access to, or feel intimidated from accessing, such services. But to lead with the slogan "It Gets Better" suggests an automatic, inevitable improvement that some queer lives, teen or adult, do not, or at least not always, bear out. Even for those of us fortunate enough to enjoy lives largely free of antigay harassment, violence, or discrimination, the culture, media, religious and political institutions, and even sometimes families, are aswim with messages of disapproval, distance, and antipathy ranging from subtle to gross. This line of thinking does not seem unwarrantably pessimistic, merely realistic.

Particularly in light of its sincere, gay-positive intent, the "It Gets Better" campaign suffers from the outset from three troubling flaws: blithe sentimentalizing, mindless heteronormativity, and harmfully misguided intentions. First, as with the majority of same-sex marriage defenses, "It Gets Better" takes the soft argumentative tack of sentiment rather than logic or ethics. In the late 1990s, with few exceptions, gay marriage advocates presented marriage as an expression of love, a way of honoring a couple's commitment rather than as a matter of equality, basic human rights, and citizenship.[3] The focus of the "It Gets Better" campaign's antihomophobic efforts on queer and straight children and teens bears out Lee Edelman's charge that the Cult of the Child, which informs nearly every cultural moment, pits hedonistic, child-endangering fags against the straights who produce and love the children that are "'our [implicitly *non*queer] future'" (143).[4] A crusade on behalf of children is always safe, always heteronormative, and always homophobic (or at least antihomosexual). It confirms deeply ingrained ideological messages equating queerness with destructive hedonism and heterosexuality with civilization-sustaining fertility. That, I would argue at least, is the video's rhetorical undercurrent.

On its face, the video associates queerness with white, adult gay male privilege and assimilationist, heteronormative vigor. Part of this union results simply from the identity of the videographers: two white gay men who are adoptive parents and who have the wherewithal, the interest, and the cultural incitement to take ski trips and travel to Paris. This is Savage and Miller's experience, a fact for which one can hardly fault them. But they do nothing in the video to address teens who might not be able to see themselves as part of a couple like Savage and Miller, teens for whom their cultural lifestyle or their ethnic, class, and socioeconomic attributes fail to resonate. Now, some might defend Savage and Miller on this count, arguing that failing to address one's demographic differences from others is understandable in urgent circumstances of reaching queer teens at imminent risk. Yet there are a number of fallacies here. Bullying is not the issue, at least not entirely. A queer child doesn't need to be called "faggot" or "dyke" (not that some aren't called such names) in order to feel him- or herself an outsider, a pariah. Furthermore, valorizing not the queer couple but the queer couple *with children* shuts out queers who may not *want* to have children. The blinkered purview of "It Gets Better" implies that bullies are the greatest problem, the source from which all homophobia emanates. Where, the campaign neglects to ponder, do bullies get their vicious ideas about their gay and lesbian peers? Put an end to bullying of queer kids, the campaign's fatuous logic runs, and the self-esteem and survival prospects of young queers will presumptively skyrocket. I have to object. Queer kids and their peers, whether they are bullied, bullying, or simply bystanders, are volubly and repeatedly indoctrinated by parents, schools, churches, media and internet outlets, by siblings, coaches, teammates. They are assailed on a daily basis, via almost any public moment or artifact they encounter, by all the rituals of the culture we all grow up in—rituals that, even if they include queers, are characteristically heteronormative in objective and tenor. And they needn't be attuned to political and legal contests at the national level or the ravings of prominent religious figures from the bully pulpit of heavily funded lobbying organizations. They merely have to be in school, where they will encounter, firsthand, controversies over queer students taking same-sex dates to prom, the omission or misrepresentation of queer sex in health class, and teachers and administrators defending or refusing to censor denigration of homosexuality on the sacred ground of religious principle (a defense made spurious by the principle of church-state separation). Targeting bullies and not the broader heteronormative cultural vectors omits the panoply of adult figures from whom young bullies absorb the idea that, in this case, gays and lesbians are not *truly* minorities and are fair game for ridicule, abuse, and intimidation. As an American media hobbyhorse that does little to address the actual deficits of the nation's educational system, bullying is extraneous, a red herring. Even if bullying could be curtailed, which is debatable, the culture would continue to bombard queer youth with signs of their unworthiness, their abnormality, and their doom.

Even within the microcosm of a week's news cycle, the vogue of "It Gets Better" typifies the refusal of media and citizens alike to meaningfully engage with homophobia, except to wield it as a wedge issue and base whip or to condone it as a religiously untouchable "expression of belief." As the protracted public wrestling over Prop 8 and DADT demonstrates, even if many Americans fail to take homophobic right-wing religious and political discourse seriously, and even if right-wing Christians comprise a small demographic relatively speaking, that discourse is still granted air time, and, with it, antigay cultural indoctrination. Allowing queer personhood to continue to be publicly contested

SLOUCHING TOWARDS GAYTHEISM

in a way that no other group's lives and rights presently are (except maybe immigrants') transmits the message of queers' questionable humanity, their inferior, deviant status, loudly and unequivocally.[5] California's Prop 8, which defined marriage heterosexually in that state and so reversed an earlier state Supreme Court ruling legalizing same-sex marriage, was overturned in August 2010 by U.S. district judge Vaughn Walker. However, Walker agreed to a temporary stay on his ruling to give Prop 8 proponents time to file for appeal. The Ninth Circuit U.S. Court of Appeals issued a longer stay, pending the outcome of that appeal. So, Prop 8 was left standing, and gay marriage—after a brief period of legalization in 2008 amounting to five months—remained illegal in California. In June 2013 the U.S. Supreme Court provided a degree of resolution on marriage equality—though without granting full equality nationwide. SCOTUS upheld the repeal of Prop 8 and rendered gay marriage once more legal in California. The Court also invalidated a key clause of DOMA, but the decision was—as some had anticipated—a legally narrow one: finding DOMA's ban on federal rights for same-sex married couples unconstitutional was qualified as applying *only* to residents of states where same-sex marriage is legal. The justices were explicit about not compelling states where gay marriage is still *illegal* to recognize such couples. Although the language of the DOMA decision rendered it almost inevitable that a subsequent legal challenge would succeed in demolishing DOMA entirely, and thus legalize gay marriage nationally instead of just in piecemeal fashion, Justice Kennedy expressed concern about the "uncharted waters" of full marriage equality—a hollow statement, given that a number of states as well as other countries had already navigated those very waters and found them free of either legal disputes or social chaos. While it was a significant advance in the American fight for gay and lesbian legal parity, the DOMA decision stopped short of instituting a change for which certain delicate citizens, implicitly those driven by antigay religious concerns, might not be ready (qtd. in Stohr par. 3).

By contrast, gay and lesbian adults may have been bewildered by the Obama administration's initial response to legal wrangling over the DADT repeal. Here it should be apparent that my focus is the administration's responses to activists' calls for repeal and legal responses to the California-issued DADT injunction. Once both houses of Congress supported repeal in December 2010—the very measure that had "twice failed to advance in the Senate" in 2010 and "was widely seen as unlikely to survive"—Obama did sign the repeal into law (O'Keefe par. 12). My focus is the administration's posturing and resistance *up to that point* and the rhetorical message it sent to queer teens and adults. Though no doubt some would excuse such posturing as understandably cautious, politically *de rigueur*, even tactically necessary, my response is that playing a safe, even reactionary, game—amid an increasingly progressive cultural climate and on an issue where the ethically just path is starkly clear—is fundamentally unnecessary. More importantly, when such tactics are deployed in deference to toxic homophobia and so-called religious freedom (freedom to dictate the law, that is), political coyness seems not only disingenuous but also frankly irresponsible.

In September 2010 California federal judge Virginia Phillips ruled that DADT was unconstitutional and issued an injunction, effectively repealing it, barring resistance from the Department of Justice. When the judge denied the DOJ's request, the following month, for a stay on her injunction (thus keeping the policy in effect), the DOJ asked the Ninth Circuit appellate court to freeze Phillips's ruling; it did, until the DOJ's appeal of the injunction could make it to court. Obama had previously stated his commitment to seeing DADT repealed "on his watch." But that commitment's credibility was weakened by the fact that the only approach he supported at this time—a lengthy review process by the military and a congressional repeal—was killed by Republican filibuster in the Senate after passing the House of Representatives. Even the most loyal of the president's gay and lesbian constituents might be excused for viewing the administration's claim that the DOJ is duty bound to appeal decisions bearing on any extant law as mere lip service. The DOJ's decision to appeal the Phillips ruling, combined with the Republican takeover of the House in the 2010 midterm election, seemed to ensure that DADT might not be repealed anytime in the near future. Just after the midterms, *New Civil Rights Movement* blogger David Badash anticipated that this might be the repeal movement's death knell: "The Senate must repeal 'Don't Ask, Don't Tell' before the next Congress begins in January, or repeal . . . will be lost until the Democrats take back the House. And even then . . ." ("'Don't Ask, Don't Tell' Repeal Dead" par. 6). It seemed Badash's dire prediction might come true when, less than a week after the election, top Armed Services Committee senators Carl Levin (D-MI) and John McCain (R-AZ) began talks with defense secretary Robert Gates to "strip . . . the proposed repeal . . . from a [pending] defense bill, leaving the repeal with no legislative vehicle to carry it" (Edwards par. 2). The Log Cabin Republicans, a conservative gay political organization and plaintiff in the original suit against DADT, filed with the U.S. Supreme Court asking it to vacate the Ninth Circuit's stay and thus uphold the repeal order. But SCOTUS refused to intervene, apparently consigning the last hope for repeal to the political ash heap. Soon afterward, fortunately, the saga took a decidedly positive turn. On its third movement through the Senate in December 2010, the legislative repeal measure passed along "mostly partisan lines" in the House (250 for, 175 against—up from a May 2010 vote of 229 for and 116 against) and by more than the requisite simple majority in the Senate (65 to 31) (CNN Wire Staff, "House Passes 'Don't Ask, Don't Tell' Repeal" [Dec. 2010] par. 2; CNN Wire Staff "House Passes 'Don't Ask, Don't Tell' Repeal" [May 2010] par. 2).[7] In September 2011 "Don't Ask, Don't Tell," despite eleventh-hour handwringing, obstruction, and gnashing of teeth from religious and political conservatives, died a relatively quiet death.

Putting an end to eighteen years of a homophobic policy with no practical motives (only conservative religious ones), this progressive turn of events was a pleasant surprise to gays, lesbians, and their supporters. Still, if the White House had elected to certify the original repeal measure by Phillips, it would have gone into effect immediately and saved a lot of worry, bile, and toxic invective. And given the fact that the repeal bill had already stalled in Congress twice that year, it might well have been voted down a third time. It's all too easy to judge the wisdom of White House caution after the fact, but one does so from the vantage point of a success that might just as easily not have come to pass. Practically speaking, the broad strokes of the final result may overwhelm the nuance of individual moments and actions; but ethically speaking, those moments of action—or of inaction—matter. The momentousness of DADT's rollback fails to countermand the force of religious homophobia and values discourse that delayed the repeal for so long, indeed, that led to the policy in the first place and that continue to wield power in other significant areas. It remains to be seen whether the ethical clarity on one point will trickle down to others. Military service is one thing. Gay marriage and full equality of access and status, while logically following suit in some countries, are not concomitant or inevitable ramifications. Even with DOMA gone, heteronormativity will endure, as will religious ire against—or at least disdain for—queers. One or two laws are not the only locus of homophobia and differential cultural treatment.

As for DADT's possible future reinstitution—by a new, more conservative Congress—one might hazard a guess based on the ongoing vicissitudes of DOMA's fate. As appeals in the Prop 8 trial continued to wend their way through the courts, Obama took a definitive step toward gay equality in February 2011 when he instructed the Department of Justice not to defend DOMA against future challenges. This positive move was surprising given the administration's previously expressed support for defending DOMA. Where one branch backed down, however, another quickly filled the vacuum. House Speaker John Boehner responded to the instruction against defending DOMA by lawyering up, declaring that he and other House members were ready to defend the law against legal challenge even if the president was not.[8] Early rumblings from the 2012 presidential primaries suggested that queers once again might be the political football of the season— through warnings about the danger of same-sex marriage, DOMA, and calls for reinstating DADT. During the 2012 primary season Republican hopefuls Rick Perry and Herman Cain promised to reinstitute the military ban. Republican nominee and former Massachusetts governor Mitt Romney, along with running mate Congressman Paul Ryan, pledged to resurrect the failed Federal Marriage Amendment, which Ryan had previously voted for in 2004.

Although the outcome of these contests has been an overall— though not complete—advance toward queer equality, it's the protracted wrestling over issues of gay rights that this book regards as particularly damaging. It's the debating of whether to give queer citizens equal rights, the constant polling to measure how many straights might feel upset by queer enfranchisement and the implication that *their* feelings matter more than anything, that evinces the discouraging, demeaning reality of queer existence in America. Wrangling over the merits of queer claims for full citizenship means simultaneously contesting queers' humanity, as if it were open to dispute. The posturing of religious and government officials on issues like DADT also disputes the claim that "it gets better" (if "it" is homophobia). The efforts of politicians and pundits to maintain antiqueer laws, along with their specious reasons for doing so, merely justify the broader cultural currents of homophobia and umbilically nourish the religious indoctrination by ex-gay ministries and purity advocates, the bullying of queer youth by peers and adults. A discussion of public and governmental debates on gay military service and marriage equality connects integrally to my point about the "It Gets Better" campaign and the wider trends of homophobia vectored around issues of queer rights and survival. Popular and political debates about DADT and Prop 8, about whether or not queers deserve the rights of other citizens, are part of the same cultural continuum as the "It Gets Better" campaign and the homophobia targeting queer teens it attempts to combat. Notwithstanding the repeal of DADT, the final death of Prop 8, and DOMA's movement toward full invalidation, the fact that queer rights are still debated (as if the political rights of citizens have to be justified, politely defended against violently antigay religious rhetoric), and the fact that political support for such rights is still often mixed or absent, helps sustain homophobia in broader, more practical ways than a movement like the oversimplified "It Gets Better" campaign may be able to overcome. My point is exemplified by Obama's verbal support for gay equality but his reluctance, until May 2012, to endorse same-sex marriage because "God is in the mix." The message here, and one of the central points of my argument, is that when politicians (or anyone, for that matter) cede ethical ground to religious belief, justice for queer citizens is gravely endangered. And this is particularly true when a religious position like conservative Christian homophobia violates core national principles like equal protection. The DOMA/DADT discussion, then, is part and parcel of this chapter's and this book's demonstration of a pernicious umbilical connection between the political and the religious and of religion's undue unethical reactionary influence on the former.

Teens may be coming out earlier, but it's still dangerous for many to do so. And one can easily see how, given the continued mixed cultural and governmental messages, they might be wary or frightened, why they might hide and even contemplate suicide. When Fred Phelps of Westboro Baptist Church appeals the Kansas Supreme Court decision ruling against his so-called right to protest at military funerals bearing signs such as "God Hates Fags" and "God Hates America," what impression does that make on queer teens and children? Keep in mind, the funerals in question are not for gay or lesbian military service members; Phelps is protesting what he regards as America's unholy love affair with homosexuality, and consequently Phelps regards any war casualty as just punishment. What message, further, does it send to queer Americans regardless of their age when SCOTUS *grants* Phelps's appeal, as it did in May 2011, and thus affirms the right to shout homophobic slurs during a funeral service?[9] What about when Michigan attorney general Mike Cox defends assistant attorney general Andrew Shirvell's so-called right to harass University of Michigan's openly gay student body president online and in person, calling him a radical queer Nazi and "Satan's representative on the student assembly"?[10] What impression is made by the mere *claim* that violent, religiously inflected antigay epithets qualify as protected speech under the First Amendment? What does it say to American teens that queer humanness and equality—queer "lives," as GLAAD president Jarrett Barrios put it—are apparently *still* "up for debate" (qtd. in Debelen par. 2)? What does it say? It legitimizes the behavior of bullies. It validates the desire of those children and adults who have not yet bullied gays or lesbians but who perhaps have thought about it. It sends as intensely negative a message to queer youth as does the legal exclusion of queer Americans.

The links between antigay bullying, homophobic religious rhetoric, and federal law were made explicit in a video released in November 2010 by NOH8, a photo campaign against Prop 8. Opening with the questions, "[H]ow can these statistics [of gay teen suicides] be so high? What's convincing these kids that things *won't* get better?" the video turns to Cindy McCain, whose husband Senator John McCain "led the GOP filibuster that prevented Congress from voting on a [DADT] repeal" and campaigned for president in 2008 on an anti–gay marriage platform (Tiku par. 1). Mrs. McCain then says, "Our political and religious leaders tell LGBT youth that they have no future. . . . They can't serve our country openly. . . . Our government treats the LGBT community like second-class citizens, why shouldn't the bullies?" (qtd. in par. 2). Simply put, discrimination against gays and lesbians by figures of legal and cultural authority actively licenses their personal harassment. The same day the video debuted, however, Mrs. McCain issued another statement via Twitter, contradicting her comment in the video about DADT and, by extension, casting doubt on the sincerity of her support for other GLBT causes like marriage equality. She wrote: "I fully support the NoH8 campaign and all it stands for and am proud to be a part of it. But I stand by my husband's stance on DADT" (qtd.

in LaVictoire par. 2). Perhaps the senator's wife composed this tweet herself. Perhaps it was an attempt by one of her husband's staff to blunt the effect of her anti-DADT comment in the video—though one wonders what relevance her opinion on the military ban has to her husband's ability to *continue* to block its repeal. In either case, the legerdemain attempted in the tweet—to separate the NOH8 campaign from the DADT debate—simply isn't credible. If Mrs. McCain had not mentioned gays' inability to "serve our country openly," then the attempt to distinguish her support of NOH8 and gay marriage from her opposition to "Don't Ask, Don't Tell" might play, if only as craven hair-splitting. But she had already mentioned DADT in the video and had done so critically. Whatever the explanation for this schizophrenic episode, the implication for queer teens and adults is the same: pledges of support don't mean much; tolerance is an emotional position of convenience, to be discarded as easily as adopted, or at least demoted under pressure from other, more meaningful commitments. The message is that queers' second-class citizenship is upsetting but not upsetting enough to be a deal breaker, to motivate storming the barricades.

Now, one may object that, in matters of purely political discrimination, religion is not solely to blame; surely politicians and the media have a good deal of blood on their hands. But that blood *comes* from kowtowing to religious biases, without which there would be absolutely no grounds for even suggesting, at least without recourse to rational debate, that queers are not citizens entitled to basic rights and protections enjoyed by other citizens. To address such an objection, I want to qualify an earlier argument, or rather, to clarify my intentions. In chapters 1 and 2 I explored the possibility that the Christian closet might hold some sustaining as well as punishing properties—sustaining in ways unintended by its keepers, ways that subvert or mockingly critique the homophobic diapason that structures Christianity's history and current practice, regardless of whether religious moderates choose to ignore it. In light of the very real violence inflicted on queers, it might seem irresponsible to suggest that any queer would want to remain in the closet of purity cults, abstinence education, or conservative Christianity if any less damaging alternative were available. That *lack* of availability is my point, and not just for queer Christians in conflict, but for the queer teens are who killing themselves. These kids don't think it's safe. And often it's not. The "It Gets Better" campaign assumes that an out and proud, rainbow-doused life is available to, and safe for, *all* queer teens and adults. And clearly it's not. Even if it is concretely safer for many to be out than in decades past, the vile phobic rhetoric swarming about us says that's not necessarily true. That rhetoric is as real as any gay-straight alliance or pride parade. If queer closeted teens can locate some pleasures, sexual or emotional, within the depths of the Christian abstinence or purity movements, they should not be denied such consolation. This is not to say that the regime they inhabit is not damaging them, but for the present it may be all they have.

To those who find criticism of the "It Gets Better" campaign harsh, I would point out that the *occasion* for the campaign clarifies the need for a deliberate, thoughtful, and less simplistic response. Despite demonstrable signs of increased tolerance, pride, and openness in many quarters, many youth still view their sexuality more as the mark of Cain than as a cause for celebration. Undoubtedly for some queer teens who commit or attempt suicide, psychological issues unrelated to being gay may bear significant weight. But for some of them, and certainly for the peers who harass them, it *is* about their queerness. I would discourage no one from trying to impart hope to gay and lesbian children. They need all the support they can get. But when fairly well-adjusted queers who have made it safely to adulthood gloss over the long years of conflict, doubt, and shame *as well as* endurance and survival with a simplistic slogan that belies the sometimes disheartening, sometimes inspiring complexity of their experiences, it does our younger compatriots in queerness an unnecessary disservice. I'm reminded of Heather Love's trenchant dissection of the sanitized, one-dimensionally sunny GLBT movement in recent politics and historiography: "Celebration will only get us so far, for pride itself can be toxic when it is sealed off from the shame that nurtured it" (127).[11] In *Feeling Backward: Loss and the Politics of Queer Shame* (2007), Love cautions that

> "Advances" such as gay marriage and the increasing media visibility of well-heeled gays and lesbians threaten to obscure the continuing denigrations and dismissal of queer existence. One may enter the mainstream on the condition that one breaks ties with all those who cannot make it—the nonwhite and the nonmonogamous, the poor and the gender deviant, the fat, the disabled, the unemployed, the infected, and a host of unmentionable others. Social negativity clings not only to these

figures but to those who lived before the common era of gay liberation—the abject multitude against whose experience we define our own liberation. Given the new opportunities available to *some* gays and lesbians, the temptation to forget—to forget the outrages and humiliations of gay and lesbian history and to ignore the ongoing suffering of those not borne up by the rising tide of gay normalization—is stronger than ever. (10)

If anything, the recent spate of gay teen suicides, not to mention those before and since *not* reported in national news, attests that "continuing denigrations"—whether the bullying of peers or the front-and-center fag-bashing sound bites pouring from pulpits and political campaign ads—have flagged little, if at all, in the face of "advances" in gay media visibility and political battles for gay rights. Against the temptation to spurn what is painful about past or present queer life, we should remember the extent to which "sexual shame" and "the closet continue . . . to operate powerfully in contemporary society and media" (147). When Love recommends that "we begin to take the negativity of negative affect more seriously," she is not asking us to wallow in grief for its own sake but rather "to turn grief into grievance—to address the larger social structures, the regimes of domination, that are at the root of the pain. . . . [R]eal engagement with these issues means coming to terms with the temporality, the specific structures of grief, and allowing these elements of negative affect to transform our understanding of politics" (151). While Love states her argument in the strongest possible terms—"the transformational possibilities of gay pride [have] been exhausted," have "instead become a code name for assimilation and for the commodification of gay and lesbian identity" (153)—she does so in order to turn queers' collective focus away from the pervasive, parochial sense, nourished by media and political address, that we "have arrived." Granted, the recent spotlight on gay suicides and the "It Gets Better" campaign puncture the supposed extent of that perception. At the same time that these videos honor the pain of young queers, and connect it to pain from the speakers' own pasts, what they elide is the path from *back there* to *here*, or, for the queer kids they're addressing, the path from *here* to *there ahead*.[12] What gets bypassed on most occasions is not just the question of how to navigate that path, indiscernible from the present and visible only in retrospect, but the question of whether that path might actually be *central* to queer understanding, whether the pain queers experience—undeserved and uncultivated yet confronted and engaged with—may be productively transformative to a sense of self and community.

Saying "it gets better" is a mantra that does little substantive good to the listener, offered on occasions like funerals, when no words can salve the gutting pain of the moment. A more useful, sustaining alternative—one that doesn't passively turn in on itself—would be to embrace confidence, even anger, to demand respect and equitable treatment for queers, to be vocal in asserting that queerness is nothing to be ridiculed but is a source of identity and pride equal to any other. Queer adults understandably have difficulty finding words appropriate to tragic events like the suicide of their teenage compatriots. But if all one says about pain and loneliness is that it will pass, one dishonors those feelings, as if they're invalid because one's only responding to discrimination or as if they are a necessary rite of passage that one just has to endure to earn later happiness. Emphasizing the ephemerality of pain, which indeed may not always be ephemeral, also neglects the varied, proscribed, and enriching ways in which, as Heather Love reminds us, feelings of exclusion, solitude, and abnormality have long funded queer identity in sustaining as well as disabling ways. The passivity radiating from "It Gets Better" implies, even if unintentionally and mutedly, that turning the other cheek is the ideal response for harassed homosexuals. For some of them, regardless of age, it *may* be, depending on how safe it is for them to come out or even address their harassers. But why not encourage those who feel safe enough to speak up and to strike out, literally and/or symbolically? This seems an equally valid course of action, and it's one that out gay rapper Cazwell recommends in his own "It Gets Better" video. Cazwell, known for rap singles such as "Get My Money Back" and "Ice Cream Truck" and music videos whose perspective on male beauty is at once impish and unabashedly gay, recounts his own experience of being harassed, not as a gay teen but as an adult:

> I'm not an advocate for violence . . . but sometimes you got to pick up a motherfuckin' rock. Sometimes you have to let them know that enough is enough . . . and you're not going to tolerate it. . . . The way to solve this problem is to do things that

give you self-confidence. . . . Things do get better once you
learn to love yourself, and you learn to love yourself by doing
what you love to do. ("Cazwell . . . It Gets Better")

What I value about Cazwell's "It Gets Better" video over others is
the way it supplies what's lacking in its predecessors. Cazwell bridges
the gap between an emotional achievement ("learn[ing] to love yourself")—which, important as it is, may not always be enough to secure
one's physical safety or dignity—and taking further steps ("let[ting
homophobes] know that enough is enough"). One might argue that
only by retaliation—not just rhetorical, but, in the absence of legal protection and adult oversight, physical or verbal retaliation—can safety
be extended to and experienced by more gays and lesbians. A less sen-
timental, more pragmatic message would be to urge the safety of the
closet when necessary but to come out in a show of strength and to
strike back whenever one feels equipped to do so. If retaliation feels too
aggressive, Cazwell also says that "it doesn't just get better 'cause you're
out of high school. Things start to get better when you start to have a
strong sense of self and love for yourself. . . . It's when you start to have
a sense of self-worth that things really start to change for you." But
this is not a concession; his central message remains undiluted. What's
crucial, from my viewpoint, is that he recommends *action*, including
*re*action. Savage and Miller recommend passivity: "just stick it out. It's
painful now, but it's going to get so much better." "Stick[ing] it out"
may be a tactic backed by good intentions, but it insinuates, even if it
does so unintentionally, that gay harassment is inevitable and even that
homophobic bullies have a right to say their piece. Cazwell's response
is substantive, proactive, in ways most other "It Gets Better" videos are
not. Rather than withdrawing and waiting out the storm of homophobia (for who's to say it will weaken, will end, of its own accord?), queers
would do better, when it does not clearly endanger their safety, to
argumentatively and physically confront the unethical denigration of
homosexuality that is writ large across our culture and to demand justice, protection, and civil equity.

   That being said, I'm hardly arguing that being oppressed or hated
should be greeted as automatic fodder for nourishing the gay self.
What disappoints me about "It Gets Better" is a failure to connect the
pain of individual queer kids with larger social entities, statements,
and acts, a failure to call out the adults who generate the hate that

these kids experience directly on the internet or through unconscious or intentional statements by people they know. It's no wonder that queer youth, despite the success of openly gay television characters on *Modern Family* and *Glee*, might still feel inferior. On the heels of California's Supreme Court order declaring Prop 8 unconstitutional, GOP platforms in Montana and Texas called for laws to *re*criminalize homosexuality, well after its explicit decriminalization by the U.S. Supreme Court in *Lawrence v. Texas* in 2003.[13] And even though Maggie Gallagher, spokesperson for the National Organization for Marriage (NOM) and one of Prop 8's most vocal champions, couches her opposition to same-sex marriage in cultural and social terms (chiefly, pseudo–social science nonsense about parenting), the basis of her argument is not ethics but religion. NOM's publicity barrage supporting Prop 8 when it was first on the ballot was funded by political and religious conservatives, a significant portion of NOM's bloated $10 million budget coming from Mormon supporters outside of California. Religion may not shoulder *all* of the blame for continuing antigay sentiment, but it arguably bears the brunt of it. Without religious rationales, proponents of antigay measures would be thrown back on logical, ethical arguments, and on *that* basis, as Judge Vaughn Walker's decision on Prop 8 resoundingly asserts, homophobia is insupportable. It's time to stop defending religion as an excuse for otherwise indefensible actions and opinions. Religion has done enough damage to the discussion of gay and lesbian rights, to queer minds and lives. And no progress can be made as long as religion is taken seriously as an argumentative platform for unethical, unequal treatment of our fellow human beings. This is part of the reason why projects of gay religion and queer spirituality are ultimately unhelpful. In fact, I would argue, they are demonstrably harmful. Regardless of their theoretical innovations, these endeavors end up merely grafting insights of political revolution, psychology, or queer theory onto the unaccommodating carapace of religious discourse, a system of thought that is elementally unreceptive and antithetical to their liberalizing priorities. In this way, the liberal religious and spiritual projects mounted by MCC, Johnson, and Althaus-Reid are actually attempts at religious moderation and thus not so liberal or transgressive as they claim or want to be. Consequently, such projects not only fall flat of transcending the errors and reach of religion, they also, by implication, justify religion as, at its base, a structure of thought worth saving. It would be more helpful, to queers in particular but to others as well, if religion was left behind as an artifact of humanity's superstitious and violent past, fundamentally inimical to tolerance and unusable as an ethical pattern for justice.

Given the ongoing brutality wrought by religious beliefs on queers, what I am advocating, for those who are ready, who are safe, is the abandonment of religion altogether. Even moderate versions of religion remain tethered and in service to heteronormative, homophobic social and ideological agendas. And that is unacceptable. Just as Christopher Hitchens argues that it is time to let go of religion as a primitive approach to the world that we have evolved beyond, the same is even truer, even more pressing, for gays and lesbians. We have nothing to gain and so much to lose by persistently seeking approval from institutions and belief systems inherently opposed to us, genetically dedicated to our erasure. It's my position that, although the queer Christian closet may afford consolation, pleasure, or subversion to some of its inhabitants, though covert maneuverings may deform neat distinctions between queer and nonqueer and thus further problematize reified notions of identity, this is a battle that cannot finally be won. It is not worth winning, much less fighting. Why try to rehabilitate an institution so imbued with reactionary, sexist, and phobic energies, with such hostile animus? In seeking to find a place for gayness within Christianity, are we just asking for acceptance from "Daddy," meaning God as well as the authoritarian figures that propagate purity culture, abstinence education, ex-gay therapy, and other crimes in God's supposed service? Speaking of ex-gay therapy: it was the sympathetic responses to Tyler Clementi's death and the general "It Gets Better" tsunami that prompted Exodus International to withdraw its sponsorship from the Day of Truth. This misleadingly named affair is an annual Christian conservative event held in American high schools and universities "on the same day as the [pro-GLBT] Day of Silence . . . 'to counter,'" in Exodus's own words, "'the promotion of homosexual behavior and to express an opposing viewpoint from a Christian perspective'" (Gilgoff par. 4). While I applaud Exodus's withdrawal of support, one wonders whether the lack of their sponsorship alone will put an end to the Day of Truth movement. And, if so, for how long? Till this election or that news cycle is past?

If my reaction seems cynical, ungenerous, or ungrateful, I would point to the statement by Alan Chambers, the most recent president of Exodus International, regarding the decision to withdraw from the

Day of Truth: "All the recent attention to bullying helped us realize that we need to equip kids to live out biblical tolerance and grace while treating their neighbors as they'd like to be treated, whether they agree with them or not" (qtd. in Gilgoff par. 2). Although tricked out in the meek sackcloth of Christian humility, Chambers's statement is noteworthy for what it does *not* do: the retraction does not negate Exodus's view that homosexuality is a sinful condition incompatible with salvation and requiring change through ex-gay therapy. Chambers extols "tolerance and grace," but those qualities are still accompanied by the qualifying adjective "biblical," as if there were no other kind. Exodus understands the Bible to condemn homosexuality as a sin, so it's difficult to understand how conservative Christians can tolerate and respect those regarded as living in defiance of biblical dictates. Likewise, encouraging tolerance for others "whether [one] agree[s] with them or not" pays lip service to tolerance without renouncing the underlying *cause* for intolerance—in this case, a disapproval of homosexuality as immoral. If the underlying motive for disagreement and intolerance remains, Chambers has no business pretending to extend tolerance or even kindness. "Liv[ing] out biblical tolerance and grace," as this organization understands it, *cannot* mean "treating [one's] neighbors" with equality and respect. And are we to believe that Exodus International has finally seen the light? If it took several gay teens killing themselves—that is, if it isn't an ethical decision Christian conservatives could reach on their own—that's sad. But Chambers's choice of words reveals the true impetus for pulling sponsorship from the Day of Truth. It was not Clementi's or any other teen's suicide or harassment. What led to the pullback was not antigay bullying but "[a]ll the recent attention to" it. One suspects that the Day of Truth was cancelled to avoid the backlash and negative publicity the event might generate in the wake of extended, high-profile media coverage of the harassment of gay teens—harassment the Day of Truth explicitly encourages. Chambers issued his statement cancelling the event in October 2010, during the height of the media blitz on gay teen suicide—reserving the right to express "disagree[ment]" with supporters of the GLBT community. Exodus claimed the event would no longer take place, at least under its sponsorship; only time will tell whether someone else takes up this particular mantle. Even if Exodus no longer promotes *this* event, it and organizations like it still promote ex-gay therapy and a message that homosexuality is a painful, abnormal, and sinful condition. In light of such insubstantial and, one has to suspect, insincere gestures of religious moderation, might queers do better to jettison the quest for religious approval and acceptance, a quest that's akin to queer efforts at mainstreaming? Might we, instead, sustain ourselves by returning to our somewhat neglected communal legacy of critical and ethical insight regarding the contingencies of desire and identity, the lure and cost of unconscious normativity? Might queers, as well as straights, not be fortified to do some of the work required to reach the point where one *can* say that "it's gotten better"—the work, the discussion, and the distance elided by the "It Gets Better" mantra—if we hold to, and continue to discover, the hard, unsentimental truths of which humans are capable without threats of spiritual or sublunary punishment?

The number of Americans who will admit to being atheists, at least when asked by pollsters, remains scant. While a 2001 American Religious Identification Survey (ARIS) found that 14.1 percent of Americans admit to being "without religion," only 0.9 percent call themselves atheists or even agnostics. Polls by the BBC and Gallup in 2004 and 2008 produced higher numbers of respondents who don't believe in God, 9 percent and 6 percent respectively. A more recent ARIS, in 2009, disclosed that 15 percent of Americans do not ascribe to a particular religion but that only 1.6 percent called themselves atheists or agnostics.[14] While this last number almost doubles that from the 2001 findings, it remains a miniscule minority. The disparity between those who see themselves as not religious but also as neither atheist nor agnostic might correspond, for some respondents, to dissatisfaction with extant religious institutions. The other possibility, however, is that, as a 2006 University of Minnesota study disclosed, most respondents are aware of how generally Americans despise and distrust atheists. By contrast, in 1996 Gallup found that 40 percent of Americans believed in creationism, in the face of the scientific rationale and evidence on the side of evolution. Many continue to do so even though creationism's latest incarnation, "Intelligent Design," failed to pass legal muster, in the 2005 Dover (Pennsylvania) Area School Board case, as anything more than biblical literalism camouflaged within a confused smattering of quasi-scientific talk. Yet despite the currency of such magical thinking, the critical and popular success of two recent critiques of religious belief and defenses of atheism suggest that logic and ethics are still able to find an audience, if not to win the day. Christopher Hitchens's *God Is Not Great: How Religion Poisons Everything* (2007) and Sam Harris's *The End of Faith: Religion, Terror, and the Future of Reason* (2004) outline a salient array of well-reasoned arguments for viewing religion as an obstacle to rational debate and progress, an impediment to the ethical, civil treatment of others, and, in much of recorded history, an incitement to mistreatment and persecution.[15] While the totality of these writers' arguments exceed the scope of my project, and while their arguments occasionally differ, in broad strokes Hitchens and Harris make the same case against the maintenance of religious belief. Religion, both agree, is not an irreplaceable moral foundation. It is not a valid basis for political policy decisions, justifying, as it often does, vicious acts of violence. And religion is not the sole or the best locus of unassailable personal or cultural values.[16] Along these lines, Harris and Hitchens make five points that are distinctly germane to the present discussion and that inform my bid for atheism for queer and queer-positive Americans' route to a productive, sane, safe, vibrant future.

(1) From a cold cost-benefit viewpoint, as well as from an ethical stance, humans have inflicted and continue to inflict enough pain, suffering, and death on one another in the name of religion to make it, objectively, a losing proposition. Affecting nonbelievers as well as adherents of its own and other faiths, most religious traditions endorse and animate all manner of damage, from genocide and armed conflict in places such as Palestine, Sudan, and the Caucasus, to lies about sex, AIDS, and contraception that endanger the health and lives of hundreds of millions around the world. Under the influence of religion, ministers, physicians, and think-tank pundits issue pronouncements that abortion causes breast cancer, sterility, and mental illness; that condoms fail to prevent and may even promote HIV transmission; and that female circumcision and infibulation among African Muslims or oral-genital contact during a Jewish Orthodox bris are, from ecumenical or multicultural standpoints, cultural traditions beyond our ability to stamp out or our right to reproach.[17] Hitchens attributes the source of such absurdities not so much to a desire to inflict harm, although they definitely do that, as to the augmentation of religious institutions'

temporal authority and an incompatibility between religion and science that has survived centuries of well-meaning but intellectually unsound avowals to the contrary.[18] As Hitchens notes, the purity fixation dear to so many religions hobbles psychological development and impairs health: "Sexual innocence, which can be charming in the young if it is not needlessly protracted, is positively corrosive and repulsive in the mature adult" (227). Sam Harris insists that, given the evidence of just how deleterious measures claiming to protect sexual and, by extension, spiritual innocence can be, the "rules of civil discourse must change":

> Faith drives a wedge between ethics and suffering. Where certain actions cause no suffering at all, religious dogmatists still maintain that they are evil and worthy of punishment (sodomy, marijuana use, homosexuality, the killing of blastocysts, etc.). And yet, where suffering and death are found in abundance their causes are often deemed to be good (withholding funds for family planning in the third world, prosecuting nonviolent drug offenders, preventing stem-cell research, etc.). This inversion of priorities not only victimizes innocent people and squanders scarce resources; it completely falsifies our ethics. (168–169)

Given queer Americans' protracted exclusion from civil parity with straights on a number of fronts (marriage, property rights, health care, death benefits, as well as adoption and custody rights), the need to argue for parity in a forum unwarped by religious opinions—opinions purporting to be inarguable matters of faith—has become increasingly pressing. To find our collective way out of the impasse between febrile crusades to safeguard innocence and sensible steps to promote health and pleasure, Hitchens recommends a "divorce between the sexual life and fear, and the sexual life and disease, and the sexual life and tyranny," a divorce made possible "on the sole condition that we banish all religions from the discourse" (283). This advice feels unusually apposite to present-day GLBT life.

(2) Just as germ theory once permitted humans to move beyond theories of humors or witchcraft in explaining disease, in evolutionary terms we have progressed beyond the point at which religion offers convincing or beneficial explanations of the natural world's mysteries.

(Religion's answers to spiritual questions, and whether they can be said to truly count as answers, will be addressed later.) As Hitchens puts it,

> Religion comes from the period of human prehistory where nobody . . . had the smallest idea what was going on. It comes from the bawling and fearful infancy of our species, and is a babyish attempt to meet our inescapable demand for knowledge (as well as for comfort, reassurance, and other infantile needs).
>
> . . . All attempts to reconcile faith with science and reason are consigned to failure and ridicule for precisely these reasons. . . . [T]here would be no such churches in the first place if humanity had not been afraid of the weather, the dark, the plague, the eclipse, and all manner of other things now easily explicable. (64, 65)

More succinctly, "We no longer have any need of a god to explain what is no longer mysterious" (Hitchens 96). Sam Harris also regards religion as constitutionally tribal and backward and its persistence as a developmental holdover. Little good, and a good deal of damage, results from hanging on to "a belief system . . . passed down to us from men and women whose lives were simply ravaged by their basic ignorance about the world. . . . If religion addresses a genuine sphere of understanding and human necessity, then it should be susceptible to *progress*; its doctrines should become more useful, not less" (Harris 21, 22). Exempting religion from the rational and evidentiary standards that we apply to and expect in every other area of discourse is "maladaptive" because, "[w]here our traditions are not supportive"—as with religiously excused homophobia—"they become mere vehicles of ignorance" (Harris 67, 171). This brings us directly to the third point.

(3) Religion's obstructiveness to health and progress stems from its thoroughgoing resistance to reason. Free inquiry undermines the hold that religious institutions and their representatives wield over us. If independent thought were not so dangerous to religious authority, the religious would not have expended so much energy over the centuries suppressing and discouraging it. Coercion, whether physical, emotional, or psychological, would not be so integral to religion's way of doing business.[19] Harris asserts: "Only openness to evidence and argument

will secure a common world for us. . . . This spirit of mutual inquiry is the very antithesis of religious faith" (48). The opposition to logic and knowledge is unacceptable in any other area (medicine, engineering, or law, for example); we reject reason *only* here. Religion authorizes and commends belief in propositions that would be judged absurd, if not a sign of mental derangement, when expressed in other contexts. To claim, against all argument, that my deceased parent has risen from the grave or that aliens are speaking to me through my television would likely earn me a stay in a mental ward or a heavy course of medication. By contrast, to claim—without even the excuse of eyewitnesses, no less—that Jesus rose from the dead over two thousand years ago and speaks to me through prayer earns me social affirmation and cultural approval. The problem with the claim about alien communiqués is not that I would necessarily be alone in my belief. Others have made this and similar claims. But claims about religious belief, *most* but not all such claims, are not cause for psychological evaluation, despite the fact that religious claims—for instance, the virgin birth of Christ, his resurrection, or the promise of eternal life on certain conditions—contradict everything we know collectively and personally about the laws of nature. Human pregnancy requires an ovum *and* a sperm to fertilize it; the body dies and, after a very short time, cannot be restored to life; and, to date, no telescope or space exploration mission has stumbled across the location of heaven. Religion remains a singularly and perilously reason-free zone, "persuad[ing] otherwise intelligent men and women not to think, or to think badly, about questions of civilizational importance. And yet it remains taboo to criticize religious faith in our society. . . . What is worst in us (outright delusion) has been elevated beyond the reach of criticism, while what is best (reason and intellectual honesty) must remain hidden, for fear of giving offense" (Harris 237). Jettisoning reason and free inquiry promises not more but *less* enlightenment: "Because each new generation of children is taught that religious propositions need not be justified in the way all others must, civilization is still besieged by armies of the preposterous" (Harris 73). Because religion "attempt[s] to assert the literal and limited mind over the ironic and inquiring one" (Hitchens 258), social and ethical development remain stalled, torn between progressive and retrograde forces. And unless our society is to become a moral dictatorship (the aspirations of Christian Dominionists being the most extreme form of such an aspiration), American—particularly *queer* American—survival mandates the exercise of rational debate.[20]

From practical as well as ethical perspectives, then, religion's refusal of reason appears troublesome. Faith is often declared to be that which is beyond fact, that which attains truth without sullying its claims by evidentiary pandering. Nonetheless, religion vitiates its claim to transcendental truth, truth produced or assured by belief alone, by trying to have it both ways. Faith has no need for evidence or logical arguments. We're assured that God moves in mysterious ways in regard to some matters, but on others—instructions on dietary or sexual behavior—he stipulates explicitly. Although religious faith often extols its independence of reason, it does engage with reason on two counts: by purporting to describe some reality about the world (such as the existence of angels, of an afterlife, or the soul-imperiling nature of certain actions) and by craving so-called proofs of God's existence (from miracles and arguments-from-design to natural disasters read as divine wake-up calls). On both counts, despite its claims to be from free of reason's confines, religion opens itself to rational critique.[21] Some may find it a humbling spiritual paradox that, to paraphrase Sam Harris, truth is both crucial to faith *and* inaccessible to it. However, by contending that its propositions apply to the real world *but* cannot be measured, tested, or held accountable to real-world standards of evidence and rational inquiry, religious faith reveals its tendency to paralyze the exercise of those faculties that have permitted civilization to survive and progress (68). Hitchens inverts the notion that, because atheists cannot *dis*prove the existence of God, God must therefore exist, and so turns the responsibility, the burden of proof, back where it belongs: "a theory [such as religion] that is unfalsifiable is to that extent a weak one" (81). "What can be asserted without evidence," he adds with finality, "can also be dismissed without evidence" (150). If we're going to live in a world where humans are marginally responsible for their behavior and their treatment of others, where words and actions cannot be bracketed as exempt from criticism because a divinity who cannot be reached for comment or held responsible says so, then religious faith and custom must no longer be taken seriously in discussions of public policy and civil law, much less be allowed to dictate or curb the rights of citizens—as it still does for queer citizens. That would seem to be what sets apart the liberal democracies of Europe and the United

States from theocracies like Iran's, whose elision of the church-state distinction is so vilified by our government.

(4) Some readers might object that the preceding describes the behavior of religious extremists, and that writing off religion altogether disregards the compensatory, leavening efforts made by religious moderates. Religious moderates tend to entreat tolerance for, and abjure criticism of, members of disparate faith traditions as well as those who hold conflicting interpretations of their own traditions. They rarely grant such quarter to atheists.[22] Tolerance might be able to smooth over theological rifts or disagreements on social policy—between Methodists and born-again Southern Baptists, for example—even though, with neither party relinquishing faith in its own position, the only agreement is to pleasantly disagree. By "put[ting] humanity ahead of their own sect or creed," however, religious moderates do plausible harm by disseminating the false idea that tolerance is a heal-all (Hitchens 27). That refusal to judge actions shielded by a mantle of cultural diversity is precisely the problem. Harris puts this in the strongest terms:

> the greatest problem confronting civilization is not merely religious extremism; rather, it is the larger set of cultural and intellectual *accommodations* we have made to faith itself. Religious moderates are, in large part, responsible for the religious conflict in our world, because their beliefs provide the context in which scriptural literalism and religious violence can never be adequately opposed. (45; emphasis added)

In eschewing criticism of other religious traditions, a moderate religious stance leaves one impotent in the face of immoderate positions staked out, say, by fundamentalist Christians. Out of tolerance, some might wish to refrain from criticizing conservative views—for instance, that "homosexuality is sinful and abnormal, corrosive to social and spiritual health of gays and straights alike"—as mere articles of faith, as texts not carrying any inherent animosity but only adopted by hateful people. But these are *not* simply some form of intellectual play; they propose to make truth statements about the world we live in and then, justified by an authority beyond reproach or recourse, to dictate the political, legal, and cultural treatment of fellow human beings. This is not how moderates behave, perhaps, but religious moderation's axiom of tolerance guts its power to persuade or oppose the extremists who *do.* Abjuring judgment or criticism of any idea or act clad in the language of religious "values"—values to which moderates have pledged undiluted respect—puts not just open-mindedness but civility and justice at significant risk. Religious moderates claim to speak for the "true" nature of their respective faiths, a core spirituality that transcends the weight of institutional misconduct past and present, yet this claim is fallacious, a reassuring, often well-meaning bit of casuistry. As historian Will Durant noted more than fifty years ago in *The Age of Faith*, "Intolerance is the natural concomitant of strong faith; tolerance grows only when faith loses certainty; certainty is murderous" (qtd. in Harris 86).[23] Ecumenicalism is demonstrably *not* the core of most, if not all, religious traditions. Believers who commit to their traditions without a dose of secular reasoning, who do not ignore wide swaths of their sacred documents, must view all other faiths as erroneous. As Harris notes, moderate Christians have much to ignore in the Bible: to begin with, the violence recommended toward non-Christians or apostate Christians in Deuteronomy 18 and 82, which parallel Koranic verses instructing Muslims to slay unbelievers blow for blow. If one wants, as a moderate, to make the argument that we live in more civilized times (and in the West the ferocity of religious persecution has lost a good deal of its former violence), it is still a matter of routine observation that thoroughgoing religious certainty is incompatible with tolerance and often leads to a desire, if not a crusade, to convert the unbelievers. In addition to moderates' problematic claim to practice the *authentic* versions of their traditions, they are really acting as humanists, not as religious adherents. At least they cannot accurately claim that their motivations are religiously grounded. Their beliefs don't have to be based in religion; indeed, arguments against religious extremism and the causes of sanity and safety would fare considerably better if religious moderates did not tie their pleas for justice and tolerance to the same sets of ideas that religious extremists have wielded, for much longer and with greater success, as weapons of unreason, alarm, and dominance.

(5) Faith is often proclaimed the vessel of indispensable truths and the source of unique elements nowhere else available. We're assured that "'people of faith' possess moral advantages that others can only envy" (Hitchens 32). Yet it's entirely possible to operate from within a serviceable, admirable code of ethics equal to that produced by religious moderates through heavy editing but *without* the confining,

backward strictures of religion. Hitchens goes even further: "[E]thics and morality are quite independent of faith, and cannot be derived from it. . . . [R]eligion is—because it claims a special divine exemption for its practices and beliefs—not just amoral but immoral" (Hitchens 52).[24] When Hitchens speaks of religion as constitutionally immoral, he refers to the amoral tendencies religion lays itself open to. Religion predisposes itself to actions that vitiate its nobler principles by placing its own moral justification beyond reproach and beyond verification: the word of God or his representatives should not be questioned and cannot be cross-checked with any accessible, independent source. Apologists who remind us that there is "much that is wise and consoling and beautiful in our religious books" might be met with the following rejoinder: "words of wisdom and consolation and beauty abound in the pages of Shakespeare, Virgil, and Homer as well, and no one ever murdered strangers by the thousands because of the inspiration found there" (Harris 35). Ethical treatment of one's fellow humans may be borne of altruism, selfishness, or some combination of the two (evolutionary biology has long claimed their interrelation), but "we simply do not need religious ideas to motivate us to live ethical lives" (Harris 172).[25] Treating religion as the best or ultimate provenance of ethics or, as often happens in secular culture, associating ethics *uniquely* with religion produces moral relativism: "Many people appear to believe that ethical truths are culturally contingent in a way that scientific truths are not. Indeed, this loss of purchase upon ethical *truth* seems to be one of the principal shortcomings of secularism" (Harris 170). And while moral relativism may seem an easy way of encouraging tolerance for other religions (though of course this is a lazy and morally problematic means to that end), it does nothing to shield queers and other demeaned groups from religious hatred. "A *rational* approach to ethics becomes possible once we realize that questions of right and wrong are really questions about the happiness and suffering of sentient creatures" (170–171; emphasis added). For example, from an ethical standpoint, as opposed to a religious one, it would be impossible to justify the practice of "honor killing" as the right or duty of men whose female relatives have been raped or have had consensual premarital sex. This horrific act against individuals one supposedly loves has been justified, barbarically, as an expression of religious respect in some cultures.[26] As opposed to religion, which offers moral "truths" that typically pose more questions than they answer, ethics can, if not resolve mysteries (a suitable task for reason), at least equip us with tools for mature, conscious interaction with others. Divorcing ourselves from the arbitrary dictates of religion liberates us from a vicious range of inexplicable behaviors and prejudices. In some Muslim countries, executing homosexuals remains a politically and religiously accepted practice. In the West, we have thankfully moved beyond punishing homosexuality with execution. Yet in America, even though sodomy laws have been declared unconstitutional, homosexuality still earns a number of legally enforced exclusions. If and when all these legal barriers are removed, as some have been, this does nothing to diminish the religiously legitimated marginalization of homosexuality—a symbolic sort of death but a compelling one. Once the behavior enjoined against a sin has been questioned as inhumane or unjustified, we must also question the associated prejudice. Both rest on the same irrational foundation: bias dressed up as custom, superstition ossified into tradition.

Ethics seeks answers to questions that religion obfuscates or simply cannot tackle. The oldest problem, for philosophers and priests alike, is theodicy: Why do evil and suffering exist? More pointedly, why do people suffer who are ethically good or religiously faithful? Ancient Greek philosopher Epicurus may have stated the problem most succinctly and in a way most damaging to religion's exclusive claim as a path to truth: "Is [God] willing to prevent evil but not able? Then he is impotent. Is he able but not willing? Then he is malevolent. Is he both able and willing? Whence this evil?" (qtd. in Hitchens 268). Most religions have been unable to solve the puzzle of theodicy satisfactorily. Some suffering may appear retributive, punishment for some misdeed. But if the sufferer has not committed a wrong, or if wrongdoers go *un*punished, the entire scheme seems senseless. Religion finesses the contradiction by telling the faithful that the divine scheme of rewards and punishments is *still* intact but that their mortal minds are simply unable to comprehend the divine plan in which their pain plays a part. This of course begs the initial question of justice, proffers ignorance as an anodyne for the curse of independent thought, and weakens the incentive for obeying the rules in the first place. Religious individuals may find a secular, philosophical response to all of this less satisfying. To *their* ears, the answers provided by ethics might sound the same: it's unlikely that meaning is predestined; pain may be often undeserved.

Yet the advantage of ethics over religion is that, by fostering the application of independent thought and free inquiry, ethics requires us to forge our own meaning, to sort out and accept the consequences of our own justice, whether they are pleasing or not. Success or blame for the human venture rests with ourselves. Under rational review, the religious justification for the condemnation of many "sins," from dietary restrictions to codes of sexual purity, falls away. Thus we can erode the detritus of custom, habit, and superstition, and leave standing only those injunctions (against murder, rape, theft, and so on) that are conducive to an ethical, safe, and equitable communal life. All we need ask is, "Does this mandate upon which salvation or divine approval supposedly depends have any rational basis? Does a reputed crime, such as homosexuality, materially injure the practitioner or anyone else?" Once we reject the shibboleth of sin—an intangible pretext whereby a certain action disqualifies one for an afterlife, yet another injurious, unprovable concept—then the distance separating religious custom from good ethical sense stands out, clear and cogent.

Religion often seems to fall short as an ethical blueprint. The Bible, for example, contains surprising gaps as a set of instructions on moral living: it "contain[s] a warrant for ethnic cleansing, for slavery, for bride-price, and for indiscriminate massacre" but no commandments against rape, slavery, or genocide (Hitchens 102). Religion's use of psychological coercion to dissuade certain behaviors and adduce others would seem to *lessen*, not augment, the worth of performing good deeds or refraining from bad ones. Hitchens notes the ethical diminishment inherent here: "By definition one may not be *compelled* into altruism. Perhaps we would be better mammals if we were not 'made' this way, but surely nothing could be sillier than having a 'maker' who then forbade the very same instinct he instilled" (214).[27] A common objection by religion's defenders is that, even if religion does not always render its practitioners more selfless or less violent, humankind would be still more grasping and barbaric *without* its restraints. The historical record fails to bear out this dodge, however. On average, Hitchens argues, religion is not morally improving; it tends to resist, not enable, progress on matters of social justice. The most compelling example he offers—regarding the role of religion in delaying the end of slavery by providing a divine endorsement for racism—seems strikingly pertinent to queer Americans' battle for equality in the face of homophobia instilled and fed by religion:

Even a glance at the record will show, first, that person for person, American freethinkers and agnostics and atheists come out the best. The chance that someone's *secular* or freethinking opinion would cause him or her to denounce the whole injustice was extremely high. The chance that someone's religious belief would cause him or her to take a stand against slavery and racism was statistically quite small. But the chance that someone's religious belief would cause him or her to uphold slavery and racism was statistically extremely *high*, and the latter fact helps us to understand why the victory of simple justice took so long to bring about. (180)

Humanism can produce unethical behavior, too, of course, but, unlike religion, humanism welcomes rather than discourages free inquiry, and so it is capable at least of self-correction. It's also true that most people are quite capable of hatred and violence without the window dressing of religion, but, when backed by divine writ, cruel and invasive acts are difficult if not impossible to impede or argue against. Some religious people are lovely, tolerant folk. But there's no evidence that their tolerance and kindness are the product of religion and not predisposition, ethical conscience, or logical reasoning. Likewise, theirs is no evidence that *not* being religious makes one any more likely to commit atrocities, immoral acts, or seek to control the lives and minds of others for temporal ends—whereas, on balance, the historical record supports the case that being religious *does* foster these tendencies. As far back as the seventeenth century, Pierre Bayle argued "it was absurd to believe that religious faith caused people to conduct themselves better, or that unbelief made them behave worse" (Hitchens 264). The examples frequently trotted out by the religious to evince atheism's moral poverty (Stalin, Hitler, and so on) prove nothing, statistically or causally. For one thing, these reputedly atheist leaders built their empires on claims to unquestioned authority that closely mirrored religious zealotry and exacting devotion; they merely substituted national leaders and states for faith in God and church as the proper objects of that zeal and allegiance. Second, Hitler's doctrine of Aryan racial purity drew much of its inspiration from a long tradition of Christian anti-Semitism. If religion doesn't necessarily make people better, the opposite does not logically follow: "There is no requirement for any enforcing or supernatural authority. And why should there be? Human decency is not derived from religion. It precedes it" (Hitchens 266). Absence of religion cannot be demonstrated, in isolation from all other factors, to make people any worse.

For religious apologists, or for those who feel it can be rescued from its homophobic practitioners, past and present, there is one inconvenient, glaring stumbling block to which these recuperative projects have yet to produce a satisfactory alternative: arguments against homosexuality are *always* religiously inflected. Whether disparaging gays and lesbians' demands for so-called special rights or forecasting the destruction of heterosexual institutions in marriage and family by queer inclusion, all antigay arguments draw their ideological water from the same wellspring of religious homophobia. This is not to say that religion invented homophobia. Within historical memory, however, it has been the first storehouse and *entrepôt* of antigay prejudice, the original disseminator of stereotypes, and either the loudest voice calling for its punishment or the strongest hand dispensing that punishment. Admittedly, the same has been true of civil authorities in most places until fairly recently. But they were merely following suit. Hitchens and Harris produce an array of convincing arguments that removing religion from the equation is necessary for progress on a multitude of fronts. It's the contention of *Slouching towards Gaytheism* that such a step is particularly pressing for queer Americans because their equality, humanity, and status as full-fledged citizens *continues* to be a subject of political and cultural debate and because, despite gay-positive pushback from other citizens and organizations, their very survival seems at stake. Continuing to hold out hope that religion can be made amenable to dignified, unthreatened lives and legal equality for gays and lesbians is to wait on a ship that is never going to come in.

CONCLUSION

Before the Cock Crows

Despite recent, hopeful political steps in the direction of gay and lesbian equality, there is ample evidence of how protracted the wait for wider cultural acceptance could be—or for a nonhomophobic inflection of religion capable of political traction. Three positive examples will suffice for now. In late October 2010, Heather Ike took a short cell phone video of students at a football game between North High School and Willoughby South High School in Eastlake, Ohio. The thirty-second clip, which Ike posted on YouTube, showed North High students chanting the phrase "powder blue faggots" at the opposing side (Willoughby's uniforms are light blue). North High principal Jennifer Chauby, who was present, claimed she "heard the . . . chanting . . . and stopped it immediately," yet, according to Ike, "no teachers or parents . . . intervened . . . and [the] chant occurred 3 times in the first 3 minutes of the game" (qtd. in J. D., "High Schoolers" par. 1). In interviews Chauby touted the existence of an anti-bullying program and a gay-straight alliance at her school, but such programs mean little in the face of administrative apathy and institutionalized homophobia. She admitted to hearing the chant once a couple of years before this incident but not since then; school records indicate, however, that it dates back to the 1970s. She did nothing about it until Ike's video hit

177

the internet. While Superintendent Keith Miller expressed disgust at the incident and promised to take disciplinary action, Chauby took the position that there were "too many people involved to suspend them all" (Valdez par. 7). Her strategy was to tell students "she was disappointed in their behaviors" and to meet with students in an attempt to identify those chanting, an approach that seems unlikely to succeed, and pointless if suspension is not on the table. "'Every student I spoke with,'" the principal told reporters, "'didn't realize gravity of that word'" (qtd. in J. D., "High Schoolers" par. 7). The superintendent, negating his official expression of disapproval, took refuge in comparable sophistry: "The students said they didn't mean anything negative by the chant" (qtd. in J. D., "High Schoolers" par 8). Though appalling, the disingenuousness of these teens, if not their outright mendacity, should not be a surprise in the face of such adult apathy. Whether Chauby and Miller *wanted* to find an excuse for absolving the students of guilt, or whether they were both naïve enough to credit such gibberish and ignorance, they set their charges a startlingly irresponsible lesson: shirk the impact of your actions—offense resides in the way others perceive your actions, or apparently in this case, in the way they misperceive them. More problematic even than the administrators' motives for absolving the students involved, or the impact of that absolution, is the claim that no harm or offense was intended. The nonsensical claim that "I didn't *mean* for anyone to get hurt"—a duplicitous claim at best—is the real culprit here.

In online reactions to media coverage of the incident, some objected that Willoughby students referred to the North High team with an equally antigay slur ("Halloween homos") yet escaped criticism. Others point out that both chants date back at least to the 1970s. Neither excuse ameliorates the situation or exonerates the parties involved. Even if antigay bullying or harassment is not occurring at either of these schools, these teens will grow up to be adults who vote on gay rights referenda. They will become adults who pass on to their children the antigay attitudes retained from uttering, or merely hearing, the "powder blue faggot" chant at football games throughout their high school years.

Also in October 2010, three separate gay bashings occurred in New York City and, perhaps given already heightened awareness of antigay harassment, received national media attention. Early in the month, a thirty-four-year-old gay man was beaten up by two assailants (aged seventeen and twenty-one) in the bathroom of the Stonewall Inn, the iconic Greenwich Village bar where, in June 1969, the Stonewall Riots touched off the modern gay liberation movement. That same weekend, two other gay men were physically attacked while "kissing and hugging goodbye" in Chelsea. Two weeks later, in the Bronx, nine gang members took a seventeen-year-old gang pledge whom they suspected of having gay sex with a thirty-year-old man to an empty apartment where they "repeatedly used anti-gay slurs as they attacked him . . . forced [him] to strip naked . . . cut [him] with a box cutter and sodomized [him] with the wooden handle of a plunger" (CNN Wire Staff and Candiotti par. 10). After letting him go, they abducted a second teenager they believed to have had sex with the same man and beat him, interrogated him, and held him hostage in the same apartment. Then, managing to lure the thirty-year-old to the scene, they "forced him to strip," bound him to a chair, and forced the second teen to strike the man as well as inflict cigarette burns. Other gang members joined in the assault, using their fists, chains, and "sodomiz[ing] him with a small baseball bat" (par. 14). The assailants completed their gay-bashing marathon by traveling to the man's own apartment where they entered, beat his roommate (who was also his brother), and demanded money in exchange for freeing the captive: "The older brother told them where they could find money, after which they tied him and left the apartment. The 30-year-old victim was later dumped outside his home" (pars. 16–17). The quick succession of these attacks attests to the perception, if not the reality, of an open season on gays—and in one of the urban areas allegedly most amenable to queers. In fact, even as nationally gay-bashing incidents declined 4 percent between 2011 and 2012, over the same period they *increased* by 4 percent in New York City. The following year, May alone saw six antigay assaults there, one of them a fatal shooting.

For a third example of what appears at times to be homophobia's redoubled cultural strength, especially when shielded by religious belief, we return to the discussion in the media of the gay teen suicides from September and October 2010. Tony Perkins, president of right-wing lobbying group the Family Research Council, wrote an op-ed for the *Washington Post* in order to rebut what he saw as unfair accusations of culpability for antigay bullying and teen suicides against Christians "who teach that homosexual conduct is wrong" and "pro-family groups such as Family Research Council which oppose elements of the homosexual political agenda, such as same-sex 'marriage'" (Perkins par. 2). His antigay stance is no surprise to those familiar with Perkins or the FRC; what's striking is the flat denial that religion disseminates hatred toward gays and lesbians and that conservative religious rhetoric has any causal or contextual relation to their depression or suicide or to the verbal and physical attacks of those who bully them. In Perkins's assessment, the cause lies elsewhere: with individual bullies whose actions lack any context or cultural example; with gays and lesbians themselves; with gay and lesbian activism—anywhere but with religious homophobes. Perkins's words have to be read to be believed, for their gelid bravado and obliviousness to contradiction and hypocrisy:

> The Christians and pro-family leaders I know are unanimous in believing that no person, especially a child, should be subjected to verbal or physical harassment or violence—whether because of their sexuality, their religious beliefs, or for any other reason. Such bullying violates the Christian's obligation to love our neighbor as we love ourselves, and receives no support from the pro-family political movement.
>
> Where bullying has occurred, the blame should be placed on the bullies themselves—not on organizations within society who clearly oppose bullying. I suspect that few, if any, such bullies are people who regularly attend church, and I would not be surprised if most of the "bullies" did not have the positive benefit of both an active mom and dad in their lives. Religious faith and a return to traditional family values are more likely to be a solution to the problem of bullying than a cause.
>
> However, homosexual activist groups like GLSEN (the Gay, Lesbian and Straight Education Network) are exploiting these tragedies to push their agenda of demanding not only tolerance of homosexual individuals, but active affirmation of homosexual conduct and their efforts to redefine the family.
>
> There is an abundance of evidence that homosexuals experience higher rates of mental health problems in general, including depression. However, there is no empirical evidence to link this with society's general disapproval of homosexual conduct. In fact, evidence from the Netherlands would seem to suggest the opposite, because even in that most "gay-friendly"

country on earth, research has shown homosexuals to have much higher mental health problems.

. . . Some homosexuals may recognize intuitively that their same-sex attractions are abnormal—yet they have been told by the homosexual movement, and their allies in the media and the educational establishment, that they are "born gay" and can never change. This—and not society's disapproval—may create a sense of despair that can lead to suicide.

. . . Since homosexual conduct is associated with higher rates of sexual promiscuity, sexually transmitted diseases, mental illness, substance abuse, and domestic violence, it too qualifies as a behavior that is harmful to the people who engage in it and to society at large. It is not loving to encourage someone to indulge in such activities, no matter how much sensual pleasure they may derive from them. It is more loving to help them overcome them. This is why, in the public policy arena, we will continue to oppose any policy or action that would celebrate or affirm homosexual conduct. (pars. 2–5, 7, 9)

Like NOM spokesperson Maggie Gallagher, Perkins turns the blame for gay suicide back on gays themselves.[1] If these teens hadn't been gay in the first place—or, by the religious right's pernicious false logic, if they hadn't persisted in being gay—they wouldn't have killed themselves. Far from queers' being hounded, through the media and in their schools and churches, with messages of their own abnormality and unworthiness, Perkins, in classic projective fashion, attributes the notion that homosexuality is abnormal to the teens themselves. Even while Perkins condemns antigay bullying, he undercuts the idea that bullies who harass queers are doing anything wrong. Putting scare quotes around "bullies" suggests the term is merely a liberal media–imposed label, not a factual descriptor. No wonder Perkins seeks to subliminally redeem harassment in this way, since that's exactly what *he* is doing. The depraved genius of Perkins's projection of blame onto gay teens is that it rhetorically clears both him and the teens' harassers of any responsibility. If, as he contends, gay teens commit suicide because they "recognize intuitively that their same-sex attractions are abnormal" despite being brainwashed by widespread secular opposition to "changing" one's sexuality, then Perkins is simply expressing Christian compassion. And those who vilify queers, he implies, are simply saying out loud what queers are already thinking.

The so-called evidence at the heart of Perkins's argument has undergone similar contortions. In order to claim that gay teens are more prone to mental health problems, and thus that homosexuality, not homophobia and harassment, leads to depression and suicide, Perkins cites a 2001 study from the Netherlands on mental health problems in GLBT populations. To claim the study as supporting his case, however, he has to make one flagrant omission. Perkins neglects to mention that the authors of the study observe that "discrimination may help fuel these higher rates" (Walker par. 7). A direct quote from the study bears this out. Finding "a higher prevalence of various psychiatric disorders in homosexual people compared with heterosexual people," Sandfort and his coauthors cite as possible causes "both . . . biological and social factors and an interaction between them" (Sandfort et al. pars. 25, 32). While they suggest that "[b]iological and genetic factors in the causes and development of homosexuality might also predispose homosexual people to developing psychiatric disorders," their example is bipolar disorder, "which is generally considered to be largely congenital." More generally, however, they conclude that

> [t]he effects of social factors on the mental health status of homosexual men and women have been well documented in studies, which found a relationship between experiences of stigma, prejudice, and discrimination and mental health status. Furthermore, controlling for psychological predictors of present distress seems to eliminate differences in mental health status between heterosexual and homosexual adolescents. (par. 32)

Perkins's conclusion that "there is no empirical evidence" linking depression among gays and lesbians to "society's general disapproval of homosexual conduct" is, in fact, contradicted by the very study his conclusion is based on. Sirdeaner Walker, the mother of a gay teen suicide, wrote a response to Perkins that the *Washington Post* printed the following day, under the title "Addressing Anti-GLBT Bullying: Something All Christians Can Support." Walker objected to Perkins's selective quoting from the study as a "serious omission—in fact . . . a gross distortion of the truth" (par. 8). It's noteworthy that, despite the religion-friendly title of Walker's response (an editorial decision, most likely), she does *not* offer Christianity as an antidote to antigay bullying. A board member of GLSEN, Walker recommends care, protection, and educational and political advocacy. Hitchens's observation about the humanist character of the religious moderate position is clearly borne out here. Contrary to any headline, Walker's strategy is ethical, not religious, and seeing it as such can clear our vision from the distorting animus of religious discourse. Not all Christians are homophobic; many may express tolerance and, unlike Perkins, sincere rather than sham compassion for gays and lesbians. The problem is that as long as religion is not removed from the discussion altogether, as long as homophobia can cling to religion as an intelligible defense, antigay harassment and discrimination will retain their most vital engine. Presbyterian pastor Dr. Fritz Ritsch, of Fort Worth, Texas, has the best of intentions when he calls on "[m]oderate Christians—the silent majority— . . . to stop being silent and speak out" against the extremists who use religion "as a justification to demean and belittle GLBT people" (Jones, "Texas Pastor" pars. 4, 3). But it's not clear how moderates, even if they speak out, can overwhelm the extremists who "dominate the airwaves, sidelining more moderate Christian voices" (par. 4). The obstacle here is not this or that interpretation of the Bible (that argument can go on interminably without either side ceding ground) but rather the intrusion of religious faith, of unadjudicable beliefs resistant to rational scrutiny, into the forum of civil debate. Although Perkins is admittedly an extremist, his pledge "in the public policy arena [to] continue to oppose any policy or action that would celebrate or affirm homosexual conduct" is an apt description of religion's deep-seated antipathy, despite the mollifications of religious moderates, to queer rights and survival.

As galling as Perkins's own malice and lies is the fact that, instead of fact-checking Perkins regarding the scientific evidence he cites, the *Post* stood back and counted on someone else, Walker, to do their work for them. What if she had not exposed his misrepresentation? Would they have stepped in editorially? Merely presenting two pieces, by Perkins and by Walker, suggests that there is a debate to be had, that there are *two sides* to the question of whether antigay harassment is a factor in gay depression and suicide. While a number of commentators quickly spoke out against Perkins,[2] the presentation of his tirade as simply another voice in the debate (much less as a coherent argument) is typical of the post-Bush media trend in which investigation and objectivity have been supplanted by undigested talking points from each side. In this instance, such a hands-off approach is more than bad journalism. It is callous quietism. It is the *condoning* of harassment, discrimination, and queer misery and death. If this seems like a harsh accusation, consider also that the *Post* chose to run Perkins's op-ed on October 11, National Coming Out Day, a day dedicated to demonstrating support for GLBT persons. It's difficult to interpret that decision as anything other than callous and hostile—at the very least, it's blithely oblivious. I'm not saying that Perkins hasn't a right to his opinion, but when a mainstream, theoretically objective news organization gives carte blanche to a homophobic demagogue interested in nothing but fomenting hate among straight readers and self-hatred among queer ones, one has to wonder about the Fourth Estate's motives.

Motives aside, the *Post*'s decision to run Perkins's editorial and then publish a series of rebuttals, which they surely must have anticipated, bears out a disheartening general trend in current news reporting: "he said, she said," with little to no fact-checking and editorial perspective. In regard to gay rights in particular, the media continue to frame this "emotional topic" as one with two legitimate sides. This is precisely my point, proof of religion's intellectual and ethical stranglehold on civic discourse in general and queer lives in particular. The religious right would be laughed off the podium of public debate in any rational country where religion and murderous tolerance for so-called difference of religious values did not have a stranglehold on the nation (Associated Press, "Schools Confront Anti-Gay Bullying" par. 3). Debating whether public school curricula addressing antigay harassment are too "adult-oriented" or political would be unthinkable if those professing religious "disagreement" with homosexuality had a shred of decency, if they did not hold dear the genocidal fantasy of a world free of queers (par. 33). Their shielding of so-called innocent children from gay issues has no objectively ethical basis. Despite their clear ideological dependence on the perverted queer other, they would like nothing better than for us to disappear, along with our filthy unnatural petition for civil rights and our humane appreciation of sexuality and nonnormativity. Religion is the only real crutch propping up their nonsensical opposition, since their so-called expert studies are either laughable or misrepresented. And they are using religion to condone violence, to shield the violent and the bigoted, and to encourage or force educators to turn a blind eye to the queer bodies piling up at our feet. If religious belief, which we supposedly must tolerate in any guise and not subject to the indignity of rational inquiry, were not used as a smokescreen, we would not be having this discussion even as queer teens and adults are being hectored and marginalized. If the bald reasoning of homophobes were put forward without religious/moral window dressing—we hate queers because they're abnormal, subhuman, and so on—the debate about addressing gay bullying would be over. The homophobic side's argument would fold immediately as it should, exposed as murderous, irrational, criminal hate that has no justification. Debating whether we have a right to intervene would seem as ridiculous as it is. If we stand accused of promoting homosexuality, that's precisely right. We *are* promoting it, promoting its protection against violence, assault, and normative slur. We are promoting reason and justice. We are making the case that queers are humans who deserve equality and common respect. Groups that are harassed, discriminated against, and legally excluded *need* their interests promoted by those with the legal rights and the cultural cachet to do so. By contrast, promoting religious values when those values "disagree" with homosexuality means promoting violence, harassment, and (self)-extermination. That diverges from what religious homophobes claim they represent. But that is the brutal, factual reality.

Hard on the heels of Perkins's op-ed, a new poll by the Public Religion Research Institute and Religion News Service appeared to suggest that most Americans failed to agree with his absolution of institutional religion from the charge of inciting homophobia. Nicole Neroulias reported that, according to the poll, "Nearly three-quarters (72 percent) of Americans say religious messages about homosexuality contribute to 'negative views' of gays and lesbians, and nearly two-thirds (65 percent) see a connection to higher rates of suicide among gay youths" (par. 5). But even though a majority think religion contributes to negative views of homosexuality, most do not think *their* churches are the ones inciting intolerance: "A plurality (45 percent) . . . give their own house of worship an 'A' or 'B' grade on how it handles homosexuality" (par. 3). Ironically, the percentage of those who blame religions other than their own for homophobic rhetoric is higher still for Catholics and evangelical Christians (nearly one-third and three-quarters, respectively). It's perhaps not coincidental, institutionally speaking, that these two groups tend to be among the most vocal in their disapproval of gays and lesbians (out of projective self-reassurance, among other reasons).[3] An optimistic take on the survey results would be that the solution lies in a renewed commitment to tolerance education, directed toward those with negative, religiously fueled views of homosexuality. Wrong: such individuals seem comfortable with their hatred. Some may come around now and then, when one of their own daughters or sons is gay-bashed or dishonorably discharged from the military or denied death benefits from a longtime partner. Even these events might not dissuade them from homophobia: violence, disgrace, and loss might only confirm their notion that homosexuality is a bad "choice." I have drawn on critiques of religion by Hitchens and Harris and analyzed the deep antiqueer animus at the heart of not just certain religions or sects but the religious enterprise per se, in order to argue that, even though some individuals who now hate gays and lesbians might be "brought over" to a more humane viewpoint, religion will not be part of such changes of heart. If we're objective about it, religion is not even germane to such transformations. Religion at its core is antithetical to enlightenment. A religious person knows what he believes and, if he's faithful to his creed, refuses to change. The poll results just cited attest to religion's power to cast blame elsewhere: over half the number of people who think religious institutions spread homophobic messages think the problem lies in an institution other than their own. As long as this paradox endures—it's someone else's church—the problem will continue to be someone else's problem, will remain unchanged. Anyone who moves from antigay hatred or apathy to acceptance and love does so as a humanist, as a person drawing on ethics and reason—principles for which religion is not necessary. Religion only makes things worse. And it makes things worse for queers in particular. Responding to a sermon by Mormon leader Boyd Packer "endors[ing] discrimination against gay people" amid the teen suicides of 2010, Truth Out founder Wayne Besen points out that the "unholy marriage of the bully and the bully pulpit is all anti-gay activists have left in their arsenal to defeat the GLBT movement. No matter how many youth commit suicide or adults are gay-bashed, don't expect our foes to give up their trump card of violence anytime soon" (par. 9).

Even if one takes issue with the assessment that religion is the *only* remaining weapon in the arsenal of antigay activists, it is indisputably the most powerful, the most pig-headed, the most destructive to civil discourse, queer dignity, and queer life itself.

It was against the background of these dispiriting incidents that President Obama released his own "It Gets Better" video, to mixed but largely positive reactions. More important than what Obama said was what he didn't say—the unspoken gap between his message to queer teens and the message sent by his administration's action or inaction in regard to queer adults up to that point. In the video Obama urges bullied kids to speak to parents and teachers but neglects the difficult reality that for some gay teens, teachers and parents may be an unsupportive, even hostile audience. Many responses from both queers and straights were enthusiastic, yet a more deliberate consideration of the video within the context of Obama's record on GLBT issues through 2010 clarifies why other queers greeted this video more ambivalently. Gabriel Arana and Ann Friedman, both writing for the *American Prospect*, distilled the ambivalence—and ultimately, the dissatisfaction—that Obama's video generated in some viewers. Arana concedes that

> the wave of . . . celebrities and straight liberals making "It Gets Better" videos just keeps growing. But there's a problem: As the discussion about gay-teen suicide has radiated outward, it's stopped being about gay teens. . . . Ezra Klein's video discusses how he was called a nerd in high school. Even Obama's video steers clear of too much talk about gay people, safely focusing on the hurt that comes with "being different or . . . not fitting in with everybody else." The public conversation and the policy response have shifted from stopping anti-gay harassment to preventing bullying in general.
>
> When kids bandy about the term "gay" as a slur—or its more derogatory counterparts, "fag" and "queer"—it bears the force of society's homophobia. It's not just the schoolyard jerk who picks on you. It's the pastor who rails against the "gay agenda" on Sunday . . . and politicians like New York's Carl Paladino, who on the campaign trail said things like "there is nothing to be proud of in being a dysfunctional homosexual." Even once you get past high school, you still can't get married

or serve in the military, and in most states, your employer can fire you just for being gay. This is the kind of "bullying" gay kids face, and it's the kind no one's standing up to. (pars. 3, 6)

As Arana implies, the omissions in Obama's statement matter as much as, if not more than, what he *does* say. Silence on the frequency of antigay verbal harassment, discrimination, and physical violence risks sending the message that American gay and lesbian adults don't matter so much and undercuts the stated investment in gay and lesbian teens. If a speech to queer youth doesn't seem the place to address the complex legal rights issues on the minds of their adult counterparts, why not a national address about what equality means for GLBT adults and the suggestion of a path for getting there? Admittedly, bullying is a problem that addresses one of heteronormativity's chief fetishes, children, without the alienating specter of queer (adult) sex.

What was most problematic about the video, however, was not its content but its timing, emerging as it did amid news of the Obama administration's bid to keep DADT alive. As the *American Prospect*'s deputy editor Ann Friedman put it,

Obama's "It Gets Better" video . . . is primarily an anti-bullying public service announcement—about as politically risky as decrying people who kick puppies or steal old ladies' handbags. In a message directed toward kids who feel constantly threatened, Obama chooses the safe path. He tells gay teens to stay strong and that "there is a whole world waiting for you, filled with possibilities"—which is true, unless they aspire to marriage, parenthood, or a career in military service. Indeed, within days of posting the president's "It Gets Better" video, the Obama administration announced it would be reinstating "don't ask, don't tell" after a recent court ruling that ordered the military to stop enforcing the policy. Obama may want things to get better for LGBT teens, but he is not working to ensure that they do. (par. 6)

It's hardly shocking or surprising for a politician to make a noncommittal statement on a public issue. As topics, teen suicide and bullying are far from controversial, but the sticking point is that this involves the suicides and bullying of *gay* teens, teens harassed and attacked *because* they were gay and for no other reason. Like many politicians before him, of both parties, Obama—at least until his May 2012 endorsement of gay marriage—was being carefully noncommittal when it came to an issue that might negatively impact approval ratings or votes. For the first two years of his first term, he held back from following through on pledges to gays and lesbians for fear of upsetting voters, such as religious conservatives and Republicans, whom he did not court and who most likely did not vote for him anyway.

The most troubling aspect of Obama's video was the clash between its tolerant, supportive message and his own policy actions on gay issues such as DADT, ENDA, and, up to that time, DOMA—either by blocking judicial and legislative attempts to repeal antigay laws or by failing to advocate or initiate progay, antidiscriminatory change. The video elides that cognitive dissonance by omitting any hint of nonsupport or opposition from a PSA for tolerance. The omission was to be expected, perhaps, lest one get an impression of the president as hypocritical, insincere, or even covertly bullying. Obama's decision, soon after the video was posted, to appeal the Phillips DADT repeal order—that is, his bid to keep DADT *alive*—betrayed the message of his video and rendered it, for the time being, an empty promise. It's as if he were saying, "it gets better, but I'm doing nothing to help that come about; in fact, I'm doing what I can to make sure 'it'"— legally sanctioned antigay discrimination and the homophobia and bullying such legalized discrimination legitimates—"stays exactly the same." Friedman makes this point more broadly, emphasizing the poor example set by Obama's video for his audience: "While I'm sure it helps gay teens to know there are straight Americans who care about them, those of us who don't experience discrimination based on whom we love are in no position to assure kids that their lives will get better without pledging to make equality a reality" (par. 7). Friedman is right: Obama's video leaves untouched the climacteric political issues facing queer Americans, the discriminatory laws that legitimate the view of bullies—a view likely to be absorbed by or at least conveyed to many GLBT youth—that queers are second-class Americans. The video dissembles the antiprogressive decisions made, from 2010 to 2012, to preserve or at least not to oppose the laws prescribing second-class status for gay Americans, laws that constitute a form of legal bullying and that endorse daily bullying in service to religious rhetoric and cultural norms.

Equally as important as what Obama *isn't* saying in the video is the audience he *fails* to acknowledge or address: the heterosexual adults whose hatred of, discomfort with, or merely misinformation about queers is underwritten—directly and consciously or not—by religious beliefs or so-called moral notions. The most significant problem with Obama's video may be its failure to address religious intolerance, that is, the religious beliefs that culturally and legally underwrite so much homophobia. Without confronting the entanglement of religion and public policy in America, Obama's video fails to move beyond his aversion, up to 2012, to taking a strong pro-marriage-equality position because "God is in the mix." "God is in the mix" became the catchphrase to denote the change in Barack Obama's statements on gay marriage before and after beginning his presidential campaign. Actually, his position began to shift even before the primaries: during his 1996 run for the Illinois state senate, Obama said he "favor[ed] legalizing same-sex marriages" (qtd. in Brayton par. 2). Two years later, he claimed to be "undecided" on whether Illinois should "recognize same-sex marriages" (qtd. in Brayton par. 4). In his 2004 senate campaign, Obama "called DOMA 'abhorrent' and its repeal 'essential'" (Greenwald par. 2).[4] That same year, however, he told the *Windy City Times* he supported civil unions but backed away from supporting gay marriage because "marriage, in the minds of a lot of voters, has a religious connotation" (qtd. in Brayton par. 6). And there it is, clear as day: civil progress held hostage by the synergistic pressure of the imbricated cultural norms of religion and heteronormativity. The same ambivalence—backing off of gay marriage in deference to religious bias while shifting support to civil unions—was repeated in Obama's 2006 book *Audacity of Hope*. By 2008, in an interview with MTV, his opposition to same-sex marriage appeared to have solidified, if in somewhat contradictory terms. On the one hand he said, "I have stated my opposition to [Prop 8]," yet his very next words were "I believe that marriage is between a man and a woman and I am not in favor of gay marriage" (qtd. in Brayton par. 15). It's possible to see this as a practical, strategic move: more voters will support rights for gay and lesbian couples if those rights are granted by civil union, an institution lacking marriage's religious connotation. To regard marriage as a primarily religious institution, of course, ignores the fact that marriage is state-regulated, and that to be legally valid it requires a civil license but not necessarily a religious ceremony. Moreover, it confers not merely religious and cultural sanction but numerous federal and state economic benefits.[5] The same move shies away from the responsibility to question the undue pressure exerted by religion, and risks strengthening that pressure, on issues of civil rights in a country founded on the separation of church and state.[6] As a defense for not acting on gay marriage, Obama's use of "God is in the mix" partakes, even if unintentionally, of the religious argument by which some homophobic ministers and politicians denigrate queers and contest their arguments for civil parity. To say "God is in the mix" is to legitimate the verbal and physical bullying of gay teens, to subordinate civil rights to the tyranny of illogical, legally unjustifiable prejudice. However, Obama did significantly move the national dialogue on gay rights forward when he reversed course, almost two years later, by unequivocally supporting marriage equality in May 2012. He at last honored the pain and despair of gay teen suicides and of queer Americans who daily confront hatred, opposition, and apathy.

Unlike the number of countries that have legalized gay marriage, gay civil unions, and military service by openly gay servicemembers, America seems unable or unwilling to separate the personal matter of religion from the ethical issue of equal treatment of its citizens. Equality and nondiscrimination are ethical issues, and hiding behind religious homophobia by calling it disagreement over personal beliefs is cowardly. Religion should not be a party to the discussion. Invoking religion to excuse legal discrimination suggests that religious opinions are enough to deny gays the civil rights and protections enjoyed by other citizens and that harassment and brutalization are merely something queers have to put up with as an unpleasant but unavoidable side effect of living in a secular democracy. Religion's imperviousness to reason and ethical interrogation is the source of the problem. At minimum, it is an accelerant. As long as the so-called right to religious beliefs about homosexuality—and thus the license to preach antigay hate—remains unquestioned and as long as American politicians, media, and citizens remain unwilling to move forward on issues of ethical justice unless supported by religious figures, then the hatred, the inequity, the bullying, and the suicides will continue. The depression, the self-hatred, the self-doubt; the lives lived closeted and ashamed and fearful; the spouses deprived of death benefits, health care, parental custody—all of this will continue unabated, condoned and provoked by our disregard, until we insist that religious discourse has no warrant to dictate or even intrude in matters of civil rights.

There *has* been hopeful movement forward on gay rights, none-theless. As already acknowledged, the Obama administration's 2011 instruction to the Justice Department to no longer defend DOMA was an important development. Between 2010 and 2012 federal judges on several occasions have ruled DOMA unconstitutional, and in June 2013 SCOTUS overturned one of DOMA's key clauses.[7] Adding to the weight of these judicial challenges, at least rhetorically, were the White House's first public statements in favor of gay marriage. In early May 2012 Vice President Joe Biden appeared on NBC's *Meet the Press*: "I am absolutely comfortable," he said, "with the fact that men marry-ing men, women marrying women, and heterosexual men and women marrying one another are entitled to the same exact rights, all the civil rights, all the civil liberties" (qtd. in Barbaro par. 4). Despite the concession that "the president, not [the vice president], sets policy on such matters," Biden had effectively upped the ante, seeming to many pundits to force the hand of a president whose position on gay mar-riage had been "evolving" (par. 4). Three days later Obama followed suit during an interview on ABC: "I have hesitated on gay marriage in part because I thought that civil unions would be sufficient. I was sensitive to the fact that for a lot of people the word 'marriage' was something that invokes very powerful traditions, religious beliefs and so forth. . . . [But now] it is important for me personally to go ahead and affirm that same-sex couples should be able to get married" (qtd. in Pace pars. 2–3). Even if the tone of Obama's statement is more moder-ate or circumspect than Biden's, a sitting president's public support for marriage equality is an indisputably historic event—a pronounced leap forward from the president's previous positions, such as advocating civil unions (but not marriage) or leaving the decision up to individual states (thus ignoring the existence of DOMA). Rumored pressure from wealthy gay and lesbian donors, as well as Biden's contradiction of the official White House line at that time, nudged the president to stop trailing majority public opinion and to join it. While it was no doubt politically necessary for Obama to trace the shift from his earlier posi-tions (refusing to endorse gay marriage yet pledging to support equality for gay Americans), the progressive moment was slightly marred by his continued invocation of religion—even as he marked an official step toward rational, civil discourse. Invoking religious objections, even when asserting a position in conflict with those objections, may be intended solely as a conciliatory move. On some level, however, it's also a concession—not to arguments against same-sex marriage but to their religious inflection. In other words, it's a concession to the *dignity* of religious arguments on public policy. Such a concession seems unnecessary and insensitive when the more conservative of those arguments trade in hatemongering and civil discrimination. It risks conceding the idea that religious beliefs have a rightful role in determining laws and rights in a diverse, secular democracy. At the very least, Obama's statement foregrounds the undue pressure religious belief has exerted on the civil rights of queer Americans and on elected officials who are expected to defer to certain opinions because of their religious pedigree. Invoking religious objections to gay marriage, or even characterizing such objections as worthy of sensitivity, even while distancing oneself from them, demonstrates that religion has not been revoked as a valid participant in debates on the rights of democratic citizens.

Lately more voices are making themselves heard, beyond Washington, in opposition to the homophobic preachments of conservative Christians and politicians. Significant work remains to be done, however, in prying apart civil rights discourse from religiously invested rhetoric. With the Obama administration's 2012 decision to take a firm stance in favor of same-sex marriage, Americans were faced with a clearer partisan difference than ever. Up to that point, there had sometimes been only subtle differences between the two parties' stances on this issue. Though George W. Bush's 2004 proposed Constitutional Federal Marriage Amendment failed to make it out of congressional committee, it succeeded as the wedge ploy it was intended to be, fomenting antigay sentiment in the base and fueling the passage of gay marriage and civil union bans in a number of states that had not already passed them. For the past two decades, both parties tended to espouse the safe position of leaving the matter up to individual states— a doubly disingenuous stance given that many states had made their own gay marriage measures or amendments, and given that Congress overstepped that ostensible state prerogative when in 1996 it *federally* codified nonrecognition of same-sex marriages through DOMA. By contrast, the Democratic National Committee included marriage equality as a plank in its 2012 national convention. Republican nominee Mitt Romney, despite his record as governor in Massachusetts, continued the GOP's policy of courting antigay and conservative religious constituents by reaffirming the party's opposition to marriage equality and even pledged to resuscitate the failed Federal Marriage Amendment if elected. Thus, while 2012 saw yet more vociferous antigay declarations (as with Chick-fil-A), it also manifested increasingly vocal counters from individuals, activists, and corporations (such as Starbucks and JCPenney). Perhaps the controversy over gay and lesbian Americans' rights is finally building toward a decisive moment. As some have opined, the nation might well be moving gradually and inevitably toward full marriage equality. Public opinion has shifted increasingly toward support; even some conservative Republicans have said opposing gay marriage is no longer the high priority it has been in the past. The remaining, vocal resistance by some conservatives may constitute the death throes of the anti–gay marriage movement. Still, it would be hasty to conclude that we have heard the last gasp of a venomous religious right, especially if they sense the battle is no longer going their way, and of a political right still courting antigay voters. It would also be foolish to assume that the cultural power of heteronorms will vanish with same-sex marriage's legalization; the law may be the visible and sometimes the most concrete embodiment of those norms, but they are hardly its sole site of enshrinement or its lone mechanism of dissemination and enforcement.

To take one example, in early January 2013 Cardinal Francis George, head of Chicago's archdiocese, issued the following statement in response to the proposed gay marriage bill then coming to the floor of the Illinois state legislature. As is typical but not universally characteristic of religious defenses of so-called traditional marriage, George's admonition depends on secular as well as sacred heteronorms and illustrates the manifold conduits by which religious, political, and cultural homophobia nourish one another's toxicity:

> Marriage comes to us from nature. . . . It provides the biological basis for personal identity.
>
> It is physically impossible for two men or two women to consummate a marriage. . . . [T]his means that marriage is what nature tells us it is and that the State cannot change natural marriage. Civil laws that establish "same-sex marriage" create a legal fiction. The state has no power to create something that nature tells us is impossible.
>
> Neither did the Church create marriage. . . . [L]ike the State, the Church cannot change the natural basis of marriage. Does this mean that the Church is anti-gay? No, for the Church welcomes everyone, respects each one personally and gives to each the spiritual means necessary to convert to God's ways and maintain friendship with Christ.

. . . Should the [Illinois legislature] take up the passage
of [this law], it will be acting against the common good of
society. We will all have to pretend to accept something that
is contrary to the common sense of the human race.

. . . [L]aws teach; they tell us what is socially acceptable
and what is not. . . .

If we ignore in law the natural complementary of man and
woman in creation, then the natural family is undermined. Our
individual lives become artificial constructs protected by civil
"rights" that destroy natural rights. Human dignity and human
rights are then reduced to the whims of political majorities.
When the ways of nature and nature's God conflict with civil
law, society is in danger. (Archdiocese of Chicago pars. 2–4,
7–9)

Of the multiple lapses in logic, taste, and integrity on display in
George's encyclical, pointing out the most glaring should suffice.
Disingenuously, he brackets "rights" in sarcastic scare quotes. More
offensive, perhaps, is the proposition that spiritual acceptance and even
salvation itself ("maintain[ing] friendship with Christ") is conditional
on gays' "conver[sion] to God's ways"—that is, to heterosexuality, or,
as George offers elsewhere in the letter, celibacy (par. 6). More oppressive still is George's facile, benighted, though apparently sincere dic-
tum that norms and the laws and valuations emanating from them are
natural—not humanly constructed but divinely ordained—and that the
law only reinforces but should not, or, even more ridiculously, cannot,
control, alter, or manufacture the "natural." As Chicago law professor
Geoffrey R. Stone wrote in the *Huffington Post*,

The plain and simple fact is that what is "natural" is deeply
vulnerable to distortion by one's own personal preferences. . . .
Cardinal George insists that same-sex marriage is incompatible with "nature." One might just as easily say the same thing
about celibacy. There is such a thing as right and wrong, but
invocations of what "nature" commands is no way to get there.
(qtd. in Gibson pars. 13–14)

Most distasteful is George's hypocrisy in claiming that religion does
not or should not influence civil policy, when it has a long history
of doing or attempting to do exactly that. Perhaps it's a case of sour
grapes on George's part: if institutional religion has the cachet to shape

political policies or cultural attitudes consistent with its own reaction-ary dogma, and as long as the moral majority polls in a conservative direction, that's all well and good. But when the moral majority seems in danger of shedding its historically homophobic trappings for a saner, more tolerant mindset, suddenly "political majorities" should no longer guide matters of policy. The vitriolic antigay libel that has long powered the machine of public opinion and civic policy, whose malign ichor still lingers, somehow doesn't qualify as a "whim"—even though, as the word "whim" implies, it serves the tendentious interests of one group to the symbolic and concrete harm of another. Of course, a statement like Cardinal George's might have little influence on marriage equality in Illinois. As David Gibson observed, "similar attempts by influential cardinals . . . in Massachusetts, New York, and Washington, D.C., have all failed" (Gibson par. 15). And certainly "not all religious leaders . . . agree with George": more than "250 Illinois clergy, mostly Protestant and Jewish . . . sent an open letter [of support] to legislators . . . and Illinois Gov. Pat Quinn and U.S. Sen. Dick Durbin, both Catholics, have endorsed the bill" (pars. 10–11). The degree of influence exerted by George remains yet unclear: after passing the Illinois senate in Feb-ruary 2013, the gay marriage bill stalled in May when the bill's sponsor predicted the necessary number of votes would not be forthcoming in the state house. The problem is not that religion necessarily or inher-ently champions antigay intolerance (though I would argue it does) but that it has a prolonged history of doing so. Even if the problem is not that homophobic religious voices are the only ones speaking or, increasingly, are the most convincing or the most conclusive, their financial backing, frenzied rhetoric, and veteran service in the annals of gay-baiting lend their ideas a force that, even if it fails to govern or dominate, nonetheless reinforces heteronormative notions about sexu-ality as the imaginative horizon for individual and communal identity. And, as queers well know, such norms don't have to be legally binding to shape, to render hostile and often lethal, one's subjective experience and treatment at the hands of others.

    In the face of this representative and—as previous examples have evidenced—far from singular instance, my own concern is that, as long as religion remains an accepted player in public policy debates, the Right's virulent rhetoric, the creation and preservation of antigay laws, and the physical and civil harm to gay persons are not going to abate any time soon. The number of states that still have antigay laws and constitutional amendments is an intimidating obstacle and in more than a merely procedural sense. It's rhetorically sound to point out the hypocrisy of biblically couched antigay arguments, of course: why is *this* abomination singled out from the laundry list of ritually unclean acts catalogued in Deuteronomy? At the same time, debating religiously funded prejudice on its own ground is on some level a zero-sum game: one is unlikely to convince the very people one needs to convince; despite its so-called moral inflection, the antigay position in America tends to be not just religiously driven but also politically and culturally motivated. What's required is to disentangle religious discourse from civil rights discourse, from the civil sphere itself. And that's a tall order, to say the least. But by jettisoning religious and spiritual models of identification and opting instead for ethical arguments, one can at least *begin* to lessen the muddied and religiously muddled character of gay rights and civil rights discourse. One can begin to show that still more rational, still stronger arguments for queer equity and justice can be made from a place where religious discourse's burdensome history and overpowering weight no longer warp the discussion, where we no longer risk conceding ground to conservative Christian bullies by engaging with religious arguments, by no longer attempting to wrest away control of what, certainly on questions of queer civil rights, is an irremediably poisoned discourse.

It seems necessary, in closing, to ask what a gay embrace of atheism might mean for the queer individual. Given that the rejection of religion, including deinstitutionalized forms of spirituality, is unlikely to happen on a national level, it's worth considering gaytheism's personal and political implications. For one thing, such a move avoids the pitfall of unwinnable arguments with ideologically intractable antigay religious views, views that remain poisonous and unanswerable no matter how long one wrangles over biblical translation or shows up the dubiousness of highlighting prohibitions against homosexuality to the exclusion of countless *other* Old Testament prohibitions. The move to gaytheism also promotes a more civil standard of debate regarding the worth and dignity of citizens than current political and social rhetoric, which tends either to be directly infused with religious homophobia or invested in paradigms, such as spirituality, monogamy, and child-rearing, that reinforce heteronormative values and preserve invidious moral distinctions hostile to nonnormative individuals and communities. It's in this way that, despite localized progay sentiment (which remains, as Mary Poovey wrote of Victorian gender ideology, an "uneven development"), homophobic attitudes can continue to pervade general social attitudes regardless of localized tolerance. Organized religion may not be solely responsible for the development and dissemination of homophobia, but religion and religiously infused political rhetoric *are* its most vocal and most damaging purveyors in American culture, its chief source and legitimating body. While removing religious arguments, whether antigay *or* gay-positive, from public debates about gay rights does not guarantee the erasure of homophobia, it would at the very least not exacerbate homophobic rhetoric and violence any further, any more than it has already done. I'm not saying that we can get rid of religion altogether, for many straights and gays will cling to it. Regardless of efforts by some queers and heterosexuals to render religion queer-friendly, religion and heteronormativity are deeply imbricated in one another, and heteronorms are not going away anytime soon. But we can try to avoid some of the worst, most direct side effects of unconsciously iterated norms by leaving religion behind. No longer accepting institutionalized or deinstitutionalized religion as valid bases for claims of political rights is likely to produce several outcomes. Because such a move would reduce—or, at the very least, make less acceptable—the dissemination of toxic homophobia, it would make, for queers as well as for heterosexuals distressed by antigay rhetoric and violence, a more civil society. It would promote personal happiness for gays and lesbians, since they would no longer spend so much energy seeking the approval of systems of belief—religion as well as heteronormativity—historically opposed to the equality and human status of queers. Such approval can only be gained from religion in modified or deinstitutionalized forms, a concession that has done little to undermine right-wing Christianity's domination of cultural and political rhetoric surrounding sexuality. Finally, such a move could only be *more* conducive to the advance of GLBT rights, and not simply because religious values have been so inhibitive by comparison. When the discussion of an individual's social value or civil rights is stalemated in disputes over religion—disputes whose relativism and appeal to authorities beyond this world make them unwinnable in either direction—queer lives are devalued. When mediated by rational and neutrally ethical considerations, the overall status of GLBT persons can only benefit. When gays sufficiently value the critical insights of their own mainstream and radical communities—including a healthy mistrust of heteronormative perspectives on the value of marriage, family, reproduction, and other systems, such as religion, generative of reactionary behavioral and ideological conformity—queer dignity and sense of worth prospers.

Having begun to clear the ground of inhibitive and injurious norms inherent to religious and spiritual endeavors, it seems possible to gesture in the direction of at least two concrete avenues for accessing the benefits of gaytheism. Lest I appear to have in mind a merely political, identity-based solution, the dimensions of the alternative space of gaytheism extend in other, distinct yet not necessarily exclusive directions. Queer community might be forged in inverted or analogical forms of the models of relation discussed in chapter 2. Ex-gay ministries, although officially inimical to homosexuality, necessarily start off by housing homosexuals. Although their intent is to disable and silence the expression of gay sexual practice and desire, such organizations still billet queerness and, therefore, may provide an environment capable of nourishing gay subjectivity and experience in concealed, denatured incarnations, in sequestered forms potentially capable—as the experience of numerous ex-ex-gays has shown—of cultivating, preserving, and (re)generating queer gestures, acts, and defections, of sustaining queer life despite the best obliterative efforts of ex-gay counselors and their clients. Similarly, the barebacking subculture discussed in Tim Dean's *Unlimited Intimacy* makes available alternative models for inhabiting a counterintuitive, ambivalent positionality where transgressive pleasures enable evasion (though hardly total escape) of heterosexual culture's ubiquitous normative pull; the questioning of heteronormativity's and even identity's numbing aspiration to being taken as given, as simply the way things are; the momentary yet surprisingly powerful figural transformation of their routinized, hierarchical degradations, their enshrining of differential power, right, and voice.

Since Dean's appreciation for the transformative potential of barebacking culture's dissent from kinship structure stems, in part, from his gay cultural appreciation for the potential of alterity and parody, it's unsurprising that a second direction for innovating gay communal forms without subscribing to social conventions like religion lies within the ambit of gay cultural practice. Gay cultural practice entails a habit of conscious playing at and with affect and gender style that, while not limited to camp, is largely embraced by it. It's a manner of playing with traditionally disparate genres, or reveling in the violation of generic boundaries normatively regarded as dividing high from low, masculine from feminine, serious from unserious, tragic from melodramatic, privileged from abject. As David Halperin elegantly elucidates in *How to Be Gay*, gay culture does not so much refer to cultural artifacts and practices one might consider gay, that is, those novels, films, and other works created by gays and highlighting gay *identity*-based lives and rituals. This would be gayness as conceived as *identity*. By contrast, gay culture is a mode of *identification*, a "distinctively gay male style of cultural dissidence, a . . . style of resistance to received mainstream values" that has to do more with "cultural affiliation" than sexual identity (179). Understanding gayness as sexual identity and not much else, as enjoying sex with men but in most other respects resembling most straight men, rose to prominence in gay American culture during the post-Stonewall era. It seemed possible, finally, to escape the essentializing or pathologizing stereotypes, such as talent or affinity for opera, theater, musical theater, fashion, interior decoration, and effeminacy, that had dogged gay men since at least the late Victorian era and the trials of Oscar Wilde. Yet here it is well after Stonewall, and "*[h]omosexuality as queer affect, sensibility, subjectivity, identification, pleasure, habitus,* [and] *gender style*" remains alive and well (86). And this is because homosexuality manifested as aesthetic sense or as withering, gender-bending sarcasm remains the way that many gay men connect to gay desire. And by gay desire Halperin means much more than sexual desire for other men. "*Gay male desire*," he posits,

> cannot be reduced either to *sexual* desire or to gay *identity*.
>
> Sexual desire is only one aspect of gay male desire. Sex is not the sum of queer pleasure. Gay desire seeks more than the achievement of gay identity. Gay identity is inadequate to the full expression of gay subjectivity. Gay identity may well register the fact of gay desire; it may even stand in for its wayward promptings, its unanticipated urges and satisfactions. But gay identity does not—it cannot—capture gay desire in all its subjective sweep and scope. *It cannot express it.*
>
> Desire into identity will not go. (69)

Although the attempt has repeatedly been made, by some gay men, to sweep those supposedly stereotypical traits under the carpet, to hide them in what Halperin calls "*homosexuality's closet*," although gay liberation characterized such interests as necessary only to pathetic, self-loathing queens in bygone times when gay desire had to hide in the shadows and speak in coded language, cultural gayness is showing no signs of withering away like a vestigial appendage (100). Despite exaggerated reports of its demise, and to the chagrin of those in the gay community embarrassed that flamboyant queens, hairdressers, and drag queens still number among their ranks, gay camp and effeminacy are alive and well, persisting not just as affects but as richly sustaining, critical, and transformative models of play, self-realization, and normative deconstruction.

Now, some straights, Halperin admits, appreciate and deploy gay culture as well as gays, whereas some queers may be just as adept at straight cultural performance and cathect to its valuations more than, or as well as, they do to gay culture. Gay cultural praxis thus resides not in persons, objects, or sexualities but in the recoding of straight artifacts to endow them with queer meanings, camp valences, and strategies. Gay reading, by queers, straights, or other adepts provides strategies for resisting (if not dismantling) the norms of heterosexual culture, the "socially constructed and asymmetrical . . . polarities [of gender, sexuality, seriousness] that demand to be taken straight" (184). Far from escaping heteronorms (this seems impossible), highlighting their arbitrary and performative character accomplishes the powerful gesture of dissent: dissent from the dictatorial givenness by which they validate normative enclosure and engender homophobic rhetoric, violence, and policy. By contrast, gay culture at its best "implie[s] a principled disrespect . . . for all social performances" and the degrees of power or powerlessness, the cultural prestige or shame, "accru[ing] to those who embody them" (184). Gay culture so defined might constitute or produce a redeeming, collective, communitarian space beyond, though not necessarily exclusive of, a political solution, an empowering space of "proxy identity" that disrupts "the unquestioning claims to seriousness and authenticity" by "heterosexual or heteronormative social roles and meanings" (318, 218). Gay male culture opens a latitude of figural play by "not taking seriously, literally, or unironically the very things that matter most and that cause the most pain" (that is, without "devalu[ing]

the suffering it also refuses to dignify") and by democratically reveling in the most abject *and* the most esteemed aspects of performance
(218, 200). Within this latitude, "dominant social roles and meanings
cannot be destroyed," but they "can be undercut and derealized," their
"preeminence eroded." They can be "deprived of their claims to seriousness and authenticity, of their right to our moral, aesthetic, and
erotic allegiance" (218). In this way, gay male cultural practices like
camp "achieve a certain degree of leverage" against heteronorms "while
also acknowledging their continuing ability to dictate the terms of
our social existence" (218). Gay cultural praxis gravitates toward irony,
excess, and inauthenticity because those are the jarring aspects that
natural identities are not supposed to elicit; to elicit *these* affects would
highlight the performative, far-from-natural character of those norms
and roles. Gay culture's embrace of "the disqualifications attached to
[stigmatized] identities" like their own problematizes the whole spectrum of heteronormative roles and valuations (195).

Reared and tutored in heteronormative culture before they learn
to access gay subculture or perform queer readings of straight culture,
gay men are still as complicit in—and, ultimately, as bound within—
heteronormative valuations as their straight counterparts, even if they
later learn to be less credulously enamored by and healthily suspicious
of them. Which is to say that they develop a sense of queer irony, an
internalized distance from the roles and rituals many heterosexuals
spend their lifetime earnestly engrossed by, as just part of life rather
than cultivated performances. Gay culture's strength as a praxis of communal belonging is its predisposition to

> a simultaneous identification with the values and perspec-
> tives of both the privileged and the abject. Inasmuch as gay
> men are empowered as men, but disempowered as gay, such
> a double identification is logical. At the same time, the para-
> doxes and contradictions it generates account for some of the
> most distinctive and pervasive features of gay male culture.
> Gay male culture typically operates in two social registers at
> once, adopting the viewpoint of the upper and lower strata
> of society, of the noble and the ignoble, and relying on the
> irony fundamental to camp to hold aristocratic and egalitarian
> attitudes together in a delicate, dynamic equipoise. The brand
> of humor that results may be demeaning, but it is not just

demeaning, or not demeaning of other people only. It is also highly self-reflexive and self-inclusive: it applies to gay subjects themselves. (182–183)

A gay cultural affinity for abjection as well as glamour, powerlessness as well as triumph, makes available an alternative space of democratizing, horizontal, nonhierarchical relations in resistance to the vertical, hierarchal values so persuasively deployed by heteronormativity.[8]

Gay culture provides gay men with the "*conscious* consciousness of [one's] social being as a performance" that straights and particularly straight men, unless they are adept at gay cultural codes, tend to lack. Straight unconsciousness of norms or their artificiality and repressive power results from the fact that

> the culture of heterosexuality, which insists on its own natural-ness, encourages straight people to endow their own desires and their ways of living with a self-evident taken-for-grant-edness. The ideological weight of normality both impedes an active awareness of the social specificity of heterosexual forms of life—it prevents heterosexuals from thinking of het-erosexuality as a profound enigma that calls for painstaking investigation—and warns heterosexuals against inquiring too deeply into heterosexuality as a specific social form. Indeed, it discourages them from inquiring into social forms in general. (453–454)

Straights may be gay-friendly, homophobic, or indifferent, but if they are deaf to the critical distancing moves central to gay culture, they tend not to peek beneath the surface of their own roles. This doesn't mean they lack intelligence or insight. Rather, it means they may tend to be more deaf to the tones of tendentious piety, the differential privileges, that many gay men hear ringing loud and clear through the norms of heterosexual society. A roster of these norms would have to include the systems of belief, like religion, that have historically been instrumental in propagating not simply homophobia but heterosexuality's general ethos, its "taken-for-grantedness" (454). Even gay-positive heterosexu-als, those who do not think of homosexuality as unnatural, do not nec-essarily think of their own desires or experiences as any *less* natural, as any more *consciously* enacted, constructed, or endowed with meaning they didn't possess inherently. For straight men in particular, "[p]art of what is involved in being straight is learning to imitate straight men, to perform heterosexual masculinity, and then forgetting that you ever learned it, just as you must ignore the fact that you are performing it" (196–197). Building on Michael Warner's acute exploration of hetero-normativity in *The Trouble with Normal*, Halperin concludes that the "very blatancy, ubiquity, prevalence, obviousness, even vulgarity of the canonical definitions of sexual attractiveness in heterosexual culture relieve straight people of the imperative to define the exact social forms that correspond to their desires [in the way that queers must learn to do]. Which is why [straights] tend not even to see those forms as *social* in the first place" (198–199).

"Queers, however," Halperin continues,

> are forced to engage in at least a modicum of critical reflection on the world as it is given. As Michael Warner says [in his introduction to *Fear of a Queer Planet*], "Queers do a kind of practical social reflection just in finding ways of being queer." That practical social reflection gives rise to a second-order processing and reprocessing of immediate experience. Queer people's distance on the social world (as defined and natural-ized by heteronorms), and the acutely *conscious* consciousness they have of the different forms in which life presents itself to different people, issue inevitably in an irreducible critical attitude. (454)

Through genre mixing, tonal ambivalence, irony, and inappropriate-ness, adepts of gay male culture tend to treat "authenticity as a *perfor-mance* of authenticity." They call into question not just the authenticity of socially privileged roles and norms but the legal privilege, cultural cachet, and social importance that typically—and tendentiously—accrue to those individuals who inhabit them seriously, without irony, as merely life rather than as a performance (192). As a dissident rela-tion to official hetero readings and uses of cultural forms that "afford . . . opportunities for colonizing [nongay artifacts and cultural forms] and making them over into vehicles of queer affirmation," gay cul-ture trains gay men and others adept at gay culture in an "anti-social aesthetic" (112, 143), a way of reading epitomized by, yet not limited to, the wide-ranging, diverse practice of camp. And an "anti-social" aesthetic, in Halperin's lexicon, means an aesthetic sense "not . . . *hostile to communal belonging . . . but contrary to social norms*" (189). Gay culture equips its practitioners with a way of reading the world, each other, and themselves (and I *do* mean *reading*, hunty). It yields a crucial, buoying affect: a way of living, of realizing gay desire in all its complexity. It provides a means of, at once, both deeply feeling and laughing off marginalization by a heteronormative world, of at once accepting and transcending the homophobia and heteronormative dictates that religion generates, fans, and deploys. It enables a "swerve away from the gravitational pull of the obvious" (455). What could be more obviously crushing, and more crushingly obvious, than the damage that religious belief, whose truths are supposedly so obvious, so given and eternal, inflicts on queers by intimidating them into shame, reparative therapy, and suicide, and on queers and queer allies by impeding rational debate, by obstructing civil rights, by indemnifying hate.

Some may object that we need not banish religion from queer life entirely. It might be enough for camp reading to derealize religion's disempowering, homophobic mandates, the dehumanizing, differential attributions of worth that religion and spirituality, in blaring or understated ways, promulgate where queers are concerned. Might we keep religion and let the gay cultural questioning of its givenness and authenticity suffice? Religious seriousness and the homophobia it so often underwrites have been ironized and recoded with queer affect before now and redeployed with queer uses. The Sisters of Perpetual Indulgence, a San Francisco group of queer men in nun's drag have been doing so since 1979, combining community service and tolerance advocacy while spoofing organized religion and repurposing its accoutrement for radical queer uses. Perhaps, however, queer cultural work and activism could accomplish even more. Perhaps queer affect and communal belonging could provide more appreciable sustenance and happiness, if religion's voice in public debate were not so rancorously self-righteous, if the historical and cultural weight it brought to bear were not still so widely unquestioned or questioned so gingerly as to be nugatory.

The time has come, for queers and queer allies tired of antigay violence and exclusion, to set aside once and for all belief's imprimatur as moral arbiter, as a personal matter that cannot be silenced, that must be heard out regardless of the inanity or hatred it propagates. Some poisons are too toxic even for the antidote of queer intervention to fully overcome or to expend energy there that might more effectively and rewardingly be deployed to other ends. Puncturing the pretended authenticity of inauthentic norms is not always enough to guarantee pleasure, equity, or survival. Authenticity and acceptance, kinship and transgression, may best be sought in less noxious venues, sought more rewardingly and with a lower figurative and literal body count. Antigay religious rhetoric, particularly from the right wing, may seem more desperately shrill, more lunatic, and increasingly less relevant with each passing year. The 2012 election was the first in some time to suggest that the voting power of evangelicals and other so-called values voters was being outpaced by new key demographics, or that some conservative Christians' attitudes toward homosexuality were beginning to shift away from the extreme right. But decreasing relevance is still relevance. Lessening political suasion does not necessarily correlate with diminishing cultural normative influence, especially when it comes to the resilience of deep-seated heteronorms and their impact on queer life. Religion of any stripe packs a moral wallop to be ignored at one's own hazard, no matter how far from the mainstream its sentiments may lie. As I've suggested, moderate and liberal incarnations of religion both carry within them and reinforce heteronormative strictures on queer parity and thus reinforce impediments to queer survival. Even though polls suggest that the American religious Right's talking points on homosexuality are becoming less amenable to an increasing number of Americans, and even to some younger evangelicals, the genius of the religious Right for the past three decades has been to parlay its fringe ideas into political and cultural influence well in excess of its numbers.[9] A handful of prominent, financially backed spokespersons, widespread grassroots activism, and moralizing rhetoric's ability to bridge the gap between far-right and mainstream religion are capable of producing pivotal leverage. Hatred does not always require numbers or relevance to inflict damage, to poison debate, and to ruin lives.

Quite simply, queer community need not endure—*no one* should have to tolerate—the murderous voltage conducted throughout American culture and politics by treating religion as an untouchable third rail in spite of all the discrimination and devastation it legitimizes. Religion can no longer be accepted as an appropriate participant in social debate. Where queer dignity, queer civil rights, and queer life are concerned, it must go. My use of the term "gaytheism," far from advocating that queers turn to religion (theism), invites gays to opt for atheism, so as to opt *out* of religious ideology and the damage that its so-called moral clout continues to inflict on queer Americans. "Gaytheism" also means to connote a project of believing in queerness, in our own subversive, nonnormative ethical cores, believing in it *more than* in the ability of religious authority, extramundane beings, or invidious normative valuations to make us whole, to sanction us in ways that queerness's best insights have taught us to question. It urges believing in gayness as the key to our centeredness and our simultaneous critical *suspicion* of claims to centeredness and importance. Gaytheism invokes a commitment, typically annulled by religious and spiritual beliefs, to questioning the *possibility and desirability* of being sanctioned, redeemed, or normalized by any authority. Being stamped as indelibly given or natural, sacred or elect, is an imprimatur—religious, cultural, or otherwise—whose cost is almost always paid by someone else.

NOTES

INTRODUCTION: WHERE GAYS LIE

1. See also Neal Broverman, "Antigay Group: DADT Will Be Back."
2. By 2013, a total of thirteen states (in addition to the District of Columbia) had legalized same-sex marriage: California, Connecticut, Delaware, Iowa, Massachusetts, Minnesota, New Hampshire, New York, Vermont, Maine, Maryland, Rhode Island, and Washington. Civil unions, though a second-class status that fails to provide either the cultural inclusion or the full slate of legal rights associated with marriage, are legal in Delaware, Hawaii, Illinois, Nevada, New Jersey, and Oregon. Most remaining states have either state laws or state constitutional bans against gay marriage.
3. These figures come from Jesse McKinley and Kirk Johnson's *New York Times* piece, "Mormons Tipped Scale in Ban on Gay Marriage."
4. For additional commentary on this story, see Michael Jones, "Walmart to Sell Book about Curing Gay People," and Ryan Tedder, "Why Is Walmart Selling Janice Barrett Graham's Ex-Gay Parenting Book?"
5. Examples of fundamentalist and evangelical Christian identity's definitional opposition to homosexuality are not hard to come by: Michael Brown, *A Queer Thing Happened to America*; Ronnie Floyd, *The Gay Agenda: It's Dividing the Family, the Church, and a Nation*;

and Alan Sears and Craig Osten, *The Homosexual Agenda: Exposing the Principal Threat to Religious Freedom*. Conservative Christian rhetoric in America addresses an audience that is more than just religious, of course, as the Christian Right has grown over the past three decades to constitute a political and cultural force as well as a major wing of the New Right. The latter includes a host of advocacy and lobbying organizations whose political aims are dictated by conservative Christian identity. The largest, most influential, and heavily funded such groups include Focus on the Family, Family Research Council, Concerned Women for America, Americans for Truth about Homosexuality, and the Traditional Values Coalition. For representative readings of the Christian Right's conflation of religious and political rhetoric and efforts to obstruct equal rights and retrench cultural support for gays and lesbians, see Cynthia Burack, Patrick Chapman, W. C. Harris, and Didi Herman.

6. Neal Broverman wrote two stories on the McCance incident, "School Official Wants Gays Dead" and the follow-up "McCance: I Have Family to Consider." For other helpful coverage, see Michael Jones, "Arkansas School Board Member," and Melanie Nathan. In all quotes from McCance's Facebook thread I have preserved the original spelling, punctuation, and other typography.

7. Given queer Americans' second-class status, "citizens" is admittedly a vexed term. In separate accounts, Margot Canaday and Amy Brandzel expertly examine the role played by the federal government in policing the confines of citizenship and its appurtenant rights and provide tremendously insightful analyses of gay and lesbian Americans' development and status as incompletely enfranchised citizens.

8. For antecedents to Christopher Hitchens, Sam Harris, Richard Dawkins, and Bertrand Russell, Will and Ariel Durant's *The Age of Voltaire* sketches many of the standard critiques of Christianity and defenses of atheism made in some of their most cogent and, figures like Epicurus and Pierre Bayle aside, their earliest forms: the European Enlightenment diatribes of Diderot, Helvetius, d'Holbach, and Voltaire.

9. Although I concur with Janet Jakobsen and Ann Pellegrini's analysis of much of the *evidence* of cultural and religious intolerance toward homosexuality, I disagree fundamentally with their proposed solution. "[E]xpand[ing] the possibilities for freedom in

America," for Jakobsen and Pellegrini, means not viewing "religion and secularism [as being] in opposition to each other" but, rather, recognizing the validity of "secular morality . . . [without] demean[ing] religion or religious people" (17, 11–12). Their project for the "development of moral alternatives" is sex-positive and antihomophobic and admirably attempts to salvage the insights of the "rich history of progressive" and "social justice movements" associated with some strains of American Christianity and Judaism (17, 12). While they admit that "Christian theological pronouncements [about homosexuality] have become so institutionalized in the official life of the nation that they can be taken for just good old American values," they hold out hope that American religious homophobia, religious tolerance, and public life can be pried apart, and that religious moralities of all stripes (tolerant as well as homophobic) and secular morality can amicably cohabit American public life and culture (3). I fail to share this optimism, obviously. Religious intolerance seems incapable of amicably cohabiting cultural space with queers and queer allies. Even if détente or armistice *could* be struck on this front, I would contend that the organic heteronormativity of institutionalized religion would continue to disseminate a toxic hostility and disregard for queer lives and to vitiate the project of recuperating and exercising tolerance via spiritual and religious mediums.

10. Jessica Valenti's *The Purity Myth: How America's Obsession with Virginity Is Harming Young Women* contains an accessible, activism-oriented dissection of how a corrosive "purity myth" and its corollary "virgin/whore straitjacket" animates conservative religious discourse as well as legislative policy and mainstream cultural attitudes. While *Slouching towards Gaytheism* shares some subject matter with Valenti's book, including abstinence-only education and purity balls, Valenti focuses almost exclusively on how the purity myth impacts heterosexual women; her discussion of masculinity is likewise heterocentric (167–183).

11. Through their website (generationsoflight.myicontrol.com), Randy and Lisa Wilson's organization sells numerous books on abstinence culture as well as a kit that provides "everything you need to start a Father-Daughter Purity Ball in your area." For news coverage of the phenomenon, see Nancy Gibbs, as well as Nancy Gibbs and Lucas L. Johnson II. See also Valenti 65–67. Although purity balls

as popularized by the Wilsons may be a fairly recent phenomenon, virginity, purity, and sexual ignorance—in young men as well as young women—have long been cultural fetishes and hardly limited to Western culture or to Christianity (see Bertrand Russell 26–30, 67–70, 166–167, 176–178).

12. Readers seeking insider accounts of the ex-gay movement may consult Jallen Rix, *Ex-Gay No Way: Survival and Recovery from Religious Abuse*, and Ben Tousey, *My Egypt: Why I Left the Ex-Gay Movement*. Generally, Rix and Tousey's observations mirror those of Erzen and Wolkomir regarding the ex-gay movement's homophobic, sex-phobic propaganda and use of religious ideology to curb nonnormative and independent thought. Aside from confirming my speculation, in chapter 2, that sexual "backsliding" does happen in ex-gay dormitory settings, Rix and Tousey focus on the narrative of addiction, abuse, and recovery—to and from religion. Their work is evidence of how painful and damaging attempts to "change" gay sexuality can be. My own analysis of ex-gay identity as a potential space for queer identitarian resistance and pleasure, even under duress, is admittedly speculative. Far from recommending the Christian closet as a space to inhabit if one has any other choices, chapter 2 seeks to explore the fissures and unresolved ambivalence in the ways in which homosexuality, and gay men themselves, are positioned within conservative Christianity.

13. Penn Bullock and Brandon K. Thorp reported on the Rekers scandal for the *Miami New Times*. Joe Jervis, of the blog *Joe. My. God.*, reprinted the Rentboys.com ad posted by Geo ("Lucien"'s real name) through which Rekers first contacted the twenty-three-year-old (Jervis, "Meet Geo, the Male Prostitute"). Geo offered "massage, good times, travel, escort for days, nights, and weekends." Other details of the ad—including penis size, the details "UNCUT, VERSATILE, NICE ASS," and "very clean, HIV and disease free"—suggest his clientele enjoyed one of his offered services ("a sensual meet") more often than the other ("companionship").

14. In *God Hates Fags: The Rhetorics of Religious Violence*, Michael Cobb mounts a provocative argument that, while divergent from my own in important respects, suggests the similar possibility that antigay ideology may yield for articulation of queer identity and desire despite itself. Cobb's analysis coincides with mine on at least three counts. He "investigate[s] the manner in which religious hatred

becomes a language through which queers strategically mediate conventional structures of national belonging" (11). He regards "American religious rhetoric [as] a sovereign language—the fundamental language of those who rule in an inequitable manner, enabling some people to count as worthwhile and some as disposable," "sanctif[ying some lives] by the right kind of national-family value while restricting others from that value" (15). Finally, Cobb asks us to "entertain the possibility that the public articulation of queerness does not mean that one must be truthful or faithful. In fact, there is dire importance in conceptualizing one's public identity as a fiction that can be manipulated for one's political and cultural advantage" (16). However, when such insights are applied to the Christian closet—home variously to pain, protection, subversion, and sacred or profane pleasure—I am less optimistic than Cobb that rhetoric's fictional, positively transformative capacities can always reliably offset its injurious material consequences.

15. In *The Queening of America*, David Van Leer honors the pull of both constructionist and essentialist influences on identity, its status as both notional category and lived experience:

> I suspect that the concept of identity cannot be fully understood as a distinction between essence and invention. . . . Much recent theory has responded to such ambiguities by deconstructing the homosexual/heterosexual binarism. Rather than explore the indeterminacy of sexual identity, I critique the ways in which sexual categories, whether real or not, have been used to misrepresent and mask an identifiable cultural difference. . . . Even on those days when I do not think the homosexual/heterosexual dichotomy is here to stay, I am not convinced of the practicality of dismantling it unilaterally. Deconstructing difference might problematize homosexual identity yet leave heterosexuality blissfully unaware that its universality was under attack. (7, 9)

Van Leer models his attention to the substance and utility of essentialist identity categories on the recuperative work of Diana Fuss who, along with other feminist as well as African American critics, argued for a reconsideration of occasions where essentialism can be descriptively true and strategically useful. In *Essentially Speaking,* Fuss questioned the feminist dismissal of essentialist categories as wholly misrepresentative, exclusionary, and politically reactionary—a move that inspired similar recuperative moves in queer studies (such as in Van Leer's text or in my own *Queer Externalities*). *Slouching towards Gaytheism* attempts to balance appreciation for the plasticity of ideological positions and identitarian modalities with a healthy respect for their very real intransigence and punishments.

16. Dean bases his usage of "post-subcultural" on the "de-essentialization of subcultural theory" proposed by David Muggleton and Rupert Weinzierl in *The Post-Subcultures Reader.*

17. In *Straight to Jesus,* Tanya Erzen notes the divergent positions on the question of "change" between grassroots movements like New Hope and national groups like Exodus and Focus on the Family.

18. In *Sin, Sex, and Democracy,* Cynthia Burack supplies a rewarding overview of the ex-gay movement, particularly its employment of development narratives and its Janus-faced "juxtapos[ition of compassionate] therapeutic discourse with brass knuckled political instruction for a conservative Christian audience" (87). She also examines Christian Right rhetoric portraying queers "as a satanic fifth column within America" (105). "Nazi" and "terrorist" being the two most prevalent comparisons, such imagery has fueled complementary narratives of a putatively straight, Christian nation under siege by enemies seeking its destruction and providing a *casus belli* for "fight[ing] . . . internal . . . threats to the American homeland by cordoning off the danger until it can, finally, be extinguished" (105, 104).

19. For additional coverage of Starbucks's same-sex marriage advocacy and responses to their position, see James O'Toole, Jeanné McCartin, and Tiffany Hsu.

20. The Southern Poverty Law Center website provides a complete listing of their designated "hate groups"; see, particularly, Evelyn Schlatter's entry titled "18 Anti-Gay Groups and Their Propaganda." The SPLC emphasizes that "viewing homosexuality as unbiblical" is not what "qualif[ies] organizations for listing as hate groups" from their perspective. Rather, SPLC restricts this categorization to groups that disseminate "demonizing propaganda aimed at homosexuals and other sexual minorities," propaganda "amplified by certain politicians, other groups, and even news

organizations, and whose "known falsehoods" (which they call "'facts'") "about homosexuality"—"claims about homosexuality that have been thoroughly discredited by scientific authorities"—amount to nothing but "groundless name-calling" (Schlatter par. 1). Retaliatory comments should come as no surprise. Yet the AFA's Bryan Fischer managed to take the trademark projective habits of religious and political conservatives further than the typical, ludicrous claim that denouncing Christian homophobia as hate speech itself constitutes persecution of Christians. In August 2012 Fischer wrote that the SPLC's

> attack on us is predicated on the fact that we tell the truth about homosexuality and oppose the normalization of homosexuality. . . . What we are for is natural marriage and the historic "laws of Nature and Nature's God" on which this nation was founded.
>   . . . Unfortunately, what the SPLC calls "myths" about homosexuality turn out to be what neutral observers call "truths" about homosexuality.
>   . . . If propagating falsehoods [about homosexuality] qualifies you as a hate group, then SPLC belongs on its own list. (Fischer, "SPLC Propagates Falsehoods" pars. 4, 6, 7)

Aside from the fallacious logic, misrepresented evidence, and outright lies that plague this passage and its supporting "proof," one has to be amused at Fischer's mistaken use of scare quotes around the "truths" offered by the AFA. Surely he understands the function of scare quotes, since in the same sentence he uses them to discredit what the SPLC refers to as "myths"—that is, the very points the AFA and similar groups regard as truths, sans scare quotes.

21. For additional representative coverage of the One Million Moms-JCPenney conflict, particularly regarding the Father's Day ad, see Heba Hasan and Neetzan Zimmerman.

22. Cathy's equation of so-called traditional or biblical marriage, as in most forms of this argument, ignores obvious evidence *against* the claim that marriage has always been, in the Bible or in American society, a union between "one man and one woman": namely, that marriage has been redefined in multiple ways just in the past

century or two (expanding women's property rights, legalizing interracial marriage) and in even more ways since the Old Testament era (when a man was allowed to marry multiple wives, slaves, concubines, and rape victims and was *commanded* to marry the childless widow of his deceased brother). In the satirical video "Betty Bowers Explains Traditional Marriage to Everyone Else," conservative religious gadfly character Betty Bowers provides a wry litany of factual biblical examples of marriage extending far beyond the monogamous, nuclear-family model mechanically adduced by gay marriage opponents touting biblical or secular historical tradition.

23. Coverage of the Chick-fil-A episode was widespread, but discussion of its various stages is available from a variety of perspectives: mainstream reporters Sarah Aarthun, Joe Howell, Elise Hu, Andrew Lu, Kate Mather and Kenny Stockdale, Jena McGregor, Laura Petrecca, Eric Pfeiffer, Kim Severson, and Elizabeth Tenety; right-wing organs like FOX News ("Chick-fil-A Confirms 'Record-Setting Day'"); liberal commentators including *Huffington Post*'s Don Babwin and Melissa Jeltsen; GLBT-centered reportage by Lucas Grindley ("My Life Isn't a Political Issue"), Jeremy Hooper, and Zinnia Jones; and bloggers Ryan Ebersole and Wayne Self. Self's "The Chick Fellatio: Stuck in the Craw" is as thoughtful as its title is playful.

24. Mel White's *Holy Terrors: Lies the Christian Right Tells Us to Deny Gay Equality* provides an exemplary dissection of the Christian Right's concerted campaign against the so-called gay agenda and its simultaneous claim that *Christians* are the persecuted party. *A Queer Thing Happened to America*, a pompous antigay screed by Michael L. Brown, exemplifies the sort of propaganda White is speaking of.

25. In a fitting instance of poetic justice, a group of GLBT Ugandans returned the favor, traveling to the United States to seek legal recompense. In January 2013 the Center for Constitutional Rights presented a lawsuit to the Massachusetts Supreme Court under the Alien Tort Statute, a "'powerful legal tool that allows foreign victims of human rights to seek civil remedies in US courts." The "first-ever sexual orientation-related lawsuit" brought under this law, *Sexual Minorities Uganda v. Scott Lively* "alleges that Lively committed crimes against humanity in his campaign urging

Uganda to implement harsh persecutions of LGBT people" (Jervis, "Crimes Against Humanity Case" par. 1). Accounts of the genesis and repercussion of the "Kill the Gays" bill are widespread, but Emily Cody provides a useful summary.

26. Sean Harris soon issued a retraction—"more [of] a legal document than an apology," as David Badash put it—"'of any and all words that suggest that child abuse is appropriate for any and all types of behaviors including (but not limited to) effeminacy and sexual immorality of all types. . . . I have never suggested children or those in the LGBT lifestyle should be beaten, punched, abused (physically or psychologically) in any form or fashion'" (Badash, "Beat the Gay Out of Kids Pastor Apology" par. 6). From there Harris's statement quickly toboggans downhill into unrepentant homophobia draped in religious privilege:

> I do not apologize for the manner in which the Word of God articulates sexual immorality, including homosexuality and effeminacy, as a behavior that is an abomination to God. Nothing in this official statement of retraction should be perceived as an apology for the overarching intent and message of the sermon and the need to define marriage as one man and one woman and to maintain the gender distinctions that God created from the beginning when He made them male and female (Genesis 1). I recognize that there are those in the LGBT community who believe that their sexual behavior is not sin. I do not agree with them and this official retraction should not be misunderstood as an apology for the gospel of Jesus Christ or the Word of God. (qtd. in Badash par. 9)

A less sincere, nonretraction retraction has perhaps yet to be written.

CHAPTER 1. "THE END OF THE RAINBOW, MY POT OF GOLD"

1. Conservative Christian ideals of purity and sanctity require not just adherence to certain theological and ideological concepts but commitment to literal productivity—that is, sexual reproduction to

create more adherents. An extreme embodiment of this commitment to fecundity is Quiverfull, an American evangelical movement proscribing any form of birth control and exhorting followers to have as many children as possible in order to secure Christianity's religious and political future. Rick and Jan Hess and Kathryn Joyce provide, respectively, insider and outsider perspectives of the movement.

2. Mike Yorkey is listed as secondary coauthor on three books in the *Every Man* series, but he seems to have done largely editorial work on these volumes; therefore, when referring to *Every Young Man's Battle*, I have used the names of the two main coauthors, Arterburn and Stoeker, as a less cumbersome shorthand. That there seems to be no shortage of Christian purity books for adults and teens surely has something to do with the cultural and political ascendancy of the Christian Right during George W. Bush's administration (from White House conference calls with evangelical ministers to federally mandated abstinence only education) as well as with the greater accessibility of erotic and pornographic material via the internet. A sampling of recent purity books includes Randy Alcorn, *The Purity Principle: God's Safeguards for Life's Dangerous Trails*; Jim Burns, *The Purity Code: God's Plan for Sex and Your Body*; Robert Daniels, *The War Within: Gaining Victory in the Battle for Sexual Purity*; Dannah Gresh, *And the Bride Wore White: Seven Secrets to Sexual Purity*; Joshua Harris, *Sex Is Not the Problem (Lust Is): Sexual Purity in a Lust-Saturated World*; Jim and Pam Koehlinger, *Protecting His Workmanship: Teaching Your Child God's Design for Sexual Purity*; Leslie Ludy, *Answering the Guy Questions: The Set-Apart Girl's Guide to Relating to the Opposite Sex*; Brienne Murk, *Eyes Wide Open: Avoiding the Heartbreak of Emotional Promiscuity*; Bill Perkins and Randy Southern, *When Young Men Are Tempted: Sexual Purity for Guys in the Real World*; Rebecca St. James, *Wait for Me: Rediscovering the Joy of Purity in Romance*; and Kris Vallotton, *Purity: The New Moral Revolution*.

3. According to its website, the Abstinence Clearinghouse "is a privately funded 501(c)3 non-profit, non-partisan international educational organization. The Clearinghouse was founded to provide a central location where character, relationship, and abstinence programs, curricula, speakers, and materials could be accessed." Involved with agencies on local, state, national, and international

levels, the organization publishes a directory of abstinence resources, a quarterly newsletter, and other abstinence materials. They also work with churches and schools to disseminate materials that are not only "age appropriate" but also—they have the gall to claim, despite House investigations to the contrary—"factual and medically-referenced." The Clearinghouse's mission is "to promote the appreciation for and practice of sexual abstinence (purity) until marriage."

4. In terms of American religious history, the purity ball's masculin- ist priorities recall such antecedents as "muscular Christianity"—a movement that, between 1890 and 1920, "transformed Jesus [from a feminized figure] into a . . . working-class carpenter" and enabled "revivalist preachers like Billy Sunday and Dwight Moody" to rese- cure patriarchal control of a church perceived as having "suffered under too much feminine influence" (Erzen 244n31). For more on the lineage of heterosexual panic over female sexual auton- omy, male impotence and effeminacy, and permeable boundaries between cultures of same-sex friendship and homosexuality, see John Donald Gustav-Wrathall and George Chauncey.

5. The "granting rules [for states receiving these funds] mandate that abstinence be defined as no sex before marriage, and they define a mutually monogamous relationship in the context of marriage as the 'expected standard of human sexuality'" (Heywood par. 2). The rules also require educators to teach that "abstinence from sexual activity is the only certain way to avoid out-of-wedlock pregnancy" and STDs and that "sexual activity outside the context of mar- riage is likely to have harmful psychological and physical effects" (Michigan Department of Community Health).

6. Elizabeth Landau reports on the 2010 Health Care Reform Bill's inclusion of $250 million (over five years) for abstinence education, despite judgments from Congress and medical professionals that such programs are ineffective, untruthful, and unethical. The study touted by abstinence education advocates as proof of the latter's effectiveness was conducted by University of Pennsylvania profes- sor Dr. John B. Jemmott III, who followed 662 African American urban middle school students for two years after their participation in weekend abstinence-only classes. The results, released in early 2010, found that "a third of the students who participated in [the] abstinence-only class started having sex within the next 24 months,

compared with about half who were randomly assigned instead to general health information classes, or classes teaching only safer sex. Among those assigned to comprehensive sex-education classes, covering both abstinence and safer sex, about 42 percent began having sex [within two years]" (par. 3). Despite abstinence advocates' rave reviews of the study, it suffers a number of flaws that render it inconclusive. The median participant age was twelve. Furthermore, "unlike the federally supported . . . programs now in use, [Jemmott's classes] did not advocate abstinence until marriage. Most significantly, Jemmott's classes—*unlike* the federally funded abstinence-only ones—"did *not* portray sex negatively or suggest that condoms are ineffective, and contained *only medically accurate* information" (pars. 14, 15; emphasis added). An instructive contrast to Jemmott's study is one conducted at Columbia University, which "found that although teenagers who take 'virginity pledges' may wait longer to initiate sexual activity, 88 percent eventually have premarital sex" (Connolly par. 17). Tracking abstinent teenagers for more than two years (the window of Jemmott's study) seems to make all the difference in terms of arriving at useful results. Not having premarital sex, period, would seem to be the ultimate proof of abstinence education's and a purity pledge's effectiveness.

7. Of the thirteen abstinence-only programs reviewed in Waxman's 2004 report, only two were providing accurate information. The other eleven programs, which were "used by 69 organizations in 25 states," "contain[ed] unproved claims, subjective conclusions or outright falsehoods regarding reproductive health, gender traits and when life begins. In some cases . . . the factual issues were limited to occasional misinterpretations of publicly available data; in others, the materials pervasively presented subjective opinions as fact" (Connolly par. 5).

8. Todd Henneman, Todd Heywood, and Abbie Kopf discuss the ways in which abstinence-only programs exclude gay youth by pathologizing or simply not addressing nonheterosexual sex. As one might expect, an organization like the Family Research Council (take, for example, their page on "Human Sexuality") is more frankly hostile about demonizing anyone who's not straight.

9. Repetition of the phrase "purity balls" evokes a crude but germane image of what purity ball culture studiously fails to reference—testicles—even as it immures filial female sexuality within the scaffolding of the parental male body. These phantom balls, conjured

but never materializing, lead one to associate purity and virginity, the twin fetishes of abstinence culture, with the Phallus. Like the Phallus, purity can never be appreciated, sensed, or truly known till it has been lost. Both provide a false sense of wholeness. In the Lacanian moment of *méconnaissance*, or misrecognition, we found our initial sense of self as infants on a mistaken sense or vision of our own integrity; from the first, our self is based on the other, on what we are not, what we lack. The *imago* of "sexual integrity," of purity as encompassing not just abstinence but also sex within marriage, is the *Gestalt* of the teen purity movement. *Losing* one's virginity can thus be likened to one's entrance into language, or the Symbolic. Abstinence culture aims to keep teens corralled within a presexual and prelinguistic state.

10. See Leslie Ludy 23–31; and Kerby Anderson passim.

11. See Erzen 202–204, 207–208; and Wolkomir 31–35. Erzen credits ex-gay John Paulk's joining Focus on the Family as effecting this shift. Whereas before 1994 Dobson and other spokespersons for Focus on the Family described gays and lesbians as perverts seeking "special rights" through the promotion of a so-called gay agenda, Paulk—unsurprisingly, given his own experience as an ex-gay—"adopted the ex-gay testimony of change and transformation to make their anti-gay agenda less overt and more palatable to a conservative Christian agenda" (203). While I'm not sure the latter is entirely incompatible with Focus on the Family's older, more aggressive rhetoric, the salient point is that even the milder approach, while no longer *openly* seeking to "'rob anyone of their rights,'" accomplishes the same objective in a quieter way (204).

12. Debates over the degree to which one can "change" one's sexuality and the duration and exact nature of such change are hardly new. Starting in the United States in the 1970s and spurred no doubt by the modern gay and lesbian liberation movement, proponents of ex-gay therapy such as Exodus and their critics have battled over these questions. This debate was reinvigorated in the early 1990s by the formation of the National Association for Research and Therapy (NARTH). Founded by psychoanalyst Dr. Charles Socarides, NARTH promotes itself as a neutral organization of unbiased mental health professionals who offer reparative (or conversion) therapy—a form of psychotherapy aimed at altering a patient's sexual orientation from gay to straight. Since 1973, when the American Psychiatric Association (APA) voted to remove homosexuality

from the DSM where it had previously been listed as a mental disorder (the 1980 edition was the first to reflect this change), a majority of mental health professionals including the APA and the American Psychoanalytic Association have disavowed reparative therapy as unethical and ineffective. NARTH's own stable of psychiatrists, psychologists, and therapists naturally argue to the contrary. The controversy escalated in 2001 when psychiatrist Dr. Robert Spitzer published a study claiming to substantiate the hypothesis that homosexual orientation can be changed. Immediately and fervently, the study was praised by organizations like NARTH and Exodus, dismissed by the major professional mental health organizations, and excoriated by gay and lesbian activists. Spitzer's claims, which were hardly new, would have garnered little attention had the author been anyone else: this was the same Robert Spitzer, who as chair of the APA's Committee on Nomenclature in 1973 was instrumental in homosexuality's declassification as a mental disorder. Queers and their supporters saw Spitzer as a turncoat; NARTH and affiliates of the religious Right celebrated him as that most fetishized of proselytes, a former heretic. In 2006 Harrington Park Press, a reputable scholarly publisher in mental health and sexuality research, published *Ex-Gay Research: Analyzing the Spitzer Study and Its Relation to Science, Religion, Politics, and Culture* (edited by Kenneth Zucker and Jack Drescher). This volume provides a broad critique of the study's methodological flaws and the biases that shaped the study and its reception. The following year, Christian publisher InterVarsity Press produced *Ex-Gays?:A Longitudinal Study of Religiously Mediated Change in Sexual Orientation*, which defended Spitzer and "religiously-informed psychotherapy" from their critics. For other examples of the ways Spitzer's data and conclusions were received on the antigay side, and often misrepresented or taken out of context, see *A Parent's Guide to Preventing Homosexuality*, by former NARTH president Joseph Nicolosi, and the Family Research Council of America's *Getting It Straight: What the Research Shows about Homosexuality*.

13. Wesley Hill's *Washed and Waiting: Reflections on Christian Faithfulness and Homosexuality* exemplifies the continuing commitment by conservative gay Christians to celibacy as well as to the tendentious equation of homosexuality with "brokenness."

CHAPTER 2. BREEDING FRATERNITIES

1. Regarding the pervasiveness and debated recalcitrance of hetero-normativity, see Michael Warner's introduction to *Fear of a Queer Planet* (Warner is credited with coining this term). See also W. C. Harris, *Queer Externalities*; and Eric O. Clarke, *Virtuous Vice.*

2. See Steven Seidman.

3. My examples of ex-gay therapy come primarily from Erzen and Wolkomir, whose thorough, even-handed analyses make them indispensable sources for any discussion of this phenomenon. Wolkomir also examines gay Christian experience. Typical partisan accounts of ex-gay therapy—that is, religious defenses of it—can be found in the work of Joe Dallas and Alan Chambers. Dallas, author of *Desires in Conflict: Hope for Men Who Struggle with Sexual Identity*, is a former chair of Exodus International's board, founder of Genesis Counseling, and leader of ex-gay workshops for Love Won Out (a collaboration of Exodus and Focus on the Family) as well as for Steven Arterburn's New Life Ministries. Chambers, coauthor of *God's Grace and the Homosexual Next Door: Reaching the Heart of the Gay Men and Women in Your World*, is the most recent president of Exodus International. Beginning in 2001, Chambers attempted to set Exodus apart from other conservative religious organizations and churches that regard homosexuals as irredeemable sinners by espousing a "compassionate" message toward homosexuals and prioritizing youth outreach. Although Chambers frames the Exodus message as one of love and emphasizes that homosexuality is no worse a sin than any other, this compassionate outreach is fundamentally co-optive and, despite its protestations to the contrary, deeply hostile and damaging. While Chambers and his coauthors admit, like Dallas, that not all ex-gays may come to feel heterosexual desire, and that many may continue to experience homosexual desires, Exodus maintains that *acting* on homosexual desires is antithetical to being a saved Christian. In this view, gays and lesbians simply need to be healed of their sin, like alcoholics—a typical conservative Christian equation of queer sex with physically and psychologically damaging behavior—in short, with disease. Exodus's pathologizing view of homosexuality puts its reputedly progressive approach on par with that of

nineteenth-century sexologists. The negative message that Exodus ascribes to *other* ex-gay organizations or conservative churches differs from its own solely in being undisguised by hypocrisy and the patina of tolerance. In general, the theories of homosexual desire's origins or causes as well as the therapeutic methodologies practiced by the ex-gay groups studied by Erzen and Wolkomir are similar if not identical to those espoused by Dallas and Chambers. Given Exodus's enormous influence on the ex-gay movement, the commonality is unsurprising. (Exodus was founded in 1976, third only to Aesthetic Realism in 1971 and Love In Action in 1973; Love In Action, started by Frank Worthen, later merged with Exodus.)

4. While my exclusive focus on male ex-gays reflects the focus of my own project, it's worth noting that the ex-gay movement in general does not have a heavy investment, either symbolically or materially, in female ex-gays. Love In Action started a program for women in 1986, but by the early 1990s its women's ministry had folded due to a leadership crisis. At present, most "residential programs still tend to be geared toward men" (Erzen 30).

5. See Donna Haraway, *Simians, Cyborgs, and Women: The Reinvention of Nature*; and Maria Pramaggiore and Donald E. Hall, eds., *RePresenting Bisexualities: Subjects and Cultures of Fluid Desire*.

6. See Wolkomir (32–35, 114) for an effective précis of ex-gay theories of homosexuality's origins and causes.

7. For another account of the erotically confused, if not downright ambivalent, male bonding that characterizes ex-gay therapies, see Ted Cox's undercover report on his participation in a weekend workshop called Journey into Manhood. Developed in 2002 by Rich Wyler (founder of the website People Can Change) and "gender affirming" therapist David Matheson, the workshop is offered several times a year.

8. As Erzen astutely remarks, the thoroughgoing identification at New Hope of heterosexuality with monogamy, and thus of homosexuality with promiscuity, is based on participants' largely minimal interaction with anything resembling a gay community—and is designed to keep it that way:

> The ex-gays' lack of involvement in gay communities and the character of their sexual relationships as anonymous or closeted bolster their idea that monogamous or long-term

relationships are impossible for gay men. . . . The work-book teaches that there is something intrinsic in being gay that prevents men from sustaining long-term relation-ships, but it rarely discusses the constraints of a homo-phobic society or the legal restrictions on gay couples. . . . The terms of the debate disallowed for the possibility of a nonpathological view of a person who had multiple rela-tionships . . . (112–113)

Erzen's final point is well taken, and meshes nicely with Eric Clarke's analysis of the public sphere in *Virtuous Vice*: to see non-monogamous relationships as inherently pathological is reductive, and to hold such a view one must be profoundly blind to the moral valuation that originally informed the bourgeois, modern notion of citizenship and that continues to restrict what sorts of persons count as acceptable members of a community. Quite apropos of my own argument, Clarke writes: "This blockage can be seen in the force with which narrow group interests, such as Evangelical fundamentalism in the United States, have been able to hinder and/or unduly affect the inclusive potential of publicity for sexual minorities in particular (often under the guise of protecting reli-gious liberty in general)" (14).

9. For straight Christian teens, abstinence is a sacrifice with a term limit. Upon getting married, they are free to fuck like rabbits; sexual purity is defined as sex with one's spouse. But abstemiousness for ex-gays, with the exception of those few who marry women and/or manage to generate hetero desire, looms as a long-term com-mitment. Defined as abstemiousness, then, ex-gay identity is an identity founded on self-denial and abnegation. If we construe this as being in any way akin to Foucauldian ascesis, might it be viewed as liberating to the extent that it denatures traditional, especially conservative, Christianity? Or is that a trap? Is it too easy to see Christian ex-gays as imprisoned and ourselves thus as liberated (the sort of trap Foucault explodes at the outset of *The History of Sexuality, Volume 1* in regard to Victorian sexuality)? The ex-gays Erzen describes seem, by and large, unhappy. But who are we to say that shedding their evangelical beliefs would eliminate their emotional, psychological, or political conflict? Does a queer critical distance from institutionalized religion, perhaps, merely bring us

back to Lee Edelman's version of the antisocial thesis in *No Future: Queer Theory and the Death Drive*? Does one risk, by such a move, overidentifying queerness with solipsism? Is it possible to think critically and not succumb to the lure and/or appearance of moral superiority (the Marxist pitfall of enlightenment—even though queers are both inside and outside in a slightly different way than Marx's intellectual is)?

10. With equal humor and seriousness, Tim Dean points out the comparable risks, typically minimized by straights, that accompany heterosexual "breeding":

> Pursuing the comparison between breeding a baby and breeding the virus, we might observe that until quite recently, childbirth endangered the mother's life and that, even today, babies make their parents more vulnerable to illness by compromising their immune systems. Despite the risks, the inconvenience, and the enormous expense involved, straight people seem unable to stop themselves from breeding. Virtually all parents insist that these inconveniences—together with a lack of sleep and the extra coughs and colds that a baby brings—pale into insignificance beside the pleasure and satisfaction of their new child. Having a baby is life transforming and absolutely worth it, my peers assure me. Then again, barebackers attest that the pleasure and satisfaction achieved through unprotected sex and cum swapping is both life transforming and absolutely worth it. The inconvenience of a few extra illnesses, as well as the expense and hassle of extra medications, pale into insignificance beside the rapture of unencumbered fucking. (87)

Chapter 3. Jesus Needs Gays, Yes He Does

1. Here Dean seems consciously indebted to Michael Warner's analysis in *The Trouble with Normal* of "in-group purification" as it applies to the present-day gay and lesbian movement.
2. See Eric Clarke 1–6, 32–46. Clarke's work is indebted to earlier queer-focused public sphere theory, such as Michael Warner's

Publics and Counterpublics, in particular, chapters 1, 2, 5, and 6. Chapter 5, titled "Sex in Public" and coauthored with Lauren Berlant, is rightfully seen as a foundational text in queer studies' concern with citizenship.

3. Robert McRuer's *Crip Theory: Cultural Signs of Queerness and Disability* (2006) and Eric Clarke's *Virtuous Vice: Homoeroticism in the Public Sphere* (2000) yield informative comparisons with elements of my own project. *Crip Theory* interrogates models of disability as opportunities for those who are viewed as socially nonnormative—because of disabilities ranging from physical handicaps and medical diagnoses like HIV to queer sexuality itself—to "come out crip." Exploring the cultural alignment between heteronormativity and able-bodiedness, McRuer calls for a "critically disabled position" that "call[s] attention to the ways in which the disability rights movement and disability studies have resisted the demands of compulsory able-bodiedness and have demanded access to a newly imagined and newly configured public sphere where full participation is not contingent on an able body" (24, 30). Just as queer studies promised to exceed the theoretical grasp and political possibilities of gay and lesbian studies, McRuer offers "crip theory" in order to interrogate the field of disability studies, which he views as still beholden to notions of able-bodiedness. Crip theory is proposed as a way to "resist delimiting the kinds of bodies and abilities that are acceptable and will bring about change," a means of "collectively transforming . . . — [of] cripping—the substantive, material uses to which queer/disabled existence has been put by a system of compulsory able-bodiedness . . . [and] of imagining bodies and desires otherwise" (31, 32). McRuer's concept of "noncompliance" seems most pertinent to my own discussion of the Christian closet's potential not simply for oppressing its inhabitants but being co-opted, reconfigured, and in some ways resisted by its inhabitants. Chapter 3 of McRuer's book in particular offers an example that resonates with my own discussion of ex-gay ministries. *The Transformation*, a documentary that "detail[s one individual's] journey from the transgender streets of New York to a housed, married, and Fundamentalist Christian life in Dallas," exemplifies the force and success of individual "*refus[als of]* rehabilitation" relative to hegemonic "rehabilitative logic[s] of identity" that attempt to discount and quell resistance by "discount[ing]

. . . difference and noncompliance" (103, 121). McRuer's view is finally more optimistic than my own perspective, which seeks to balance speculative optimism with cautious realism when parsing the potential successes *and* the intransigent antagonisms that noncompliant identities may face in their bids to defuse, evade, and transform the punitive, inflexible properties of spaces like the Christian closet.

4. Admittedly, Eric Clarke would balk at the suggestion that queers ever could be meaningfully included within Western social and political culture, given the deep heteronormative biases underwriting Western notions of liberal pluralism that exclude what is nonnormative and dissident about queers even as (in some cases) they extend to queers certain delimited democratic rights. Legal and even cultural inclusion, Clarke argues, can thus ever only be partial because it fails to resolve much that remains problematic about mainstream heterosexual and queer notions of identity and community. I am inclined to agree with Clarke, which would seem to problematize my recommendation that queers distance themselves from religion, and that religion be barred from civil rights discourse, as being an incomplete solution. Certainly the problems facing queer inclusion extend beyond the damage inflicted by religious rhetoric and belief. And from some perspectives, like Clarke's, "inclusion" is a vexed term to use regarding queers and their actual or potential relation to mainstream culture. Despite my sympathy for Clarke's theoretical critique, however, practical legal, social, and cultural inclusion is a pressing matter for American queers at present. The end results of such a bid for inclusion may be fairly criticized as problematically normalizing; I would agree with such a critique and hold it to be especially fair in regard to same-sex marriage. Regardless, however, of the vexed implications of queer inclusion in such a normative institution, the fact remains that within the current legal reality, by which innumerable material rights and benefits are bundled with the institution of marriage, marriage is the simplest, though not unfreighted, means to queer civil parity. It seems disingenuous to ignore these material realities for a largely theoretical, rhetorical victory, or to dismiss out of hand the ethical parity, emotional dignity, and cultural inclusion queers may desire and find in both mainstream and more radical modes of queer belonging. While religion is certainly not the only obstacle

to such projects of communal realization nor the only problematically heteronormative aspect of civil discourse and society, this is
the scope to which I have confined my efforts. There is enough
work to be done within these limits, and enough convincing that
needs to be done, such that moving beyond religion is an indispensable first step.

5. George Rekers's outing is discussed in the introduction to the present volume. Ted Haggard, an evangelical minister and the president of the National Association of Evangelicals who was regularly
consulted by the Bush White House on policy matters and who
advocated a gay marriage ban in his home state of Colorado, was
outed in 2006 by the gay escort with whom he had been having sex
for three years. For more on Haggard and other prominent outings
of conservative religious and political operatives in the early 2000s,
see W. C. Harris, *Queer Externalities*, 143–175.

6. Additional coverage of the Brock scandal appeared on Queerty.
com and *Huffington Post* (the latter being a repost of the Associated
Press story).

7. In addition to the gay religious and spiritual endeavors referenced
here, additional sources may be of interest. *Authorizing Marriage?
Canon, Tradition, and Critique in the Blessing of Same-Sex Unions*,
ed. Mark Jordan, Meghan Sweeney, and David Mellott, scrutinizes
the Judeo-Christian tradition so often invoked by opponents of gay
marriage and finds it to be far from singular and not exclusively
proscriptive of same-sex unions. Justin Lee's *Torn: Rescuing the
Gospel from the Gays-vs.-Christians Debate* urges gay inclusivity on
Christians in the name of authentic faith. *Gay Religion*, ed. Scott
Thumma and Edward Gray, ranges usefully through the diversity
of religious communities and experiences within the American
GLBT community, from evangelicals, Seventh-Day Adventists,
and Latter-Day Saints to radical faeries, leathermen, and circuit
queens.

8. Eric Clarke (10–16, 19–20, 50–67) delivers a subtle analysis of
public sphere value determination as it affects queers and results
from a "confusion between . . . economic and political equivalence"
(55).

9. Wolkomir offers a variety of sociological explanations for whether
participants choose to follow the ex-gay or the gay Christian path.
Yet the fundamental reason may be simply that they want to be

one, gay or Christian, *more* than they want to be the other (see Wolkomir 89). The religious environment in which ex-gays may have been raised or which they later seek out arguably shapes their willingness and perhaps ability to weigh the two components of their identity with objectivity and full autonomy. Even so, enough individuals have abandoned ex-gay therapies—becoming "ex-ex-gays"—to suggest that such approaches fail to foreclose identity integration altogether. Similarly, Melissa Wilcox concludes that, while organizations such as MCC or Dignity may support queers in their reconciliation with a religious identity, the initial steps to integration are typically taken *outside* the church. Churches or other religiously affiliated groups are approached once the individual has already taken steps toward developing his or her own gay-positive religious identity (see 13, 117–124). Wilcox asserts that, in contrast to ex-gays, most gay Christians in her study made "the shift on their own," "not at the urging of a religious leader or based upon changing teachings in their church or denomination" (157). Of the five patterns of GLBT religious identity integration identified by Wilcox, only one "relies significantly on community *during* the coming-out process as well as after the fact"; "in four out of five patterns, the main events take place outside of religious communities, sometimes but not always culminating in a return to congregational attendance" (63).

10. Tolerance or rejection of either homosexuality or gay and lesbian congregants is rarely uniform within single denominations or faith traditions. While this variation may occur in moderate sects, it tends to be more noticeable, and perhaps surprising, in traditions whose popular image or loudest public voice is conservative, such as evangelical Christianity or the Catholic Church. For instance, Courage and Dignity are two groups catering to gay Catholics. Courage preaches acceptance of homosexual congregants on the condition that they abstain from gay sex; although this group does not consider itself an ex-gay ministry, the terms of its tolerance, conditional on not acting on one's sexual desires, bears an inescapably heteronormative bias. Straight Catholics don't have to stop having sex because, implicitly, their kind of sex is not sinful. The group Dignity, by contrast, embraces the sexual *and* the religious identity of gay Catholics. Not officially endorsed by

the Catholic Church, which still holds to the sophistic distinction between sin and sinner, Dignity does not preach abstention and also endorses social and political activism. Consequently, many chapters of Dignity meet by choice or necessity in non-Catholic facilities. Some dioceses do allow chapters of Dignity to meet at Catholic churches and even welcome gays and lesbians to services. As might be expected, however, tolerance from officially intolerant institutions is subject to abrupt reversal: in 2010 the interim head of the San Antonio, Texas, archdiocese ended the previous archbishop's fifteen-year policy of welcoming GLBT Catholics, claiming that "simply allowing LGBT Catholics to worship as a group made Jesus weep, and could . . . not be tolerated" (Jones, "San Antonio Archdiocese" par. 3). By contrast, MCC does not represent the only attempt to forge a liberal path for religious gays and lesbians. Former Jesuit priest John McNeill offers a synthesis of progay theology, sex positivity, pastoral care, and psychotherapy in *The Church and the Homosexual* and *Taking a Chance on God: Liberating Theology for Gays, Lesbians, and Their Lovers, Families, and Friends*. Regardless of my own position, it can be a matter of individual taste whether or not these efforts to embrace queers remain hampered by religion's record on homosexuality and by its doctrinal touchstones (reliance on scripture, liturgy, and Mariology, for example).

11. Joe Dallas, *Desires in Conflict* (209–227) and Kerby Anderson (65–75) provide representative ex-gay and straight conservative Christian rebuttals of the idea that condemnation of homosexuality is not original to biblical texts but the result of human prejudice and errors in translation. The debate over whether or not homosexuality is biblically proscribed continues with strenuous contributions from both sides. Other contributions from the antigay side include Joe Dallas, *The Gay Gospel? How Pro-Gay Advocates Misread the Bible*; Joe Dallas and Nancy Heche, *The Complete Christian Guide to Understanding Homosexuality: A Biblical and Compassionate Response to Same-Sex Attraction*; and Robert J. A. Gagnon, *The Bible and Homosexual Practice: Texts and Hermeneutics*. Significant progay volumes that refute antigay scriptural exegeses by those like Dallas and Gagnon are Linda J. Patterson, *Hate Thy Neighbor: How the Bible Is Misused to Condemn Homosexuality*; Jack Rogers, *Jesus,*

the Bible, and Homosexuality: Explode the Myths, Heal the Church; and R. D. Weekly, *The Rebuttal: A Biblical Response Exposing the Deceptive Logic of Anti-Gay Theology.*

12. In *Regulating Aversion: Tolerance in the Age of Identity and Empire*, Wendy Brown observes that even "an individual bearing of tolerance in nonpolitical arenas carries authority and potential subjection through unavowed norms. Almost all objects of tolerance are marked as deviant . . . by virtue of being tolerated, and the action of tolerance inevitably affords some access to superiority" (14). As a "disciplinary strategy of liberal individualism," tolerance's

> [d]esignated objects . . . are invariably marked as undesirable and marginal, as liminal civil subjects or even liminal humans; and those called upon to exercise tolerance are asked to repress or override their hostility or repugnance in the name of civility, peace or progress. . . . This regulatory individuation of the deviant, the abject, the other, suggests a further implication of the normalizing work of contemporary tolerance discourse. Tolerated individuals will always be those who deviate from the norm, never those who uphold it, but they will also be further articulated as (deviant) individuals through the very discourse of tolerance. (28, 44)

13. See Sedgwick 87–90 for further discussion of these distinct yet overlapping and sometimes cross-pollinating trains of queer thought.

14. Toby Johnson's paean to gay sex is likewise overeffusive: "In our homosexuality itself is our experience of 'God'": "all sex is sex with God" (xvi, 36). While in some quarters gay sex remains a target for expressions of disgust or outrage, and while romanticizing gay sex and desire makes for a pleasant change from its cultural erasure and vilification, the amount of energy *Gay Spirituality* spends making gay sex feel normal verges on idealizing it as superior. Not only does such a move merely invert the dynamic of heteronormativity instead of seeking to even the balance, it also counterproductively distracts us from the very real and malign sway of heterosexuality's culturally comprehensive—and in the United States, legally exclusive—imprimatur.

15. Sedgwick is quoting, respectively, Don Mager, "Gay Theories of Gender Role Deviance," *SubStance* 46 (1985): 36; and James D. Steakley, *The Homosexual Emancipation Movement in Germany* (New York: Arno, 1975), 24.

16. See, for example, Johnson 7–8, 267–268.

17. A complicity in Johnson's work between spirituality and religion can be further deduced from his repeated, haphazard equivalence between two terms that so many religious moderates or spiritual seekers attempt to strongly differentiate. Contrary to this frequent distinction, Johnson describes *spirituality* as "the positive aspects of religion"—a notion he ascribes to unnamed "contemporary religious revolutionaries" [xiii]. For instance, he states that "the primary focus of religion is the experience of consciousness," but he also regards broadening one's consciousness as requisite to spiritual enlightenment (87). *Gay Spirituality*'s avowed hope is the formation of a "pro-gay, life-positive religion"—in short, "homosexuality *as* religion" (261; emphasis added). This doesn't seem to solve the problem of the normative values and rigidity that tend to accompany institutionalization.

18. Noteworthy predecessors in this progressively minded, anti-essentialist tradition include gay and lesbian liberation writers Carl Wittman and Martha Shelley, semioticians of AIDS and HIV such as Paula Treichler and Douglas Crimp, and the rich proliferation of queer theory catalyzed by three seminal works published in 1990: David Halperin's *One Hundred Years of Homosexuality*, Eve Sedgwick's *The Epistemology of the Closet*, and Judith Butler's *Gender Trouble*. A valuable instance of queer theory's "first wave" in the early 1990s remains the anthology *Fear of a Queer Planet*, ed. Michael Warner.

19. See Marjorie Garber, *Vice Versa: Bisexuality and the Eroticism of Everyday Life*; Christopher James, "Denying Complexity: The Dismissal and Appropriation of Bisexuality in Queer, Lesbian, and Gay Theory"; and Maria Pramaggiore and Donald E. Hall, eds., *RePresenting Bisexualities: Subjects and Cultures of Fluid Desire*. In *Queer Externalities* (178–188) I address the benefits and the costs of a sexual identification such as bisexual that *resists* identification in the ostensibly narrow, essentializing terms by which, the bisexual argument goes, most gays, lesbians, and straights identify.

20. At times *The Queer God*'s defense of bisexuality's radicalness is

more cryptic than it is convincing: "This is obviously not a question of an individual sexual identity, but of an epistemological identity which considers bisexuality critically, that is, not assuming that bisexuality *per se* is a liberative force unless there is a critical reflection of its relation to other sexualities" (15). Similarly, Althaus-Reid's elaboration of a "truly Trinitarian [extra-dyadic] sexual identity" fails to distinguish satisfyingly between a bisexuality that is "disjunctive [and] unstable," never ossifying into routine, and a bisexuality that's just as liable to oppositionality as either homosexuality or heterosexuality (59).

21. See also Foucault 41–43, 155.

22. For other instances of queer theology's non- or extra-institutional ambitions, see Althaus-Reid 37–38, 43, 74–75, 168.

CHAPTER 4. SLOUCHING TOWARDS GAYTHEISM

1. In *The New Gay Teenager*, Cornell University psychologist Ritch Savin-Williams discusses flaws and assumptions in the most frequently cited statistics for suicide risk among gay and lesbian youth. In a brief article for *Live Science*, Benjamin Bradford reviews methodological critiques by Savin-Williams as well as Joel Best (University of Delaware professor of sociology and criminal justice and author of *Damned Lies and Statistics*).

2. In March 2012 Clementi's roommate, Dharun Ravi, was sentenced to a thirty-day jail term, three hundred hours of community service, three years' probation, and a $10,000 fine to go to a hate-crime victims' fund. The sentence "divided many gay rights activists, with some arguing that 30 days was little more than a slap on the wrist, and others arguing that his conduct, while despicable, did not merit the same punishment as the kind of violent or threatening behavior typically associated with bias crimes" (Zernike pars. 6). Sentencing judge Glenn Berman described Ravi's actions as "unconscionable" yet said he could "not find it in me to remand him to a state prison that houses people convicted of offenses such as murder, armed robbery and rape" (par. 2). Hate crime laws typically recommend five- to ten-year sentences. Although Ravi was "found 'guilty of all 15 charges against him (including invasion of privacy and anti-gay intimidation),'" he "was not charged with

causing Clementi's death. And while the jury was told Clementi had taken his life, prosecutors did not argue directly that the spying led to his suicide" (Mulvihill pars. 2, 17).

The 2010 suicides of Clementi and other gay teens were covered by numerous alternative and GLBT media organizations, bloggers, and, in some but not all cases, national media outlets. The accounts I referenced include those by Advocate.com editors ("Gay R.I. Student Commits Suicide"), Associated Press ("US Student Tyler Clementi"), J. D. ("Oakland University Student Corey Jackson"), Jesse McKinley ("Suicides Put Light on Pressures"), Max Simon ("Teenager Justin Aaberg Killed Himself Over Gay Bullying"), and John Wright.

3. For a thorough analysis of the most common arguments for same-sex marriage and a run-through of their flaws, see chapter 3 of Michael Warner's *The Trouble with Normal.* As Warner observes, the most woeful deficit in same-sex marriage defenses is not sentimentality or blind heteronormativity but the failure to discuss the prejudicial bundling of innumerable economic rights, social benefits, and cultural cachet with the institution of marriage. Permitting gays and lesbians to marry would extend those benefits to a slightly larger number of Americans, but only to those who wished to get married. Same-sex marriage would do little to alter the tendentious restriction of benefits to certain groups of people, married individuals, but not others.

4. For a fuller discussion of "the Child" as the engine of heteronormativity and of queerness's opposition to "reproductive futurism," see chapter 1 of Edelman's *No Future: Queer Theory and the Death Drive.*

5. For a clear-eyed analysis of President Obama's options according to military and constitutional legal experts, see Ben Adler. David Badash ("'Don't Ask, Don't Tell' Repeal Dead") speculated on the fate of the repeal after the 2010 midterms.

6. By the end of 2012, eight federal courts (in California, Connecticut, Florida, Massachusetts, New York, and Washington) had found section 3 of DOMA, which defines marriage heterosexually, unconstitutional on issues regarding immigration, employee benefits, and estate taxes.

7. Legislative and executive stonewalling of efforts to repeal DADT were made more bewildering by the Pentagon's own survey of

400,000 active-duty and 150,000 military spouses. The survey found that "more than 70 percent of respondents . . . said the effect of repealing the . . . policy would be positive, mixed, or nonexistent" (O'Keefe and Jaffe par. 2). The strongest opposition came from the Marine Corps, and even there opponents of repeal were in the minority at 40 percent. "The survey results led the report's authors to conclude," the *Washington Post* reported, "that objections to openly gay colleagues would drop once troops were able to live and serve alongside them" (par. 2). Of course, straight military personnel were *already* living and serving alongside them.

My focus on the DADT repeal, Proposition 8, and gay teen suicide—issues much in the news between 2010 and 2013—is not meant to elide other pressing issues facing the GLBT community, such as affordable access to HIV medication. As Michael Warner writes in *Publics and Counterpublics*, an exclusive turn to "state-oriented politics in the American gay movement, always a danger in the public-sphere discourse, represents a real loss of insight and action in dominant circles of gay and lesbian organizing" (223). Warner's comment refers specifically to the 1993 march on Washington whose organizers "pushed the gays-in-the-military issue, rather than AIDS, into the spotlight." First made in 1995, this comment remains a salubrious reminder of the power of state-oriented issues to incite "amnesia" about other, more personally threatening circumstances and to impede queers' ability or desire to find alternative models of social and political relation: "What besides patriotism could smother the antinational sensibilities of queers who have seen so many die for no country? What could more affirm the state's expression of the nation? What could more weaken the culture of resistance to a state that has added AIDS inaction to its earlier history of heteronormative policing? . . . It's possible to oppose the ban on gays in the military and still believe that this sentiment costs too much" (223).

For coverage of the repeal's near-failure on the floor of Congress in December 2010, see Andy Towle ("Senate Rejects Defense Bill"). A piece by Servicemembers Legal Defense Network details pushback during senate repeal hearings against Senator John McCain's vehement anti-repeal position by figures like Joint Chiefs of Staff chairman Admiral Mullen and Secretary of Defense Robert Gates. The repeal's successful passage only days later was reported

NOTES TO CHAPTER 4

on by sources such as Ed O'Keefe and CNN Wire Staff ("House Passes 'Don't Ask, Don't Tell' Repeal" [Dec. 2010] and "Senate Votes to Repeal Ban on Gays Openly Serving in Military"). Negative reactions to the repeal were heard almost immediately, as one might expect, from McCain, Rep. Louie Gohmert (R-TX), Marine Corp commandant General James Amos, and the American Family Association's Bryan Fischer. For coverage of these reactions, see, respectively, "Jon Kyl: DADT Repeal Could Cost Lives"; Elyse Siegel; Advocate.com editors, "Rep. Gohmert on Oversexed Gay Soldiers"; Chip Somodevilla; Bryan Fischer, "Benedict Arnold Republicans Destroy Military." Liberty Counsel's Matthew Staver called for DADT's reinstitution "in the next Congress" (Advocate.com editors, "Antigay Group: DADT Will Be Back" par. 5).

8. For discussion of Obama's instruction for nondefense of DOMA, see Associated Press, "Obama: DOMA Unconstitutional, DOJ Should Stop Defending in Court"; Chris Cassidy; and Kerry Eleveid. Joe Sudbay reports on the first DOMA challenge—issued to Congress, not the president, since the DOJ was not to defend the law. Responses from Boehner and other House Republicans are addressed by Chris Geidner ("Speaker Boehner's DOMA Defense Lawyer"), Linda Hirshman, and Ryan J. Reilly.

9. For the 8–1 SCOTUS decision in favor of Westboro Baptist Church's First Amendment rights (Justice Alito was the lone dissenter), see Sean Gregory.

10. On September 13, 2010, University of Michigan student assembly president Chris Armstrong filed for a PPO (personal protection order, popularly known as a restraining order) against Assistant Attorney General Shirvell, and the university followed by banning Shirvell from campus. Less than three weeks later, Shirvell took a leave of absence from his post at the state attorney general's office; he was fired soon afterward. In late October, Armstrong and his lawyers requested that the PPO be dropped—perhaps, one speculates, out of concern that the order might be a liability if Shirvell later wanted to claim infringement of free speech rights. Although at this time cyberbullying was not illegal in Michigan, Shirvell was not just any citizen engaged in antigay harassment: he held a federal government appointment as a state prosecutor. His boss, Michigan attorney general Mike Cox, initially criticized Shirvell's actions but quickly reversed himself and asserted his underling's

"right to free speech outside working hours" (qtd. in Steve Williams par. 43). Cox is right in one regard: the online harassment occurred on Shirvell's "non-work related blog"—a blog titled, one should note, "Chris Armstrong Watch," a blog created and devoted to the harassment of one person (qtd. in Steve Williams par. 38). Although Shirvell's homophobic words and deeds may not be legally actionable (I leave the subtleties of free speech arguments to others), what I find disheartening is that neither the attorney general (who did comment) nor *his* superior, President Obama (who did not), saw nothing inappropriate in Shirvell conducting antigay tirades while sitting as a representative of the Department of Justice, even on his own time. Developments in the case were tracked by Advocate.com editors ("Michigan Pol on Antigay Harassment"), Rachel Brusstar, David Jesse, and Steve Williams. There were two encouraging footnotes to the incident. In March 2012 Shirvell lost the appeal to have his firing overturned; according to "William Hutchens of the Michigan Civil Service Commission . . . Shirvell was justly dismissed after engaging in 'hate speech' and 'physical and mental harassment'" ("Michigan Civil Service Commission Upholds Firing"). Then in August 2012 a Michigan jury "ordered [Shirvell] to pay $4.5 million in damages" for "harassing" and "stalking" Armstrong. The fervency of Shirvell's homophobia can be gauged by his refusal to accept a plea bargain according to which charges would have been dropped had he simply apologized (Grindley pars. 1, 2; see also Jeff Karoub).

11. A clear antecedent for Love's book is Michael Warner's *The Trouble with Normal*, particularly chapter 2, which explores the modern gay and lesbian movement's assimilationist shame over nonnormative elements of its own community and identity. More recently, *Gay Shame* (2010), edited by David M. Halperin and Valerie Traub, looks "beyond gay pride"—beyond "liberation, legitimacy, dignity, acceptance, and assimilation"—to typically spurned yet potentially enriching and critically enabling aspects of queer identity such as abjection (3).

12. The video made by Fort Worth, Texas, councilman Joel Burns during a city council meeting stands out as a notable exception to this trend; there may be others.

13. On calls to recriminalize homosexuality as part of the GOP platform in Texas, see Aliyah Shahid; for similar efforts in Montana,

see Associated Press, "Montana Republican Party Wants to Make Homosexuality a Crime."

14. The 2001 and 2008 ARIS surveys can be accessed through the organization's website, www.americanreligionsurvey-aris.org. "UK among Most Secular Nations" reviews the findings of the 2004 survey of 10,000 people in ten countries as part of the BBC program "What the World Thinks of God"; Frank Newport discusses the 2008 Gallup poll findings.

15. As touchstones for recent defenses of atheism and critiques of religion, Harris's *The End of Faith* and Hitchens's *God Is Not Great* seem natural choices. In addition to their mainstream notoriety and accessibility, these books capture elegantly and in fairly condensed fashion the points about religion most relevant to my argument. Similar points, as well as others not immediately pertinent to my own purposes (such as refutations of intelligent design arguments), can be found in the following recent volumes: Dan Barker, *Godless: How an Evangelical Preacher Became One of America's Leading Atheists*; Richard Dawkins, *The God Delusion*; Sam Harris, *Letter to a Christian Nation*; Jennifer Michael Hecht, *Doubt: A History*; John Loftus, ed., *The Christian Delusion: Why Faith Fails*; John Loftus, *Why I Became an Atheist: A Former Preacher Rejects Christianity*; and Daniel Sennett's *Breaking the Spell: Religion as a Natural Phenomenon*. Bertrand Russell's *Why I Am Not a Christian* remains a valuable repository of masterly, still quite timely, polemics against religion's excesses, irrationality, and moral corrosiveness.

16. One notable difference is the disagreement between Harris and Hitchens on, respectively, religion's basic usefulness or toxicity. Contrary to Harris, who contends that mysticism, meditation, and certain strains of Eastern religion offer possibilities for ethical development (40–41, 43, 214), Hitchens views Hinduism and Buddhism as being no more conducive to ethical behavior or happiness than other traditions (199).

17. Numerous European and American advocacy groups, of course, vocally oppose the brutish custom of female genital mutilation, and many countries with Muslim populations have outlawed these practices. The point is that, for those individuals who still practice it, religion's mandate must be followed, regardless of civil law or rational argument. Hitchens dissects religious misinformation about AIDS and HPV (human papillomavirus) (46–48) and attacks

defenses of and/or refusals to criticize practices such as female and male circumcision because they are religiously prescribed in spite of their damage to one's psychological and physical health (50–51, 226).

18. On the accretion of temporal authority to religious leaders who are putatively more interested in nonworldly, spiritual matters, see Hitchens 103; on the objectively irreconcilable conflict in goals and methodology between religion and science, see Hitchens 64–65, 149–151, 260.

19. Bertrand Russell forcefully summarizes religion's long working relationship with coercion, intimidation, and the suppression or discouragement of dissent: "the three human impulses embodied in religion are fear, conceit, and hatred. . . . It is because these passions make, on the whole, for human misery that religion is a force for evil, since it permits men to indulge these passions without restraint, where but for its sanction they might, at least to a certain degree, control them" (44).

20. This point has been made before, of course. Bertrand Russell's version of it, in "What I Believe" and "Can Religion Cure Our Troubles," remains as urgent as the more recent polemics of Christopher Hitchens and Sam Harris. Rational review, evidence, and open-minded debate, Russell insists, will separate empty superstition from ethical guidelines *independent* of religion. Contrary to the objections of religious apologists, "the dependence of morals upon religion is [not] nearly as close as religious people believe it to be. . . . [V]ery important virtues are more likely to be found among those who reject religious dogmas than among those who accept them . . . [such as] truthfulness [and] intellectual integrity. . . . As soon as it is held that any belief . . . is important for some other reason than that it is true, a whole host of evils is ready to spring up. Discouragement of inquiry . . . is the first of these" (194, 197).

21. Unshakeable certainty of an afterlife inspires all manner of irresponsible, cruel, and barbarous behavior. Muslim suicide bombers are, for Harris, the most extreme example, but the promise of an afterlife kindles, if not logically demands, violent words and acts in adherents of any faith. As Harris observes, "A single proposition—*you will not die*—once believed, determines a response to life that would be otherwise unthinkable. . . . While religious people are not generally mad, their core beliefs absolutely are" (36, 73).

Of religion's self-undermining exertions to prove itself, Hitchens writes: "Religion doesn't in fact rely on 'faith' at all but instead corrupts faith and insults reason by offering evidence and pointing to confected 'proofs' [such as] arguments from design, revelations . . . and miracles. . . . [I]t is within the compass of any human being to see these evidences and proofs as the feeble-minded inventions that they are" (71). Harris similarly notes that religion's truth claims make it vulnerable to logical challenge (63, 68, 95).

22. For further commentary on religion's unique status as exempt from criticism, see Harris 13–14, 20, 27, 36, 46, 223, 237; on the impact of religious moderates on social and political debate, see Harris 15, 23, 45.

23. The original passage comes from Will Durant, *The Age of Faith* (1950, reprint, Norwalk CT: Easton Press, 1992), 784.

24. For further analysis of religion's immoral predisposition, see Hitchens 203–205, 210, 242. Ethics, by contrast, can be derived from reason and, argues Harris, from science as well (220). Bertrand Russell (56–76) stresses the importance of working out ethics in common, not as matters of individual interest (as religion encourages), balancing conflicting desires as much as possible, and subjecting traditions like religious guidelines, which are so often founded on superstition rather than practicality or utility, to rational review.

25. For further commentary by Sam Harris on the externality of ethics to religion, see 78, 106, 169–72, 179, 182, 185–87, 191, 226.

26. Although Western media coverage tends to describe honor killings as "'tribal' practice[s] . . . they almost invariably occur in a Muslim context" (Harris 187).

27. Given its predilection for rules that are "[im]possible to obey," "revelation from absolute authority," and "enforce[ment] by fear," Hitchens regards religion as a "totalitarian" and "stupefying dictatorship" (212).

CONCLUSION: BEFORE THE COCK CROWS

1. Like Perkins, Gallagher argues that her crusade against same-sex marriage does not foster an environment conducive to antigay bullying (see J. D., "Maggie Gallagher Blames Gay Teens' Homosexuality for Their Deaths").

NOTES TO CONCLUSION

2. Perkins's op-ed, and the *Post*'s decision to run it, raised the quickest objections from the alternative press, mainly in gay and straight blogs and forums (Jeremy Hooper, "And Now in Undeserved Credence News"; Evan Hurst, Andrew Marin, Rick Rosendall, Joe Solomonese, and Nick Wing). K. Debelen's coverage for *Mass Live* was an early mainstream response.

3. David Badash ("Poll: Vast Majority of Americans Blame Churches for Gay Teen Suicides") also discusses the poll results.

4. For additional coverage of Judge Tauro's anti-DOMA ruling, see Michael Levenson and Rachel Slajda.

5. Where federal protections for gays and lesbians existed (before the 2013 SCOTUS decision on DOMA, that is), they were still quite limited: hospital visitation rights and, for federal employees only, partner benefits and employment discrimination. Even these marginal advances have been fiercely decried by the religious and political Right, see Americans for Truth about Homosexuality; Eric W. Dolan; Joe Jervis, "American Family Association and Liberty Counsel"; and Max Simon).

6. Despite routine claims to the contrary by conservative pundits and news organizations, the U.S. Constitution is fairly clear on church-state separation: Article VI protects officeholders from having to ascribe to any religion to qualify for public office; the First Amendment prohibits the government establishment of a state religion and protects citizens' freedom of religious exercise. From the late nineteenth century onward, the U.S. Supreme Court case has upheld this separation.

7. For sample coverage, see, respectively, Carol Williams and Chris Geidner ("Massachusetts Wants Supreme Court").

8. Halperin cites the origin of "horizontal" versus "vertical" social relations as Guy Hocquenghem's *Le Désir homosexuel*, a foundational work of French Marxist/gay liberation theory originally published in 1972.

9. A November 2012 poll conducted by LifeWay Research (which, along with the Christian bookstore chain LifeWay, is owned by the Southern Baptist Convention) showed that a mere "37 percent [of respondents] affirm a belief that homosexual behavior is a sin—a statistically significant change from . . . 44% percent" one year earlier (Rankin par. 2). However, the finer details of the survey, while encouraging to queer Americans and their allies, and, one

imagines, discouraging for most of LifeWay's customer base, show slow but not irreversible progress toward greater tolerance. Only 2 percent of those who viewed homosexuality as a sin in the first survey shifted to the "not a sin" column in 2012; the rest of the decrease in the "not a sin" column responded "I don't know." Life-Way Research president Ed Stetzer pointed to Obama's change in his position on same-sex marriage as a catalyst in the "evolution of cultural values" (par. 4). Most relevant to my argument are the disaggregated 2012 survey numbers showing a high correlation between antigay sentiments and religious beliefs and habits. Seventy-three percent of respondents identifying as "born-again, evangelical, or fundamentalist" viewed homosexuality as sinful; for respondents who attend religious services weekly, the figure was 61 percent. Even if LifeWay is oversampling conservative Christians compared to other demographics, the numbers indicate that attitudes regarding homosexuality, while definitely shifting toward greater tolerance, have not yet undergone a sea change. The numbers also suggest that religion is one of, though arguably not the only, stumbling block to further change. (See also the *Huffington Post* piece, "Americans Who Believe Homosexuality Is a Sin Decreases Significantly.")

WORKS CITED

Aarthun, Sarah. "Chick-fil-A Wades into a Fast-Food Fight over Same-Sex Marriage Rights." CNN. 27 July 2012. Web. 16 Aug. 2012.

Adler, Ben. "Is Obama's Excuse for Not Repealing 'Don't Ask, Don't Tell' Legitimate?" *Newsweek*. 19 Oct. 2010. Web. 22 Oct. 2010.

Advocate.com editors. "Antigay Attack at 7-Eleven in Colorado." *Advocate*. 25 Oct. 2010. Web. 25 Oct. 2010.

Advocate.com editors. "Gay R. I. Student Commits Suicide." *Advocate*. 1 Oct. 2010. Web. 22 Oct. 2010.

Advocate.com editors. "Michigan Pol on Antigay Harassment: 'It's Nothing Personal.'" *Advocate*. 29 Sept. 2010. Web. 26 Oct. 2010.

Advocate.com editors. "Rep. Gohmert on Oversexed Gay Soldiers." *Advocate*. 21 Dec. 2010. Web. 21 Dec. 2010.

Alcorn, Randy. *The Purity Principle: God's Safeguards for Life's Dangerous Trials*. New York: Waterbrook Multnomah-Random House, 2003. Print.

Althaus-Reid, Marcella. *The Queer God*. London: Routledge, 2003. Print.

Americans for Truth about Homosexuality. "Should Gay TSA Agents Be Barred from Giving 'Same-Gender Pat-Downs?'" Americans for Truth about Homosexuality. 16 Nov. 2010. Web. 21 Nov. 2010.

"Americans Who Believe Homosexuality Is a Sin Decreases Significantly: LifeWay Research Poll." *Huffington Post*. 11 Jan. 2013. Web. 11 Jan. 2013.

Anderson, Kerby. *A Biblical Point of View on Homosexuality*. Eugene: Harvest House, 2008. Print.

Archdiocese of Chicago. "'Same-Sex Marriage': What Do Nature and Nature's God Say?" Rpt. in *Chicago Sun Times*. 3 Jan. 2013. Web. 5 Jan. 2013.

Arana, Gabriel. "Giving Bullies a Pass." *American Prospect*. 9 Nov. 2010. Web. 11 Nov. 2010.

Arterburn, Stephen, and Kenny Luck. *Every Day for Every Man: 365 Readings for Those Engaged in the Battle*. Colorado Springs: Water-Brook, 2008. Print.

Arterburn, Stephen, and Kenny Luck. *Every Young Man, God's Man: Confident, Courageous, and Completely His*. Colorado Springs: WaterBrook, 2010. Print.

Arterburn, Stephen, and Fred Stoeker. *Every Man's Marriage: An Every Man's Guide to Winning the Heart of a Woman*. Colorado Springs: WaterBrook, 2010. Print.

Arterburn, Stephen, Fred Stoeker, and Mike Yorkey. *Every Man's Battle: Winning the War on Sexual Temptation One Victory at a Time*. Colorado Springs: WaterBrook, 2009. Print.

Arterburn, Stephen, Fred Stoeker, and Mike Yorkey. *Every Young Man's Battle: Strategies for Victory in the Real World of Sexual Temptation*. Colorado Springs: WaterBrook, 2002. Print.

Associated Press. "Obama: DOMA Unconstitutional, DOJ Should Stop Defending in Court." *Huffington Post*. 23 Feb. 2011. Web. 23 Feb. 2011.

Associated Press. "Montana Republican Party Wants to Make Homosexuality a Crime." *RawStory*. 18 Sept. 2010. Web. 21 Oct. 2010.

Associated Press. "Schools Confront Anti-Gay Bullying Across the Country." Fox News. 9 Oct. 2010. Web. 21 Oct. 2010.

Associated Press (Minneapolis). "Tom Brock, Hope Lutheran Church Reverend Who Attends Gay Support Group While Advocating against Gay Clergy Expected to Keep Job." *Huffington Post*. 27 June 2010. Web. 27 June 2010.

Associated Press. "US Student Tyler Clementi Jumps to His Death over Sex Video." *The Guardian (UK)*. 30 Sept. 2010. Web. 12 Oct. 2010.

Babwin, Don. "Chicago Alderman to Block Chick-Fil-A Expansion." *Huffington Post*. 25 July 2012. Web. 19 Aug. 2012.

Badash, David. "Beat the Gay Out of Kids Pastor Apology Attacks Homosexuality as 'Abomination.'" *The New Civil Rights Movement*. 2 May 2012. Web. 19 Aug. 2012.

Badash, David. "'Don't Ask, Don't Tell' Repeal Dead—Unless Reid Acts Immediately." *The New Civil Rights Movement*. 4 Nov. 2010. Web. 5 Nov. 2010.

Badash, David. "Herman Cain: Chick-fil-A Donating Up to $30 Million to Anti-Gay Groups." *The New Civil Rights Movement*. 3 Aug. 2012. Web. 4 Aug. 2012.

Badash, David. "Poll: Vast Majority of Americans Blame Churches for Gay Teen Suicides." *The New Civil Rights Movement*. 21 Oct. 2010. Web. 24 Oct. 2010.

Bannerman, Lucy. "The Camp That 'Cures' Homosexuality: At a Christian 'Boot Camp' in the US, Those Struggling to Reconcile Faith and Sexuality Are Taught to Overcome Gayness." *Times Online*. 7 Oct. 2008. Web. 25 May 2010.

Barbaro, Michael. "A Scramble as Biden Backs Same-Sex Marriage." *New York Times*. 6 May 2012. Web. 16 Aug. 2012.

Barker, Dan. *Godless: How an Evangelical Preacher Became One of America's Leading Atheists*. Berkeley: Ulysses, 2008. Print.

Besen, Wayne. "Gay Conversion: The Religious Right's Violent Bully Pulpit." *Huffington Post*. 11 Oct. 2010. Web. 22 Oct. 2010.

Best, Joel. *Damned Lies and Statistics: Untangling Numbers from the Media, Politicians, and Activists*. Berkeley: U of California P, 2001. Print.

Blume, K. Allan. "'Guilty as Charged,' Cathy Says of Chick-fil-A's Stand on Biblical and Family Values." *Baptist Press*. 16 June 2012. Web. 18 June 2012.

Bowers, Betty. "Betty Bowers Explains Traditional Marriage to Everyone Else." 2 June 2009. Online video clip. YouTube. 17 Aug. 2012.

Bradford, Benjamin. "Is There a Gay Teen Suicide Epidemic?" *Live Science*. 8 Oct. 2010. Web. 23 Oct. 2010.

Brandzel, Amy. "Queering Citizenship? Same-Sex Marriage and the State." GLQ 11.2 (March 2005): 171–204. Print.

Brayton, Ed. "Obama on Gay Marriage." Dispatches from the Creation Wars. ScienceBlogs. 25 Aug. 2010. Web. 15 Oct. 2010.

Broverman, Neal. "Antigay Group: DADT Will Be Back." Advocate. 20 Dec. 2010. Web. 21 Dec. 2010.

Broverman, Neal. "Hateful Pastor Sean Harris Thinks Effeminate Children Are Ungodly." Advocate. 2 May 2012. Web. 16 Aug. 2012.

Broverman, Neal. "School Official Wants Gays Dead." Advocate. 26 Oct. 2010. Web. 27 Oct. 2010.

Broverman, Neal. "McCance: I Have Family to Consider." *Advocate.* 27 Oct. 2010. Web. 27 Oct. 2010.

Brown, Michael L. *A Queer Thing Happened to America: And What a Long, Strange Trip It's Been.* Concord: Equal Time, 2011. Print.

Brown, Wendy. *Regulating Aversion: Tolerance in the Age of Identity and Empire.* Princeton: Princeton UP, 2006. Print.

Brusstar, Rachel. "AG's Office: Shirvell Took Leave of Office on Own Accord, Will Be Subject to Disciplinary Hearing upon Return." *Michigan Daily.* 30 Sept. 2010. Web. 26 Oct. 2010.

Bullock, Penn, and Brandon K. Thorp. "Christian Right Leader George Rekers Takes Vacation with 'Rent Boy.'" Miami New Times.com. 6 May 2010. Web. 18 May 2010.

Burack, Cynthia. *Sin, Sex, and Democracy: Antigay Rhetoric and the Christian Right.* Albany: SUNY P, 2008. Print.

Burns, Jim. *The Purity Code: God's Plan for Sex and Your Body.* Grand Rapids: Bethany House, 2008. Print.

Butler, Judith. *Gender Trouble.* New York: Routledge, 1990. Print.

Canaday, Margot. *The Straight State: Sexuality and Citizenship in Twentieth-Century America.* Princeton: Princeton UP, 2009. Print.

Cassidy, Chris. "Obama: Down with DOMA." *Huffington Post.* 23 Feb. 2011. Web. 23 Feb. 2011.

"Cazwell . . . It Gets Better." YouTube. 20 Oct. 2010. Web. 22 Oct. 2010.

Chambers, Alan. "I Am Sorry." Exodus International.org. 19 June 2013. Web. 13 July 2013.

Chambers, Alan, Randy Thomas, Mike Goeke, Scott Davis, and Melissa Fryrear. *God's Grace and the Homosexual Next Door: Reaching the Heart of the Gay Men and Women in Your World.* Eugene: Harvest House, 2006. Print.

Chapman, Patrick M. *"Thou Shalt Not Love": What Evangelicals Really Say to Gays.* Foreword by Daniel A. Helminiak. New York: Haiduk, 2008. Print.

Chauncey, George. *Gay New York: Gender, Urban Culture, and the Making of the Gay Male World 1890–1940.* New York: Basic Books, 1994. Print.

"Chick-fil-A Confirms 'Record-Setting Day' on 'Appreciation Day.'" FOX News. 2 Aug. 2012. Web. 16 Aug. 2012.

Clarke, Eric O. *Virtuous Vice: Homoeroticism and the Public Sphere.* Durham: Duke UP, 2000.

CNN Wire Staff. "Arkansas School Board over Anti-Gay Post." CNN. 29 Oct. 2010. Web. 29 Oct. 2010.

CNN Wire Staff. "House Passes 'Don't Ask, Don't Tell' Repeal." CNN. 15 Dec. 2010. Web. 19 Dec. 2010.

CNN Wire Staff. "Houses Passes 'Don't Ask, Don't Tell' Repeal." CNN. 28 May 2010. Web. 19 Dec. 2010.

CNN Wire Staff. "Senate Votes to Repeal Ban on Gays Openly Serving in Military." CNN. 18 Dec. 2010. Web. 19 Dec. 2010.

CNN Wire Staff and Susan Candiotti. "Eight Arraigned in String of Anti-Gay Hate Crimes in New York City." CNN. 10 Oct. 2010. Web. 11 Oct. 2010.

Cobb, Michael. *God Hates Fags: The Rhetorics of Religious Violence.* New York: NYU P, 2006. Print.

Cody, Emily. "American Culture Wars in Uganda." *The Mantle: A Forum for Progressive Critique.* 17 Apr. 2012. Web. 3 Jan. 2013.

Connolly, Ceci. "Some Abstinence Programs Mislead Teens, Report Says." *Washington Post.* 2 Dec. 2004. Web. 20 May 2010.

Cox, Ted. "What Happened When I Went Undercover at a Christian Gay-to-Straight Conversion Camp." Stinque.com. 13 Apr. 2010. Web. 10 October 2010.

Crimp, Douglas. *Moralism and Melancholia: Essays on AIDS and Queer Politics.* Boston: MIT P, 2004. Print.

Dallas, Joe. *Desires in Conflict: Hope for Men Who Struggle with Sexual Identity.* 1991. Rev. ed. Eugene: Harvest House, 2003. Print.

Dallas, Joe. *The Gay Gospel? How Pro-Gay Advocates Misread the Bible.* Eugene: Harvest House, 2007. Print.

Dallas, Joe, and Nancy Heche. *The Complete Christian Guide to Understanding Homosexuality: A Biblical and Compassionate Response to Same-Sex Attraction.* Eugene: Harvest House, 2010. Print.

Daniels, Robert. *The War Within: Gaining Victory in the Battle for Sexual Purity.* Wheaton: Crossway, 2005. Print.

Dawkins, Richard. *The God Delusion.* New York: Houghton Mifflin, 2008. Print.

Debelen, K. "Bullying News Links: Tony Perkins Draws Fire on Column about Bullying of Gays." *Mass Live.* 15 Oct. 2010. Web. 21 Oct. 2010.

Dean, Tim. *Unlimited Intimacy: Reflections on the Subculture of Barebacking.* Chicago: U of Chicago P, 2009. Print.

Dolan, Eric W. "Anti-Gay Group: "'Homosexual' TSA Staff 'Secretly Turned On' by Patdowns." *Raw Story.* 17 Nov. 2010. Web. 21 Nov. 2010.

Ebersole, Ryan. "Chick-Fil-A Debate Largely Misses the Point." *Open Salon.* 2 Aug. 2012. Web. 16 Aug. 2012.

Edelman, Lee. *No Future: Queer Theory and the Death Drive.* Durham: Duke UP, 2004.

Edwards, David. "Top Democrat Ready to Kill Effort to Ban 'Don't Ask, Don't Tell." *Raw Story.* 8 Nov. 2010. Web. 8 Nov. 2010.

Eichler, Alex. "Critiquing 'It Gets Better Project' for Gay Teens." *The Atlantic Wire.* 8 Oct. 2010. Web. 23 Oct. 2010.

Eleveid, Kerry. "Obama and DOMA: The Unspoken Truth and How We Got Here." *Equality Matters.* 24 Feb. 2011. Web. 24 Feb. 2011.

"Ellen DeGeneres' JCPenney Partnership Slammed by Anti-Gay Group One Million Moms."*Huffington Post.* 1 Feb. 2012. Web. 17 Aug. 2012.

Erzen, Tanya. *Straight to Jesus: Sexual and Christian Conversions in the Ex-Gay Movement.* Berkeley: U of California P, 2006. Print.

Ethridge, Shannon. *Every Woman's Battle: Discovering God's Plan for Sexual and Emotional Fulfillment.* Colorado Springs: Waterbrook, 2009. Print.

Ethridge, Shannon, and Stephen Arterburn. *Every Young Woman's Battle: Guarding Your Mind, Heart, and Body in a Sex-Saturated World.* Colorado Springs: Waterbrook, 2004.

Family Research Council of America. *Getting It Straight: What the Research Shows about Homosexuality.* Washington: Family Research, 2004. Print.

Femmephane. "FAQ of Savage Dissent." *Tempcontretemps.* Wordpress. com. 6 Oct. 2010. Web. 11 Oct. 2010.

Femmephane. "Why I Don't Like Dan Savage's 'It Gets Better' Project as a Response to Bullying." *Tempcontretemps.* Wordpress.com. 30 Sept. 2010. Web. 11 Oct. 2010.

Fischer, Bryan. "Benedict Arnold Republicans Destroy Military and Our National Security."*Rightly Concerned.* American Family Association. 18 Dec. 2010. Web. 19 Dec. 2010.

Fischer, Bryan. "SPLC Propagates Falsehoods about Homosexuality;

Belongs on Own List." American Family Association. 17 Aug. 2012. Web. 17 Aug. 2012.

Floyd, Ronnie W. *The Gay Agenda: It's Dividing the Family, the Church, and a Nation*. Green Forest: New Leaf, 2004. Print.

Foucault, Michel. *The History of Sexuality, Volume 1*. 1976. Trans. Robert Hurley. New York: Vintage, 1990. Print.

Friedman, Ann. "Straight Talk." *American Prospect*. 9 Nov. 2010. Web. 11 Nov. 2010.

Fuss, Diana. *Essentially Speaking: Feminism, Nature, and Difference*. New York: Routledge, 1989. Print.

Gagnon, Robert J. A. *The Bible and Homosexual Practice: Texts and Hermeneutics*. Nashville: Abingdon Press, 2001. Print.

Garber, Andrew. "Starbucks Supports Gay Marriage Legislation." *Seattle Times*. 24 Jan. 2012.Web. 17 Aug. 2012.

Garber, Marjorie. *Vice Versa: Bisexuality and the Eroticism of Everyday Life*. New York: Simon and Schuster, 1995. Print.

Geidner, Chris. "Massachusetts Wants Supreme Court to Hear DOMA Challenge." *Buzzfeed*. 24 July 2012. Web. 16 Aug. 2012.

Geidner, Chris. "Speaker Boehner's DOMA Defense Lawyer, Paul Clement, Is Announced—and Faces Questions." Poliglot. *Metro Weekly*. 18 Apr. 2011. Web. 19 Apr. 2011.

Gibbs, Nancy. "The Pursuit of Teen Girl Purity." *Time*. 17 July 2008. Web. 20 May 2010.

Gibbs, Nancy, and Lucas L. Johnson II. "The Ick Factor Regarding Purity Balls." HamptonRoads.com. 19 Feb. 2010. Web. 20 May 2010.

Gibson, David. "Cardinal Francis George Launches Effort against Illinois Same-Sex Marriage." *Huffington Post*. 2 Jan. 2013. Web. 3 Jan. 2013.

Gilbert, Mitchell. "Pastor Orders His Flock to Beat Gay People Arriving at Church." Addicting Info. 4 Oct. 2011. Web. 16 Aug. 2012.

Gilgoff, Dan. "Christian Group Pulls Support for Event Challenging Homosexuality." *CNN Belief Blog*. CNN.com. 6 Oct. 2010. Web. 7 Oct. 2010.

Greenwald, Glenn. "Inhumane Impact of DOMA." *Salon*. 26 Oct. 2010. Web. 26 Oct. 2010.

Gregory, Sean. "Why the Supreme Court Ruled for Westboro." *Time*. 3 Mar. 2011. Web. 30 Jan. 2013.

Gresh, Dannah. *And the Bride Wore White: Seven Secrets to Sexual Purity.* Chicago: Moody, 2004. Print.

Grindley, Lucas. "Andrew Shirvell Ordered to Pay Millions for Defaming Gay Student." *Advocate.* 16 Aug. 2012. Web. 16 Aug. 2012.

Grindley, Lucas. "My Life Isn't a Political Issue." *Advocate.* 2 Aug. 2012. Web. 16 Aug. 2012.

Gustav-Wrathall, John Donald. *Take the Young Stranger by the Hand: Same-Sex Relations and the YMCA.* Chicago: U of Chicago P, 2000. Print.

Hall, Donald. *Queer Theories.* New York: Palgrave, 2003. Print.

Halperin, David M. *How to Be Gay.* Cambridge: Harvard UP, 2012. Print.

Halperin, David M. *One Hundred Years of Homosexuality and Other Essays on Greek Love.* New York: Routledge, 1990. Print.

Halperin, David M., and Valerie Traub, eds. *Gay Shame.* Chicago: U of Chicago P, 2010.

Haraway, Donna. *Simians, Cyborgs, and Women: The Reinvention of Nature.* New York: Routledge, 1990. Print.

Harris, Joshua. *Sex Is Not the Problem (Lust Is): Sexual Purity in a Lust-Saturated World.* New York: Waterbrook Multnomah-Random House, 2005. Print.

Harris, Sam. *The End of Faith: Religion, Terror, and the Future of Reason.* New York: Norton, 2004. Print.

Harris, Sam. *Letter to a Christian Nation.* New York: Knopf, 2006. Print.

Harris, W. C. *Queer Externalities: Hazardous Encounters in American Culture.* Albany: SUNY P, 2009. Print.

Hasan, Heba. "Anti-Gay Group Slams JCPenney over Father's Day Ad." *Time.* 3 June 2012. Web. 17 Aug. 2012.

Hecht, Jennifer Michael. *Doubt: A History.* New York: HarperOne-HarperCollins, 2003. Print.

Henneman, Todd. "Sex, Lies, Teenagers: Abstinence-Only Sex Education Erases the Existence of GLBT Youth and Fills Kids' Heads with Untruths. Some Parents Have Had Enough." *Advocate.* 16 Aug. 2005. Web. 20 May 2010.

Herman, Didi. *The Antigay Agenda: Orthodox Vision and the Christian Right.* Chicago: U of Chicago P, 1998. Print.

Hess, Rick, and Jan Hess. *A Full Quiver: Family Planning and the Lordship of Christ.* Brentwood: Wolgemuth and Hyatt, 1990. Print.

Heywood, Todd A. "Gay Leaders Concerned about Abstinence-Only Education Grants." *The Michigan Messenger.* 13 Jan. 2009. Web. 20 May 2010.

Hill, Wesley. *Washed and Waiting: Reflections on Christian Faithfulness and Homosexuality.* Grand Rapids: Zondervan, 2010. Print.

Hirshman, Linda. "DOMA Laid Bare: House Republicans Defense of DOMA Will Be Rooted in Their Own Ugly History." *Slate.* 10 Mar. 2011. Web. 16 Mar. 2011.

Hitchens, Christopher. *God Is Not Great: How Religion Poisons Everything.* New York: Grand Central, 2007. Print.

Hooper, Jeremy. "And Now in Undeserved Credence News: WaPo Gives Anti-Bullying Ink to Man Who Says Gays Are 'Held Captive by the Enemy.'" *Good As You.* 12 Oct. 2010. Web. 21 Oct. 2010.

Hooper, Jeremy. "With Latest Comments, Chick-fil-A Can No Longer Deny Anti-LGBT Feelings." *Good As You.* 18 July 2012. Web. 19 Aug. 2012.

Howell, Joe. "Free Speech, Free Enterprise, and Chick-Fil-A." *Seattle Times.* 16 Aug. 2012.Web. 19 Aug. 2012.

Hsu, Tiffany. "Gay Activists Counter Chick-fil-A with Starbucks Appreciation Day." *Los Angeles Times.* 6 Aug. 2012. Web. 16 Aug. 2012.

Hu, Elise. "Chick-fil-A Gay Flap a 'Wakeup Call' for Companies." NPR. 27 July 2012. Web.16 Aug. 2012.

Hughes, Thomas. *The Manliness of Christ.* Boston: Houghton Mifflin, 1879. Print.

"Human Sexuality." Frc.org. Family Research Council, n.d. Web. 20 May 2010.

Hurst, Evan. "Dear *Washington Post*: Tony Perkins' Bigotry Is Not 'Faith.'" *Truth Wins Out.*12 Oct. 2010. Web. 21 Oct. 2010.

"It Gets Better: Dan and Terry." YouTube. 21 Sept. 2010. Web. 11 Oct. 2010.

Jakobsen, Janet R., and Ann Pellegrini. *Love the Sin: Sexual Regulation and the Limits of Religious Tolerance.* 2003. Boston: Beacon, 2004. Print.

James, Christopher. "Denying Complexity: The Dismissal and Appropriation of Bisexuality in Queer, Lesbian, and Gay Theory." *Queer Studies: A Lesbian, Gay, Bisexual, and Transgender Anthology,* ed. Brett Beemyn and Michelle Eliason. New York: NYU P, 1996. 217–231. Print.

J. D. "High Schoolers Behind 'Powder Blue Faggots' Chant Won't Be Suspended ('Cause There's Too Many of Them)." *Queerty.* 20 Oct. 2010. Web. 21 Oct. 2010.

J. D. "Lutheran Pastor Tom Brock Gets 2 Weeks Off for Having Sex in Slovakia." *Queerty.* 18 June 2010. Web. 27 June 2010.

J. D. "Maggie Gallagher Blames Gay Teens' Homosexuality for Their Deaths." *Queerty.* 20 Oct. 2010. Web. 21 Oct. 2010.

J. D. "Oakland University Student Corey Jackson, 19, Hangs Himself. Was Bullying a Factor?"*Queerty.* 20 Oct. 2010. Web. 24 Oct. 2010.

Jeltsen, Melissa. "Chick-fil-A Has 'Record-Setting Day' While Embroiled in Anti-Gay Controversy." *Huffington Post.* 2 Aug. 2012. Web. 16 Aug. 2012.

Jervis, Joe. "American Family Association and Liberty Counsel Object to Hospital Rights for Gays." *Joe. My. God.* 19 Nov. 2010. Web. 20 Nov. 2010.

Jervis, Joe. "Crimes against Humanity Case against Scott Lively to Begin Monday." *Joe. My. God.* 3 Jan. 2013. Web. 3 Jan. 2013.

Jervis, Joe. "Meet Geo, the Male Prostitute Hired by NARTH Member and Family Research Council Co-Founder Dr. George Rekers." *Joe. My. God.* 4 May 2010. Web. 18 May 2010.

Jervis, Joe. "Predictable: Navel-Gazing Over-Intellectualizing Queer Theorists Attack Dan Savage's 'It Gets Better.'" *Joe. My. God.* 6 Oct. 2010. Web. 7. Oct. 2010.

Jesse, David. "U-M Student Body President Armstrong Drops Restraining Order Request against Andrew Shirvell." AnnArbor. com. 25 Oct. 2010. Web. 26 Oct. 2010.

Johnson, Lucas L., II. "Purity Balls Feature Lessons on 'Appropriate' Dance Moves." *Huffington Post.* 20 Jan. 2010. Web. 20 May 2010.

Johnson, Toby. *Gay Spirituality: Gay Identity and the Transformation of Human Consciousness.* 2000. Maple Shade: White Crane, 2004. Print.

"Jon Kyl: DADT Repeal Could Cost Lives." *Huffington Post.* 19 Dec. 2010. Web. 19 Dec. 2010.

Jones, Michael A. "Arkansas School Board Member Says Gay Students Should 'Get AIDS and Die.'" *Gay Rights.* Change.org. 26 Oct. 2010. Web. 27 Oct. 2010.

Jones, Michael A. "San Antonio Archdiocese Says No More Gays at Mass." *Gay Rights.*Change.org. 23 Oct. 2010. Web. 27 Oct. 2010.

Jones, Michael A. "Texas Pastor: Christians Have a Moral Obligation to Stop Anti-Gay Bullying." *Gay Rights.* Change.org. 26 Oct. 2010. Web. 27 Oct. 2010.

Jones, Michael A. "Walmart to Sell Book about Curing Gay People." *Gay Rights.* Change.org. 8 Oct. 2010. Web. 11 Oct. 2010.

Jones, Stanton L., and Mark A. Yarhouse. *Ex-Gays? A Longitudinal Study of Religiously Mediated Change in Sexual Orientation.* Downers Grove: InterVarsity, 2007. Print.

Jones, Zinnia. "Chick-Fil-A: Because It's Only 'Free Speech' If You Agree with Homophobes." *The New Civil Rights Movement.* 2 Aug. 2012. Web. 19 Aug. 2012.

Jordan, Mark D., Meghan T. Sweeney, and David M. Mellott, eds. *Authorizing Marriage? Canon, Tradition, and Critique in the Blessing of Same-Sex Unions.* Princeton: Princeton UP, 2006. Print.

Joyce, Kathryn. *Quiverfull: Inside the Christian Patriarchy Movement.* Boston: Beacon, 2009. Print.

Karoub, Jeff. "Andrew Shirvell, Lawyer Ordered to Pay $4.5M to Gay University of Michigan Student Christopher Armstrong." *Huffington Post.* 16 Aug. 2012. Web. 17 Aug. 2012.

"Kleefisch's Comments Draw Protest." *Channel3000.* 28 Oct. 2010. Web. 7 Nov. 2010.

Koehlinger, Jim, and Pam Koehlinger. *Protecting His Workmanship: Teaching Your Child God's Design for Sexual Purity.* Midland: Search for the Truth, 2005. Print.

Kopf, Abbie. "Gay Teens Ignored or Misled Through Abstinence-Only Sex Ed. Change.org. 17 Feb. 2010. Web. 20 May 2010.

Kors, Joshua. "Q & A with Dan Savage: On Obama, Fox News' Shepard Smith, and Success of 'It Gets Better' Campaign." *Huffington Post.* 10 May 2011. Web. 10 May 2011.

Landau, Elizabeth. "$250 Million for Abstinence Education Not Evidence-Based, Groups Say." CNN. 31 Mar. 2010. Web. 21 Oct. 2010.

LaVictoire, Bridgette. "Cindy McCain Contradicts NoH8 PSA with Tweet Backing Sen. McCain on DADT." *Lezgetreal.* 12 Nov. 2010. Web. 12 Nov. 2010.

Lee, Justin. *Torn: Rescuing the Gospel from the Gays-vs.-Christians Debate.* New York: Jericho, 2012. Print.

Levenson, Michael. "Judge Declares US Gay Marriage Ban Is Unconstitutional." Boston.com. 8 July 2010. Web. 26 Oct. 2010.

Lewin, Tamar. "Quick Response to Study of Abstinence Education."
    New York Times. 2 Feb. 2010. Web. 9 Oct. 2010.

Loftus, John W., ed. *The Christian Delusion: Why Faith Fails*. Amherst:
    Prometheus, 2010. Print.

Loftus, John W. *Why I Became an Atheist: A Former Preacher Rejects
    Christianity*. Amherst: Prometheus, 2008. Print.

Lorde, Audre. "The Master's Tools Will Never Dismantle the Master's
    House." 1979. *Sister Outsider: Essays and Speeches*. Berkeley: Cross-
    ing Press, 1984. 110–114. Print.

Love, Heather. *Feeling Backward: Loss and the Politics of Queer Shame*.
    Cambridge: Harvard UP, 2007. Print.

Lu, Andrew. "Chick-fil-A's Gay Marriage Fight Hits Boston, Chi-
    cago." *Reuters*. 26 July 2012.Web. 16 Aug. 2012.

Ludy, Leslie. *Answering the Guy Questions: The Set-Apart Girl's Guide to
    Relating to the Opposite Sex*. Eugene: Harvest House, 2009. Print.

Marin, Andrew. "No 'Christian Compassion' in Tony Perkins' Response
    to Anti-Gay Bullying."*Religion Dispatches*. 18 Oct. 2010. Web. 21
    Oct. 2010.

Mather, Kate, and Jenny Stockdale. "Chick-fil-A 'Kiss In' Protest Tries
    to Challenge Appreciation Day." *Los Angeles Times*. 3 Aug. 2012.
    Web. 16 Aug. 2012.

McCartin, Jeanné. "Starbucks' Support for Gay Marriage Divides
    Consumers." *Seacoast Online*. 29 Mar. 2012. Web. 16 Aug. 2012.

McGregor, Jena. "Amid Chick-fil-A Uproar, Amazon CEO Jeff Bezos
    Takes a Stand on Gay Marriage." *Washington Post*. 27 July 2012.
    Web. 16 Aug. 2012.

McKinley, Jesse. "Suicides Put Light on Pressures of Gay Teenagers."
    New York Times. 3 Oct.2010. Web. 11 Oct. 2010.

McKinley, Jesse, and Kirk Johnson. "Mormons Tipped Scale in Ban on
    Gay Marriage." *New York Times*. 14 Nov. 2008. Web. 5 Nov. 2010.

McNeill, John J. *Taking a Chance on God: Liberating Theology for Gays,
    Lesbians, and Their Lovers, Families, and Friends*. 1988. Boston:
    Beacon, 1996. Print.

McNeill, John J. *The Church and the Homosexual*. 1976. 4th ed. Boston:
    Beacon, 1993.

McRuer, Robert. *Crip Theory: Cultural Signs of Queerness and Disability*.
    New York: NYU P, 2006. Print.

"Michigan Civil Service Commission Upholds Firing of Assistant AG over Anti-Gay Bullying." *ThinkProgress.* 28 Mar. 2012. Web. 17 Aug. 2012.

Michigan Department of Community Health. "Michigan Abstinence Program." Michigan.gov, n.d. Web. 3 June 2010.

Mordden, Ethan. "The Straight; or, Field Expedients." *I've a Feeling We're Not in Kansas Anymore: Tales from Gay Manhattan.* 1985. New York: St. Martin's, 1996. 10–21. Print.

MSJacks. "Dan Savage's 'It Gets Better' Project: A Counter-Response." *The Bitter Buffalo.* Wordpress.com. 3 Oct. 2010. Web. 23 Oct. 2010.

Muggleton, David, and Rupert Weinzierl, eds. *The Post-Subcultures Reader.* Oxford: Oxford UP, 2003. Print.

Mulvihill, Geoff. "Dharun Ravi Found Guilty in Webcam Spying Trial." WABC. *ABC Local.* 16 Mar. 2012. Web. 18 Mar. 2012.

Murk, Brienne. *Eyes Wide Open: Avoiding the Heartbreak of Emotional Promiscuity.* Ventura: Regal, 2007. Print.

Nathan, Melanie. "Aftermath for McCance, Midland Arkansas School District Board Bully." *Lezgetreal.* 26 Oct. 2010. Web. 27 Oct. 2010.

Neroulias, Nicole. "Americans Say Religious Messages Fuel Negative Views of Gays." Religion News Service. *Huffington Post.* 21 Oct. 2010. Web. 22 Oct. 2010.

Newport, Frank. "Belief in God Far Lower in Western U.S." *Gallup.* 28 July 2008. Web. 22 Oct. 2010.

Nicolosi, Joseph. *A Parent's Guide to Preventing Homosexuality.* Downers Grove: InterVarsity, 2002. Print.

O'Keefe, Ed. "'Don't Ask, Don't Tell' Is Repealed by Senate; Bill Awaits Obama's Signing."*Washington Post.* 19 Dec. 2010. Web. 19 Dec. 2010.

O'Keefe, Ed, and Greg Jaffe. "Sources: Pentagon Group Finds There Is Minimal Risk to Lifting Gay Ban During War." *Washington Post.* 11 Nov. 2010. Web. 11 Nov. 2010.

"One Millions Moms Condemns JCPenney Again for Same-Sex Mother's Day Catalog Photo." *Huffington Post.* 3 May 2012. Web. 17 Aug. 2012.

"'One Million' Moms Responds to JCPenney's Gay Dads Ad." *Huffington Post.* 31 May 2012. Web. 17 Aug. 2012.

O'Toole, James. "Starbucks Supports Gay Marriage." CNN. 25 Jan. 2012. Web. 16 Aug. 2012.

Pace, Julie. "Obama ABC Interview: President Voices Support for Gay Marriage." *Huffington Post.* 9 May 2012. Web. 16 Aug. 2012.

Patterson, Linda J. *Hate Thy Neighbor: How the Bible Is Misused to Condemn Homosexuality.* New Conshohocken: Infinity, 2009. Print.

People Can Change. "Founding and Growth." PeopleCanChange.com. n.d. Web. 13 Oct. 2010.

Perkins, Bill, and Randy Southern. *When Young Men Are Tempted: Sexual Purity for Guys in the Real World.* Grand Rapids: Zondervan, 2007. Print.

Perkins, Tony. "Christian Compassion Requires the Truth about Harms of Homosexuality." *On Faith.* Washington Post.com. 12 Oct. 2010. Web. 12 Oct. 2010.

Petrecca, Laura. "In Gay Marriage Fight, Some Companies Take a Stand." *USA Today.* 29 July 2012. Web. 16 Aug. 2012.

Phillip, Abby. "Gay Marriage Advocates Gain Corporate Support." *Politico.* 3 June 2012. Web. 16 Aug. 2012.

Pfeiffer, Eric. "Jim Henson Company Breaks Ties with Chick-fil-A over Gay Marriage Stance." *Yahoo News.* 23 July 2012. Web. 16 Aug. 2012.

Poovey, Mary. *Uneven Developments: The Ideological Work of Gender in Mid-Victorian England.* Chicago: U of Chicago P, 1988. Print.

Pramaggiore, Maria, and Donald E. Hall, eds. *RePresenting Bisexualities: Subjects and Cultures of Fluid Desire.* New York: NYU P, 1996. Print.

QSaltLake staff. "Walmart Carrying Antigay Book for Children." *QSaltLake.* 7 Oct. 2010. Web. 11 Oct. 2010.

Rankin, Russ. "Fewer Americans Believe Homosexuality." *LifeWay Research.* LifeWay, 10 Jan. 2013. Web. 11 Jan. 2013.

Reilly, Ryan J. "Lamar Smith Says Founding Fathers Didn't Want Gay Marriage." *TPM Muckraker. Talking Points Memo.* 18 Apr. 2011. Web. 19 Apr. 2011.

Rix, Jallen. *Ex-Gay No Way: Survival and Recovery from Religious Abuse.* Forres, Scotland: Findhorn, 2010. Print.

Rogers, Jack. *Jesus, the Bible, and Homosexuality: Explode the Myths, Heal the Church.* Louisville: Westminster John Knox, 2009. Print.

Rosendall, Rick. "Why Does *WaPo* Give Tony Perkins a Platform for His Filth?" *GLAA Forum.* 12 Oct. 2010. Web. 21 Oct. 2010.

Rubin, Gayle. "Thinking Sex: Notes for a Radical Theory of the Politics of Sexuality." *Pleasure and Danger*, ed. Carol Vance. London: Routledge, 1984. Print. 267–319.

Rubin, Gayle. "The Traffic in Women: Notes on the 'Political Economy' of Sex." *The Second Wave: A Reader in Feminist Theory*, ed. Linda Nicholson. New York: Routledge, 1997. 27–62.

Russell, Bertrand. *Why I Am Not a Christian and Other Essays on Religion and Related Subjects*. New York: Touchstone-Simon and Schuster, 1957. Print.

Sandfort, Theo G. M., Ron de Graaf, Rob V. Bijl, and Paul Schnabel. "Same-Sex Sexual Behavior and Psychiatric Disorders: Findings from the Netherlands Mental Health Survey and Incidence Study (NEMSIS)." *Archives of General Psychiatry* 58 (2001): 85–91. Web. 4 Nov. 2010.

Savage, Dan. "In Your Image." *The Stranger.* 14 Oct. 2010. Web. 22 Oct. 2010.

Savin-Williams, Ritch C. *The New Gay Teenager.* Cambridge: Harvard UP, 2006. Print.

Schlatter, Evelyn. "18 Anti-Gay Groups and Their Propaganda." *Southern Poverty Law Center Intelligence Report* 140 (Winter 2010). Web. 17 Aug. 2012.

Sears, Alan, and Craig Osten. *The Homosexual Agenda: Exposing the Principal Threat to Religious Freedom.* Nashville: B & H, 2003. Print.

Sedgwick, Eve Kosofsky. *Epistemology of the Closet.* Berkeley: U of California P, 1990. Print.

Seidman, Steven. "Identity and Politics in a 'Postmodern' Gay Culture: Some Historical and Conceptual Notes." *Fear of a Queer Planet: Queer Politics and Social Theory*, ed. Michael Warner. Minneapolis: U of Minnesota P, 1993. 105–142. Print.

Self, Wayne. "The Chick Fellatio: Stuck in the Craw." *Owldolatrous.* 30 July 2012. Web. 16 Aug. 2012.

Sennett, Daniel C. *Breaking the Spell: Religion as a Natural Phenomenon.* New York: Penguin, 2006. Print.

Servicemembers Legal Defense Network. "Update: Gates, Mullen, Johnson, Hamm All Push Back on McCain in U.S. Senate Hearing." *Servicemembers Legal Defense Network.* 2 Dec. 2010. Web. 3 Dec. 2010.

Severson, Kim. "Chick-fil-A Thrust Back into Spotlight on Gay Rights." *New York Times.* 25 July 2012. Web. 16 Aug. 2012.

Shahid, Aliyah. "Texas GOP Platform: Criminalize Gay Marriage and Ban Sodomy, Outlaw Strip Clubs and Pornography." *New York Daily News.* 22 June 2010. Web. 21 Oct.2010.

Shelley, Martha. "Gay Is Good." *Out of the Closets: Voices of Gay Liberation*, ed. Jay Karla and Allen Young. 1972. 2nd edition. New York: NYU P, 1992. 31–34. Print.

Siegel, Elyse. "John McCain DADT Repeal Reaction: 'Today Is a Very Sad Day." *Huffington Post.* 18 Dec. 2010. Web. 19 Dec. 2010.

Simon, Max. "Peter LaBarbera Worries He Won't Be Sexually Molested During TSA Screening." *Queerty.* 17 Nov. 2010. Web. 21 Nov. 2010.

Simon, Max. "Teenager Justin Aaberg Killed Himself Over Gay Bullying: His Mom Won't Let Anyone Forget." *Queerty.* 14 Sept. 2010. Web. 11 Oct. 2010.

Slajda, Rachel. "Federal Judge Rules Part of DOMA Unconstitutional." *Talking Points Memo.* TPMlivewire.com. 8 July 2010. Web. 26 Oct. 2010.

Solomonese, Joe. "Enough of Tony Perkins." On Faith. *Washington Post.* 14 Oct. 2010. Web. 16 Oct. 2010.

Somodevilla, Chip. "DADT: Now the Really Hard Part Begins." *Newsweek.* 19 Dec. 2010. Web. 19 Dec. 2010.

"Starbucks Shareholders Ask CEO Schultz about Controversial Gay Marriage Stance." 21 Mar. 2012. Online video clip. YouTube. 24 Mar. 2012.

Steveningen. "A Demoralized James Dobson Admits His Defeat." *Daily Kos.* 7 Jan. 2013. Web. 7 Jan. 2012.

St. James, Rebecca. *Wait for Me: Rediscovering the Joy of Purity in Romance.* Nashville: Thomas Nelson, 2008. Print.

Stoeker, Fred, Brenda Stoeker, and Mike Yorkey. *Every Heart Restored: A Wife's Guide to Healing in the Wake of a Husband's Sexual Sin.* Foreword by Stephen Arterburn. Colorado Springs: WaterBrook, 2010. Print.

Stohr, Greg. "Kennedy Questions Whether Court Should Rule on Gay Marriage." *Bloomberg.* 26 Mar. 2013. Web. 12 July 2013.

Sudbay, Joe. "Judge Gives Congress until April 18 to Intervene in NY DOMA Case." *America Blog Gay.* 15 Mar. 2011. Web. 16 Mar. 2011.

Tedder, Ryan. "Why Is Walmart Selling Janice Barrett Graham's Ex-Gay Parenting Book?" *Queerty.* 8 Oct. 2010. Web. 11 Oct. 2010.

Tedder, Ryan. "WI Lt. Gov. Hopeful Rebecca Kleefisch: Gay Marriage Leads to Dog Marriage, but I'm Not Being Insensitive." *Queerty.* 27 Oct. 2010. Web. 27 Oct. 2010.

Tenety, Elizabeth. "Chick-fil-A Appreciation Day' Announced by Mike Huckabee amidst Gay Marriage Debate." *Washington Post.* 23 July 2012. Web. 16 Aug. 2012.

Thumma, Scott, and Edward R. Gray, eds. *Gay Religion.* Lanham: Altamira, Rowman & Littlefield, 2005. Print.

Tiku, Nitasha. "Cindy McCain Blames Gay Teen Suicides and Bullying on DADT, Her Husband." *New York Times.* 12 Nov. 2010. Web. 12 Nov. 2010.

Tousey, Ben. *My Egypt: Why I Left the Ex-Gay Movement.* Bloomington: AuthorHouse, 2006. Print.

Towle, Andy. "Ohio H. S. Targets Rival Team with Chant: 'Powder Blue Faggots.'" *Towleroad.* 18 Oct. 2010. Web. 21 Oct. 2010.

Towle, Andy. "Senate Rejects Defense Bill, 'Don't Ask, Don't Tell' Repeal in 57–40 Vote." *Towleroad.* 9 Dec. 2010. Web. 19 Dec. 2010.

Townsend, John. "Antigay Lutheran Pastor Protests Too Much." *Lavender* 18 June 2010. LavenderMagazine.com. Web. 27 June 2010.

Treichler, Paula. *How to Have Theory in an Epidemic: Cultural Chronicles of AIDS.* Durham: Duke UP, 1999. Print.

"UK among Most Secular Nations." *BBC News.* 26 Feb. 2004. Web. 22 Oct. 2010.

Valdez, Emily. "Gay Slurs Chanted at Football Game; School Under Fire." *Fox 8 Cleveland.* 19 Oct. 2010. Web. 1 Nov. 2010.

Valenti, Jessica. *The Purity Myth: How America's Obsession with Virginity Is Hurting Young Women.* Berkeley: Seal, 2009. Print.

Vallotton, Kris. *Purity: The New Moral Revolution.* Shippensburg: Destiny Image, 2008. Print.

Van Leer, David. *The Queening of America: Gay Culture in Straight Society.* New York: Routledge, 1995.

Walker, Sirdeaner. "Addressing Anti-GLBT Bullying: Something All Christians Can Support." On Faith. *Washington Post.* 12 Oct. 2010. Web. 12 Oct. 2010.

Warner, Michael, ed. *Fear of a Queer Planet: Queer Politics and Social Theory.* Minneapolis: U of Minnesota P, 1993. Print.

Warner, Michael. *Publics and Counterpublics.* New York: Zone, 2002. Print.

Warner, Michael, ed. *The Trouble with Normal: Sex, Politics, and the Ethics of Queer Life.* Cambridge: Harvard UP, 1999. Print.

Weekly, R. D. *The Rebuttal: A Biblical Response Exposing the Deceptive Logic of Anti-Gay Theology.* St. Louis: Judah First, 2011. Print.

"What Is a Purity Ball?" GenerationsofLight.com. Generations of Light, n.d. Web. 20 May 2010.

White, Mel. *Holy Terrors: Lies the Christian Right Tells Us to Deny Gay Equality.* New York: Magnus, 2006. Print.

Wilcox, Melissa M. *Coming Out in Christianity: Religion, Identity, and Community.* Bloomington: Indiana UP, 2003. Print.

Williams, Carol. J. "Defense of Marriage Act Ruled Unconstitutional by Judge." *Los Angeles Times.* 23 Feb. 2012. Web. 16 Aug. 2012.

Williams, Steve. "Asst. Attorney General Cyber-Bullies Gay College Student." Care2.com. N. d. Web. 26 Oct. 2010.

Wing, Nick. "Tony Perkins: Gay Teens Resort to 'Depression or Suicide' because They Know They're 'Abnormal.'" *Huffington Post.* 27 Oct. 2010. Web. 28 Oct. 2010.

Wittman, Carl. "Refugees from Amerika: A Gay Manifesto." *San Francisco Free Press.* 22 Dec.–7 Jan. 1970. Rpt. in *The Homosexual Dialectic*, ed. Joseph A. McCaffrey. Englewood Cliffs: Prentice Hall, 1972. 157–171. Print.

Wolkomir, Michelle. *Be Not Deceived: The Sacred and Sexual Strategies of Gay and Ex-Gay Christian Men.* New Brunswick: Rutgers UP, 2006. Print.

Wright, John. "Gay Oklahoma Teen Commits Suicide Following Toxic City Debate over GLBT History Month." *Dallas Voice.* 10 Oct. 2010. Web. 15 Oct. 2010.

Zernike, Kate. "Judge Defends Penalty in Rutgers Spying Case, Saying It Fits Crime." *New York Times.* 30 May 2012. Web. 1 Apr. 2012.

Zimmerman, Neetzan. "JCPenney Responds to Homophobic Boycott Calls with Gay Father's Day Ad." *Gawker.* 31 May 2012. Web. 17 Aug. 2012.

Zucker, Kenneth, and Jack Drescher, eds. *Ex-Gay Research: Analyzing the Spitzer Study and Its Relation to Science, Religion, Politics, and Culture.* London: Routledge, 2006. Print.

INDEX

abstinence education, 15–16, 45–49, 62, 80, 90, 156, 162

Accept (pro-gay Christian groups), 20, 100–103, 106–108

AIDS. *See* HIV/AIDS

Althaus-Reid, Marcella: 22, 94–95, 117–137, 161; misuse of Foucault, 131–132

Althusser, Louis, 19, 106, 135, 137

American Family Association (AFA), 7, 30, 117, 214 n. 20

American Religious Identification Survey (ARIS), 164

Americans for the Truth about Homosexuality, 30

Arana, Gabriel, 187–188

assimilation, gay, 104, 112, 135, 148, 158, 238 n. 11

Associated Press, 142, 184

Arterburn, Stephen, 42–43, 45, 48–58, 83

atheism: 14, 23, 26, 99, 144, 165, 175, 197, 206–207. *See also* Sam Harris; Christopher Hitchens

Badash, David, 33, 36, 151

Bakke, Christine, 67

Barbaro, Michael, 192

barebacking: 14, 18, 65, 77, 86, 91, 199; alternative models of relation, 78–86, 91, 139; comparison to ex-gay ministries, 84, 91; gay versus straight breeding, 78–80, 226n. 10; parody of incest, 79–80, 84; redefining family and erotic roles, 79–85

Bayle, Pierre, 175

Besen, Wayne, 186

Beyond Ex-Gay, 67

Biblical translation, arguments over regarding homosexuality, 101, 231 n. 11

Biden, Joe, 3, 37, 192

biosociality, 81, 84–85

bisexuality, 118, 120–121, 123, 125–126, 128–129, 233 n. 19, 233 n. 20

Blume, Allan K., 31–32

Bowers, Betty, 215 n. 22

boycotts of companies by antigay groups, 28–31

Brandzel, Amy, 210 n. 7

Brayton, Ed, 190

breeding. *See* barebacking

Brock, Tom, 97–98

Broverman, Neal, 10–11, 36

Brown, Wendy, 102–103, 232 n. 12
bullying, antigay, 10, 23, 142–153, 155, 158, 163, 177–185, 187–188, 191
Burack, Cynthia, xii, 14
Bush, George W., 1–2, 16, 45, 184, 193
Bussee, Michael (Exodus International co-founder), 66–67
Butler, Judith, 233 n. 18

Cain, Herman, 3, 33, 153
Canaday, Margot, 210 n. 7
Cathy, Dan (Chick-fil-A CEO), 31–36
Cazwell, 159–160
Chambers, Alan, 23, 38, 67, 162–163
Chauby, Jennifer, 177–178
Chauncey, George, 219 n. 4
Chick-fil-A: 31, 192; antigay donations, 33–35; antigay views of CEO, 31; antigay consumer support for, 33; politicians vow to ban expansion of, 36; progay consumer boycott of, 28
Christian closet, 14, 19, 21, 62–63, 66, 77, 82–83, 85, 87, 89, 96, 98, 129, 138–139, 146, 156, 162
Christian purity culture. *See* purity culture
Clarke, Eric, 91–93, 224 n. 8, 228 n. 4
Clementi, Tyler, 10, 12, 142, 162–163
Clinton, Bill, 16, 45
CNN, 152, 179
Cobb, Michael, 212 n. 14
Concerned Women for America, 30, 117
Connolly, Ceci, 46
conservative Christianity. *See* right-wing Christianity
Cooper, Gary (Exodus International co-founder), 66
Courage International, 20
Crimp, Douglas, 233 n. 18

"Daddy's Little Girl" (song), 43–44
Day of Truth, 162–163
Debelen, K., 155
Dean, Tim, 18–19, 47–48, 77–85, 87–88, 90–91,131, 139, 199, 226 n. 10

Defense of Marriage Act (DOMA): 2–4, 144, 152–154, 189–190, 192, 196; defense by US House of Representatives, 39, 153; state court decisions against, 28; US Supreme Court decision (2013) on, 38–39, 150, 192
DeGeneres, Ellen, 30–31
Dignity USA, 20
disability studies, 227 n. 3
Dobson, James, 18, 38, 53
"Don't Ask, Don't Tell" (DADT), 2–4, 144, 149–156, 188–189
Durant, Will and Ariel, 171

Ebersole, Ryan, 33
Edelman, Lee, 114–115, 148, 226
Edwards, David, 152
Eichler, Alex, 147
Eleveid, Kerry, 237
Employment Non-Discrimination Act (ENDA), 2, 189
Epicurus, 173
Erzen, Tanya, 14, 67–75, 214 n. 17, 221n. 11
Ethridge, Shannon, 48
Evangelical Lutheran Church of America (ECLA), 97
Every Young Man's Battle, 42–43, 48–52, 91
Exodus International: 23, 34, 100, 107, 223 n. 3; dissolution of, 38; sponsorship of Day of Truth, 162–163
Expell (ex-gay ministries), 20, 100–103, 106–108

Family Research Council (FRC), 15, 18, 23, 30, 33, 35, 38, 141, 179–180
Federal Marriage Amendment (FMA), 2, 153, 193
Femmephane (blogger), 147
Fischer, Bryan, 214 n. 20. *See also* American Family Association
Focus on the Family (FOF), 7, 38, 56, 221 n. 11
Foucault, Michel: 72, 92, 106, 131–133,

135, 225 n. 9, 234 n. 21; concept of counterdiscourse, 108–111, 132, 137
FOX News, 33
Freud, Sigmund, 15, 49, 51, 57
Friedländer, Benedict, 112
Friedman, Ann, 187–189
Fuss, Diana, 111, 127, 213 n. 15

Gallagher, Maggie, 161, 181
Garber, Andrew, 29
gay bashing, 7–8, 37, 55, 115, 144, 158, 178–179
gay liberation, 5, 118, 122, 126–127, 158, 179, 201
gay male culture. *See* Halperin, David: *How to Be Gay*
gay marriage, 3–9, 23, 26, 29–31, 35–39,78, 81,143, 148–157, 161, 189–196, 228 n. 4, 235 n. 3
gay religion, 22, 87, 94–95, 99, 109, 118, 139, 161
gay spirituality, 14, 22, 94–95, 109–117, 130–134
gaytheism, 24, 26–27, 138, 144, 197, 199, 206–207
Generations of Light, 15
George, Cardinal Francis, 194–196
Gibbs, Nancy, 44–45
Gibson, David, 195–196
Gilbert, Mitchell, 37
GLSEN (Gay, Lesbian, & Straight Education Network), 141, 180, 183
Grace Fellowship Church, 37
Graham, Janice Barrett, 8, 12
Greenwald, Glenn, 190
Grindley, Lucas, 33
Gustav-Wrathall, John Donald, 219 n. 4

Haggard, Ted, 97, 229 n. 5
Hall, Donald E., 125
Halperin, David M.: *Gay Shame*, 238 n. 11; *How to Be Gay*, 4–6, 200–205; *One Hundred Years of Homosexuality*, 126–127
Harris, Sam, 13, 22, 77, 99, 144, 165–169

Harris, Sean, 36
Harris, W. C.: *Queer Externalities*, 229 n. 5
Henson, Lisa, 35
Hirschfeld, Magnus, 112
Hitchens, Christopher, 13–14, 22, 27, 77, 99, 144, 162, 165–176, 183, 186
Hooper, Jeremy, 33
HIV/AIDS, 33, 46–47, 77, 79–80, 85, 165
Howell, Joe, 36
Huckabee, Mike, 33

Ike, Heather, 177

Jakobsen, Janet R., 14
JC Penney, 28, 30–31, 194
J.D. (blogger), 177–178
Jervis, Joe, 147
Jim Henson Company, 35
Johnson, Toby, 22, 94–95, 109–110, 113–115, 117, 130–131
Jung, Carl, 95, 109–110, 114–115

Kato, David, 34–35
"Kill the Gays" Bill, 34–35
Kinsey, Alfred, 142
Kleefisch, Rebecca, 8–12
Kopf, Abbie, 46

LaVictorie, Bridgette, 156
Lawrence v. Texas, 161
Levi-Strauss, Claude, 15, 41
Lewin, Tamar, 46
LGBTQ Spirit Day, 10
liberation theology, 103–104, 117, 125–126
Lifeway Research, 242 n. 9
Lively, Scott, 34–35
Lorde, Audre, 135
Love, Heather, 157–159
Love in Action, 69, 100
Love Won Out, 66
Luck, Kenny, 42

McCain, Cindy, 155–156

McCain, John, 151, 155
McCance, Clint, 10–12
McRuer, Robert, 92–93, 227 n. 3
Metropolitan Community Church
    (MCC), 20–24, 94–95, 100, 103–108
Mordden, Ethan, v
Mormons: 8, 161, 186; involvement in
    Proposition 8, 7
Morris, Paul, 79
MsJacks (blogger), 147
muscular Christianity, 219 n. 4

National Association for Reparative
    Therapy (NARTH), 18, 221 n. 12
National Coming Out Day, 184
National Organization for Marriage
    (NOM), 7, 29–30, 161, 181
Neroulias, Nicole, 185
New Hope Ministries, 19–20, 67,
    69–70, 72, 74–75, 89
New Life Ministries, 42–43
Nicolosi, Joseph, 221 n. 12
NOH8, 155–156

Obama, Barack, 1–4, 24, 37–38, 46,
    150–151, 153–154, 187–193
One Million Moms, 30–31
outings, 96–97, 229 n. 5

Paulk, John, 66
Pellegrini, Ann, 14
Perkins, Tony, 23, 179–185
Perry, Rick, 3, 153
Perry, Troy, 103–104
Petrecca, Laura, 216 n. 23
Pfeiffer, Eric, 36
Phelps, Fred, 55, 154–155
Phillip, Abby, 29
Phillips, Judge Virginia (DADT repeal),
    151–152, 189
Poovey, Mary, 198
Prayers for Bobby, 61
Proposition 8, 3–4, 7, 38–39, 146,
    149–150, 153–155, 161, 190
Public Religion Research Institute and
    Religion News Service, 185

purity culture, 15–17, 42–43, 47–48, 55,
    60–63, 88, 162

QSaltLake, 8
queer theology, 122, 124, 127–131

ReconcilingWorks, 20
Rekers, George, 18, 97
Restored Hope Network, 38
right-wing Christianity, 8, 14, 21,
    24–27, 61–62, 70–71, 91, 98, 105,
    117, 156, 198
Romney, Mitt, 38, 153, 193
Rubin, Gayle, 15, 41
Russell, Bertrand, 240 n. 19, 240 n. 20,
    241 n. 24
Ryan, Paul, 153

same-sex marriage. See gay marriage
Sandfort, Theo, G. M., 182
Santorum, Rick, 9–10
Savage, Dan, 23, 142–148, 160
Savin-Williams, Ritch C., 234 n. 1
Schultz, Howard, 29
Sedgwick, Eve, 44, 58, 61–62, 75, 93,
    112
Shelley, Martha, vii, 123–125
Shirvell, Andrew, 155, 237 n. 10
Southern Poverty Law Center (SPLC),
    30, 33–34, 214 n. 20
Spitzer, Robert, 221 n. 12
Starbucks, 28–29, 31, 194
Steveningen (blogger), 38
Stoeker, Brenda, 42
Stoeker, Fred, 42, 48–58, 83
Stohr, Greg, 150
Supreme Court, California, 6, 38–39,
    150, 161
Supreme Court, Massachusetts, 216 n.
    25
Supreme Court, Wisconsin, 9
Supreme Court, US, 3, 38–39, 150, 152,
    155, 192

Taylor, Edward, 48
Tiku, Nitasha, 155

tolerance, regulatory function of. *See* Brown, Wendy
Toscano, Peterson, 67
Townsend, John, 97
Traditional Values Coalition, 20
Treasure Island Media, 79
Treichler, Paula, 233 n. 18

Uganda, 34–35, 216 n25
Union of Orthodox Jewish Congregations of America, 7

Valdez, Emily, 178
vanguardism, gay, 95, 109–112, 130
Van Leer, David, 19, 213 n. 15

Walker, Judge Vaughn (DOMA repeal), 3, 150, 161

Walker, Sirdeaner, 182–183
Walmart, 8
Warner, Michael, 92; *Fear of a Queer Planet*, 204; *Publics and Counterpublics*, 226–227, 235 n. 7; *The Trouble with Normal*, 5, 26, 204, 235 n. 3, 238 n. 11
Washington Post, 179, 182
Waxman, Henry 24
Westboro Baptist Church. *See* Fred Phelps
Wilcox, Melissa, 22, 103–105, 229 n. 9
Wilson, Randy and Lisa, 15, 44–45
Wittman, Carl, 122–125
Wolkomir, Michelle, 14, 20, 22, 68, 70, 73, 99–108, 229 n. 9
Worthen, Frank and Anita, 74